A Tiger's Tale

The Story of Battle of Britain Spitfire Ace Wing Commander John Connell Freeborn DFC*

by
Bob Cossey

*In peace there's nothing so becomes a man
As modest stillness and humility:
But when the blast of war blows in our ears,
Then imitate the action of the tiger:
Stiffen the sinews, summon up the blood,
Disguise fair nature with hard-favour'd rage:
Then lend the eye a terrible aspect*

William Shakespeare
King Henry The Fifth, Act III

---

*Dedicated to the memory of
Margaret Ena Freeborn
– John's beloved Peta
who passed away 18th January 2001*

First Published in Great Britain in 2002 by
J&KH Publishing
PO Box 13, Hailsham,
East Sussex BN27 3XQ England
Tel/Fax: 01323 843871
E-mail : enquiries@jkhpub.co.uk
www.aviationbooks.co.uk

Copyright   ©   **Bob Cossey (2002)**

ISBN   1 900511 64 9

British Library Cataloguing-in-Publication Data. A catalogue record for this book is available from the British Library.

All rights reserved. No part of this publication may be reproduced, stored in a retrieval system, or transmitted, in any form, or by any means, electronic, mechanical, photocopying, recording or otherwise, without the prior permission of the publishers.

This book is sold subject to the condition that it shall not, by way of trade or otherwise, be lent, re-sold, hired out or otherwise circulated in any form without the publisher's prior consent and without a similar condition, including this condition, being imposed on the subsequent purchaser.

Contents

	Foreword	v
	Prologue	vii
Chapter One	In The Beginning …	1
Chapter Two	Tigers	7
Chapter Three	Preparation For War?	17
Chapter Four	Battle of Barking Creek	27
Chapter Five	Dunkirk	35
Chapter Six	Battle of Britain	45
Chapter Seven	From Defence to Offence	71
Chapter Eight	57 OTU	89
Chapter Nine	The States	95
Chapter Ten	602 Squadron	109
Chapter Eleven	118 Squadron Coltishall	119
Chapter Twelve	118 Squadron North of the Border	131
Chapter Thirteen	Italian Wing	141
Chapter Fourteen	Italian Wing Operations	151
Chapter Fifteen	Final Years	163
	Retrospective	171
	Index of Aircraft Types	176
	Index of Personnel	176
	General Index	178
	Index of Place Names	180

FOREWORD

by Air Marshal C. R. Spink CBE, FCMI, FRAeS, RAF

All stories of courage are worth telling and the story of John Freeborn's path through the Second World War merits particular attention. Not a person to shun danger or controversy, he impresses as a straight talking and straight acting man who quite clearly would not fit into any politically correct mould as defined by modern criteria. John was no saint by any yardstick. Nonetheless his professional integrity was absolute: even when he found great difficulty liking a comrade he never lost his objectivity or his regard for their own professional skills.

In this book Bob Cossey brings out the human side of flying for a protracted period in the many roles to which John and his beloved Spitfire were tasked during this long conflict. From the early days of honing his skills in the immediate pre-war period and through the frenetic and gallant period of the Battle of Britain one is carried along by the personal battles of this brave young Yorkshireman.

The now infamous Battle of Barking Creek is covered in some detail but John Freeborn is the first to admit that this is his recollection of events: for some it will dent their perceived and rather glossy image of heroes. They were of course all men possessed of the same fallibilities and weaknesses that beset the rest of the human race. But despite these frailties they were magnificent in their resolve not to be overcome by the terrible threat to our freedom in the dark days of 1940.

74 Squadron, 'The Tigers', was the Squadron I commanded some 15 years ago and I still experience an enormous welling up of pride when I read of the central part this famous unit played in the defence of Great Britain. John Freeborn was, for his part, central to this great Squadron and he was to take his skills on to other units operating in equally hazardous arenas. Still a young man, he was like so many others shaped on the unforgiving anvil of operations and became old beyond his years. A hard taskmaster, but utterly respected by his crews, he too eventually paid the emotional price for such constant exposure to the dangers and rigours of fighter operations. However, he did not submit to these pressures and gave one hundred percent to the last.

I commend this book on Wing Commander John Freeborn DFC* to you as a story of courage and fortitude. Today we can be thankful that we live in freedom as a consequence of the bravery of men like him.

London
May 2002

Prologue

John Freeborn DFC and bar has elected only recently to tell of the part he played within the Royal Air Force of the wartime years – a decision prompted in many ways by growing exasperation at the many inaccuracies he considers to have been published about life as it really was and events as they really were. John is the first to acknowledge that memory can be fickle as years progress but in the times I have spent with him it seems to me that he can recall with exceptional clarity the people he encountered during his service career and furthermore memory of them prompts recollection of the day to day life of a fighter pilot with equal perception. John is a forthright but fair character who never has suffered fools gladly but who is quick to praise where praise is due. Not averse to sometimes regarding rules as an inconvenience if it suited his purpose, he was nonetheless a stickler for discipline, recognising its need if units were to survive the intolerable pressures often placed on them. A natural born pilot, John could handle the aircraft he flew almost as an extension of himself – an often overworked cliché which nevertheless so often holds true.

Much of what John told me relates to his days with 74 Squadron and its participation in the Battle of Britain. This he is very well qualified to do for he flew more hours in the Battle than any pilot in any squadron. He has some interesting views on famous names of the Battle – not least Sailor Malan. John's war got off to an inauspicious start for he was in the thick of the Battle of Barking Creek and it is in the aftermath of this that his attitudes to many around him began to be formulated. But John freely admits that he has himself always been something of a blackguard and thus the stage is set for a conflict of personality between those for whom the body chemistry just doesn't work.

In terms of detail as to dates and so forth, the telling of this story has been hampered by the loss of John's log books – he no longer has his medals either although he does have replicas and knows where the originals are – so alternative, sometimes conflicting, sources have been consulted in this respect. It is not a story in which plaudits are issued just because there is an expectation that they ought to be. If no plaudits are deemed to be deserved then they are certainly not given. As such this is not just another recounting of the RAF at war. In the beginning it is the story of a Squadron at war both with the enemy and sometimes, it would seem, within itself. Which is not to say that 74 didn't emerge from the Battle with all the credits which are most definitely its due. Made up of some very tough individuals 74 lived up to its soubriquet of Tigers in all respects. The Squadron was assuredly a close and cohesive unit, for a quality possessed of all Tigers was the ability to put aside personal differences when it came to working together in the face of the enemy. Fully aware of its history during the 1914-1918 war and with its reputation yet to be made during the Battle of Britain, 74 was very proud of its expertise and professionalism from the time of its reincarnation in 1935 and the time that John joined it at Hornchurch in 1938. This was down to the strength of its pre war leaders – 'Brookie' Brooks and Sammy Sampson.

After 74 John was to serve for a further five years. He moved first to 57 OTU at Hawarden, spent a year test flying in the States, enjoyed a short stint with the Ministry of Supply, served with 602 Squadron, commanded 118 Squadron and then was posted to 286 Wing in Italy where he was Wing Commander Flying. He concluded his extremely active wartime RAF career in an administrative position at Netheravon on Salisbury Plain, at which stage he decided he had had enough and left the service. In all these postings he was to find colleagues whom he regarded highly as being the very essence of the RAF: but inevitably he found those too who he considers to have been a blight on his career.

John instinctively knew that he would survive the war and in many respects that gave him the confidence to fly and fight in the way that he did. He confesses to prescient capabilities although not of a specific kind. Thus he was aware that within the early stages of war he would be in trouble. How he was not able to discern although he did know it wouldn't be something of the nature of landing with his undercarriage up! And once he knew his colleagues on 74 he could foresee who would survive and who would not – although he certainly would never discuss this with those concerned.

This, then, is the wartime story of John Freeborn – as told to me by John Freeborn. Points of view and opinions expressed, particularly those regarding the colleagues with whom he fought, are John's and John's alone and at times they offer a rather different appraisal and interpretation of people and events than those to which we are used. As the following pages testify, there is much of interest to tell.

– o O o –

A few acknowledgments must be made at this point. The primary source for this book has of course been John Freeborn himself and I would like to pay tribute to his generosity and hospitality during the many conversations that we have had. He has been an inspiration – a man of principle and of commitment and a man with firm views on many issues (confirmed by the many topics we covered as our conversations drifted from the subject in hand!). I am honoured to count John as a personal friend.

I must also thank the staff of the Public Record Office at Kew for their unfailing help. And members of the 74 (F) Tiger Squadron Association who have recalled John's time in those early days on the Squadron, in particular Colin Hales, Derek Morris and Eden Webster. The Association is a very active one with a Reunion held at the beginning of March each year. Any former Tigers who may read this book and are interested in joining should contact Bob Cossey at 16 Pine Road, Thorpe, Norwich, NR7 9LE (E Mail *bobatsne@aol.com*) or look at the Association's website – *www.74squadron.org.uk*

Select Bibliography
Fighter Station by Mick Jennings (*1994*)
I Fear No Man by Doug Tidy (*1998*)
The Right of the Line by John Terraine (*1985*)
A World in Flames by Martin Kitchen (*1990*)
Kent Airfields in the Second World War (*1998*)
and the *Action Stations* series of books published by PSL (*1990 - 1993*)

The photographs are from John's own collection or have come via The 74(F) Squadron Association and its members and The History Room at RAF Coltishall.

Bob Cossey
Norwich
April 2002

Credits: All photographs are credited to John Freeborn unless otherwise indicated

Chapter One
In the Beginning...

Until it actually happened John had no idea that he wanted to fly let alone join the RAF. In fact he was for a long time not sure what he wanted to do and couldn't see with any clarity the direction his life was going to take – a not uncommon phenomena for young boys struggling with their schooling as John did.

Born in Middleton in North Yorkshire on December 1st 1919 in an area of then open farming which is now a huge Leeds housing estate, John's mother, Jean, came from agricultural stock: father Harold was a bank manager with the Yorkshire Penny Bank. There were two sisters and three brothers. Mother was a dour Scot – a hard woman whom John recalls as only occasionally smiling. A stickler for the proprieties of life who was rarely if ever given to showing her emotions, John recalls his mother's reaction to his first car, a Talbot 90. The HP Company rejected his application for financial help: so mother paid for it and John repaid her – with 10% interest! She knew she would get the money as John banked with his father! Nonetheless she was always quietly supportive of John and his siblings despite the fact that she didn't get along particularly well with John's sisters.

Displaying typical patriarchal attitudes of the day father Harold used to literally wield a big stick and whack John and his brothers with it if they transgressed. Not that he needed the stick for reasons of disability, it was merely an affectation. Sunday mornings demonstrates very well the ethos of parenthood as adopted by the senior Freeborns – attendance at church, all dressed in Sunday best, with mother and father at the end of the pew and their offspring sitting in strict age order alongside them. But despite their tough authoritarian and uncompromising approach to their children's upbringing – everything was done to order and for a purpose – John cared very much for his parents.

The Freeborn family always had a comfortable living – with a maid and nurse to hand and summer holidays in Bridlington every year. Harold Freeborn died at the grand old age of 97 (having sadly been knocked down by a motor cycle) and Jean peacefully in her sleep at 93. They were both quietly proud of John's success in the RAF – although mum's view in the end was, typically, that he was doing no more than his duty and he shouldn't be surprised if he were to earn a medal or two along the way! Father, who might have expected John to follow him into the bank, had not been opposed to John's decision to join. Mother initially wasn't so keen – but at the same time was undoubtedly pleased to get John out from under her feet and was not slow in telling him so!

The family moved from Middleton to Headingley where John attended Leeds Grammar School. He hated his schooldays and the prime reason for this was a growing aversion to authority – something which was to stay with him throughout his life and which in truth has led him into many a sticky situation with his superiors both in his military service and indeed in civvy street. Authority assuredly has its place and its uses: but it is the abuse of authority by those who should know better or by those who contrive to exercise and manipulate it for their own ends that John despises. This is still the case. If he thinks something is not right or if he thinks he has been treated wrongly he says so and when young would sometimes react in an physically aggressive way – at school hobnailed boots were painful when applied forcibly to shins as teachers often found out to their cost. John was not a natural scholar – he felt he simply didn't sit comfortably within the schooling system and consequently he was treated as a rebel by teaching staff, often with some justification. On one occasion he was assaulted by a teacher who persistently knocked him over the head with the edge of a ruler. John retaliated and both ended up on the floor with fists flying. John's father was called to account for his son's actions: but Harold doggedly backed John once he found out the reason for the brawl. This adds something to our understanding of the relationship between father and child. Disciplining John when necessary and often severely, Harold was nevertheless totally supportive of his son if right was on his side: John repaid this support by adoring his father.

He was always to be grateful for what his mother and father did for him, and instilled in him, as a youngster. They taught him that patriotism was important and there should be no shame in fighting for the flag of one's country. They taught him that rules were there for a purpose and should be obeyed – which is subtly different from rebellion against authority which was so often misused – and this is something that John's troubled schooldays taught him also. In the years ahead John would often be asking himself the question 'what would mother and father have done in a situation like this or when confronted with a problem like this?' Having decided on what the answer would have been John did his best to emulate it.

Freeborn junior left school at 16 and was very glad to do so. Many of his peers had successively tried to reform him from the earliest days of his education but without success. It's interesting though to note that during the war years John returned to Leeds Grammar now and again, on one occasion borrowing a Gloster Gauntlet and touching down on the cricket pitch after an aerobatic display. By now he was being held up as an example to the other pupils – as somebody making use of his life. And masters who not so long previously had been belting the living daylights out of John were now quite affably lunching with him. He found this ironic twist in attitudes mildly amusing.

As a palliative to the misery of school John's great love was, and indeed still is, the railways. Harold would take him to see the trains thundering along the lines that passed close to the house where they lived. As a youngster John visited Leeds station (a favourite place) and once he became known to drivers and firemen he would hitch lifts on the footplate – on one occasion in particular when he was nine on an Atlantic class locomotive pulling a Pullman train to the next station to collect carriages. John was allowed to drive – or at least hold the regulator! When the family were in Bridlington on their annual holidays John used to get rather bored with the beach and so would sidle off to the station to watch the trains instead at what was a busy station in those days. In later years, when in the RAF, John managed a Newcastle to London ride on the footplate.

This was on an evening express. I arrived early and got chatting to the driver. I asked whether I could ride on the footplate with him. He said provided the supervisor didn't find out it was alright by him – so I threw my bags into a carriage and at the opportune moment climbed onto the footplate. What a journey! I have never been so uncomfortable in my life. I was burned, battered and bruised. I was also cold but scalding tea from a billy-can helped in that department. There was really no room for three of us up there – I was constantly in the fireman's way. Every time the engine gathered water from the trough I got soaked. But what professionals these men were! They could tell their exact location at night by the sound of the tracks, by the sequencing of signals and so forth.

When we got to King's Cross I was in a dreadful mess – covered in coal dust, black as the ace of spades and very wet! I booked into the station hotel. The staff there were amazing. They took my uniform and handed it back to me the following morning as good as new. These were another group of people who had to put up with a lot of obstructive and offensive people during the war. But for me they were in the main unfailingly helpful and courteous.

For years John collected engine names although his railway log books, along with his aeronautical ones, have long since disappeared. John continues to derive a great deal of pleasure from the railways, diesel and electric traction notwithstanding. It's the smell and look of trains, their speed and power – as well as the statistics – that excites him. He can recite facts and figures even now – steamers, for example, used to burn 7 tons of coal on the London to Crewe run: and the engines could scoop up 600 gallons of water a minute whilst on the move. Diesels and electrics don't quite have the same fascination for him – Deltics he considers nasty, noisy beasts!

– o O o –

As is often the case, there can sometimes be an inbuilt reluctance to translate a hobby into a career and it never did occur to John that he would make a career on the railways. In fact he wasn't sure at all what he wanted to do. In the end it became a choice between the armed forces or the pits and with no inclination to become a Bevin Boy (he says the only bright spot about going down the mines would have been the money to be made on the black market selling coal during the war!), at the age of 17 John joined the ranks of the Reserve of Air Force Officers. His experience of the military up to this date had been his role as drummer and bugle boy in the OTC (Officer Training Corps). He had decided he wanted to fly and was quite simply recruited through the power of the poster. No one person influenced John in his choice of the RAF. It was a combination of circumstances. He had no romantic notions about being a flyer but didn't like the turn of events with Mussolini's involvement in East Africa and started to feel that something would have to be done about it. Interviewed by a Board of Selection (civil servants all) at the Air Ministry in Aldwych, searching questions were asked of the young Freeborn. Having endured the cumbersome and sometimes inappropriate interview process, the fact that John was suffering from a heavy cold meant that he failed his medical. Returning a month later he succeeded and was accepted into the Reserve of Air Force Officers which effectively meant that he had a year to decide whether he liked what he was doing and wanted to stay in or not. Having learnt to fly he would then join a squadron – or leave if he was not cut out for the RAF (or indeed if the RAF felt that it was not cut out for him). If he had left he would probably have applied for the Navy – he had sat an exam previously to be an Artificer's Apprentice but had failed it. But that is mere hypothesis. John took to the RAF immediately and in particular to flying.

It is worth pausing briefly here to consider the wider view and look at the Royal Air Force into which John was about to be initiated. From the perspective of the 21st century, a look at the names the service bestowed on its aircraft of the 1930s says something about the anachronistic nature of both machines and doctrine. Woodcock, Gamecock and Siskin: Heyford, Vildebeest and Wapiti summed up the spirit of the age somehow, particularly when compared with the aggressively named Hurricane, Spitfire, Tempest and Typhoon that followed them. Post World War One was a difficult time militarily and as the newcomer to the military establishment, the future of the RAF was in the greatest balance. There was a strong lobby for the abolishing of the Service altogether: this was staved off by cutting costs to the bone, by soldiering on with outdated aircraft, by reducing squadron strength and manning resources to a barely acceptable level. But slowly, perhaps in the wake of events on the other side of the world when Japan went to war with China and pictures appeared in the British press of the devastation caused by the bombing of Shanghai, the power of the bomber and the need to be able to counter its threat became an increasingly decisive factor when formulating government policy. Closer to home Hitler's Chancellorship of Germany led to the beginnings of the blatant rearming of that country's armed forces in contravention of the Versailles Treaty.

Thus from the mid-1930s there were some significant moves made. Here at home the Air Ministry specification, for example, from which came the Spitfire and Hurricane was written in 1934 followed two years later by the specification which led to the Stirling, Halifax and Manchester: the construction of new airfields: the creation of the Command system which was to take the RAF into and through the Second World War: the creation of the RAFVR: and the first of the expansion schemes by which the RAF prepared for war. Between 1934 and 1939 there were eight such schemes. The first, announced in July 1934, proposed the spending of £20 million to produce an Air Force of 84 squadrons and 1,252 front line aircraft in response to Germany's rearmament programme. In 1935 the Abyssinian crisis reared its head and, contrary to the Treaty of Versailles, the Luftwaffe was established with Goering at its head – a Luftwaffe which by this stage had already reached parity with the RAF in terms of numbers of aircraft. In response, new objectives were set in Britain and the expansion scheme was amended to create a Royal Air Force of 123 squadrons to be realised by the end of March 1937. But this was to be further modified in the light of a General Election and a February 1936 Defence White Paper which called for 124 Squadrons and 1,736 aircraft. Of the schemes promulgated in the 1930s this is the one which was actually more or less completed. Furthermore the idea of a strategic bomber force was conceived. Light bombers such as the Hawker Hind were consigned to the history books and a new generation of medium and heavy medium bombers were specified – these would be the Blenheim, Hampden, Whitley and Wellington. Then came the heavies – Stirling, Halifax and Manchester, the latter of course leading directly to the Lancaster. In October 1937 a bomber force of 90 squadrons was proposed

In addition to the home defence squadrons, overseas forces were to be increased to 37 squadrons. This increased the need at home and abroad for adequate airfields to house the new aircraft. New Royal Air Force Stations steadily came into being – by 1938 there were 89 of them. Not all the aircraft would be able to be supplied by British industry in so short a space of time – and so orders went to the USA (not a popular move back home!). The first manifestation of this was 200 desperately needed Hudsons for Coastal Command (2,000 were eventually delivered to the RAF). Of course, with the greatly expanded capacity and capability of the RAF, personnel issues needed to be addressed as well – and indeed were. In 1936 it had been realised that if things continued as they were, particularly in the light of expansion, there would not be enough men and women in the RAF. The Royal Air Force Volunteer Reserve was created to teach young men with no previous service experience to fly in their spare time. Recruitment of tradesmen and administrative people gathered pace too.

– o O o –

Such was the changing Royal Air Force that John was to join. Amazingly up to the time he reported to the Tiger Moth equipped Elementary Flying Training School at Sywell on 17th January 1938 he had never seen an aircraft close to on the ground! The Tiger Moth was the outstanding trainer in the RAF's inventory, the first examples of which had been delivered six years previously. The initial order for thirty five was quickly followed by increasing orders for the improved Tiger Moth II (with ply decking on the rear fuselage and a blind flying hood for the rear cockpit). This became the definitive trainer version and by 1939 over a thousand had been delivered to Elementary and Reserve Flying Training Schools providing *ab initio* instruction. By August 1945 over 8,000 had been built.

Initiation in this trusty trainer was a frightening experience – taken up on a familiarisation flight the instructor spun, rolled, looped and stopped the Tiger Moth's prop. John was petrified although he largely managed to hide his fear knowing that his reactions were being watched in the pilot's mirror. He was accepted on to the course. Thus began a period which are recalled as being wonderful days. Training was undertaken by a civilian company (Brooklands Aviation) and was a serious business both for the student and for Brooklands as they made a lot of money out of it. The contracting out of certain aspects of the RAF's activities is certainly not a modern phenomena. There were thirty in John's entry. One week they flew in the mornings and were in the classroom in the afternoons – on alternate weeks this schedule was reversed. The course lasted three months with a total of 50 hours flying. John confidently went solo after just 4 hours 20 minutes. The average was 7 to 8 hours and thus he was rated as an above average pilot. But although he may have shown early signs of being a natural born pilot, halfway through the course John was told he was not doing so well in the classroom. Fellow pupils Ron Courtenay, 'Butch' Surtees and Jack Caslaw got to grips with this by making John work every night at his studies and then persuaded the instructors that he should take the exam – well before his fellow students had to. John passed and thus at the end of the course was able to sit back whilst the rest went through the examination process, safe in the knowledge that he had already done so. Not unsurprisingly there were twenty or so other individuals who weren't too impressed with this and considered John to be a 'sneaky little bastard' who curried favour with those in authority! His due reward was to be dumped into the Emergency Water Tank! Actually John, the youngest on the course, and his fellows got along well together. They were, he recalls, a good bunch.

After Sywell John moved to No. 8 Flying Training School at Montrose where he flew the Hawker Hart – a proper aeroplane (as he describes it) and a real beauty to look at: indeed Sydney Camm's masterpiece and its successors are regarded as amongst the most elegant aeroplanes ever – and huge compared with the Tiger Moth: as was the Fury which had similar lines to the Hart. The principle RAF interceptor during the inter war years it was light, fast and for its time possessed an outstanding rate of climb. Those who were to go on to bombers flew the Audax: although not intended to follow this path John had the opportunity of flying it from time to time as well. The only problem with any of these types for John was that they were built for six footers which he never was – and judicious use of cushions was necessary to allow a comfortable and controlled flight for him!

The regime under the Sergeant Instructors at 8 FTS included blind flying on instruments only under a hood, reconnaissance and navigation exercises and even some rudimentary simulator work. Time was spent at the Air Firing School at Catfoss (on average an hour a day in the air – weather permitting), not only for air firing but dive bombing too, a skill which was expected of a fighter squadron in the pre war years. Air firing was done on Fairey Swordfish towed drogues with bullets dipped in paint so that hits could be marked. The average accuracy was a mere 7%. John managed 15%.

Training eventually came to an end and Acting Pilot Officer Freeborn, earning the princely sum of 11/10d a week (and this after a universally applied 10% pay cut as part of the government's strategy for combating the effects of recession and for raising money for the build up for the war effort), was assessed as having gained his wings as a continuing above average pilot. Now it was time for the front line and all at 8 FTS eagerly waited news of their postings. For John it was to be Hornchurch and 74 Squadron – the famous Tigers.

Chapter 2
Tigers

The squadron to which John was posted on 29th October 1938 was even then, prior to its exploits during the Battle of Britain, regarded as one of the RAF's premier units and this reputation rested solely on its record during the war in 1918 and its associations with Mannock, Jones and Caldwell. Formed in July 1917 at Northolt, 74's officers and men went through a somewhat protracted period of training at London Colney and Ayr. It was at Ayr in March 1918 that New Zealander Keith Caldwell became CO (the fledgling squadron's fourth in ten months!). Caldwell was to be the inspiration behind 74's phenomenal success once they moved to the front line in France at the end of the month. Between then and the cessation of hostilities in November their record (flying the SE5A) stood at 140.5 enemy aircraft and 15 balloons destroyed with 68.5 probables – 224 victories in just seven months. So ferocious had been their fighting and so determined were they as a unit to see the better of the Hun, they became known as the Tigers.

From amongst a long list of courageous pilots two names stand out alongside Caldwell himself. Mick Mannock had joined 74 in February to command A Flight. As with Caldwell he inspired his fellow pilots by personal example. He was considered to be in the top five of British aviators and was probably the finest patrol leader that the RAF had. By May 1918 he was destroying at least one German aircraft a day, shooting down his fortieth aircraft of the war on the 17th of that month. He died in combat having left 74 to command 85 Squadron. And Taffy Jones – a charismatic character who became an almost legendary figure in his own right. Another aggressive Tiger he finished the war with 26 victories. A great admirer of Mannock he was determined to emulate his success. Held in high esteem by all his colleagues he was reckoned to be the best flyer on the Squadron after his hero – and once Mannock had gone the best. To Taffy, who succeeded Keith Caldwell as CO in December 1918, fell the job of disbanding his beloved Squadron in July 1919. In later years and determined that the events of the Tigers' first two years existence be recorded in detail, Taffy wrote the first 74 Squadron history in 1954.

The Tigers lay dormant until September 1935 when the troopship *Neuralia* set sail from Southampton with the men who were to constitute a reformed 74 Squadron. On board another ship, the *Maihar*, were the Demon aircraft they were to fly. No one knew of their destination other than the CO elect, 'Jim' Crowe. Indeed the Squadron didn't actually reform until they were at sea: prior to this they were simply listed as three Demon Flights. The reason for the secrecy was an attempt to hide the fact that the RAF were sending a squadron of fighters to Malta to defend that island against possible air attacks were Mussolini's ambitions in East Africa to expand to encompass new areas. This was the time that the schoolboy John Freeborn began to be aware of possible trouble brewing in the Mediterranean area. In the event, in less than a year 74 were on their way back to the UK, a policy of appeasement having been adopted by the British government with Mussolini, not to mention Hitler, having been given *de facto* leave to pursue their aggressive policies.

The RAF in England to which 74 returned after just eleven months in Malta included a Fighter Command of just sixteen squadrons, only some of which flew the Gloster Gauntlet, the most modern fighter then in service. 74 had been posted to Hornchurch and, having had their Demons unpacked and reassembled at Sealand, they gradually built themselves back up to strength on this aircraft. Sqn Ldr D S 'Brookie' Brookes was now CO. He and Taffy Jones, who was making a point of keeping in touch with his former command, took a drawing of the tiger's head which had been used unofficially on the Squadron's aircraft in 1918 to the Chester Herald who sought the approval of the King for its adoption as 74's official crest together with the inspired motto *I Fear No Man*.

Hornchurch was a typical peacetime RAF station with grass runways, three C type hangars in a crescent and an approach path straight over Ford's Dagenham factory. It had started life as Sutton's Farm in 1915, had closed between wars and reverted to farmland and had then been developed as part of the RAF's ever changing expansion plans. On April 1st 1928 it reopened as RAF Sutton's Farm but was renamed Hornchurch two months later. Its grass landing area allowed for a 3,600ft run from north to south and 3,400 ft from north east to south west. There was also a 2,500 ft strip from south east to north west and from east to west – so virtually every direction of wind was catered for! The first incumbent squadron was 111, its CO being Sqn Ldr Keith Park – who within eleven years would be AOC 11 Group and fighting the Battle of Britain. Indeed Hornchurch became part of 11 Group of the newly formed Fighter Command in 1936.

The working week was one of Monday to Friday and Saturday mornings. Each day started with the colour hoisting parade at 0830, a rather cursory inspection of airmen by each of the incumbent squadron's Adjutants (74 were sharing Hornchurch with 54 and 65 Squadrons), the raising of the RAF ensign, prayers and a march off to places of work. Squadron routines were leisurely. Aircrew would gather in their respective Flight Commander's offices for tea and a chat whilst airmen moved the Demons out of the hangar to the flightline. Flying would start somewhere around 1000. Lunch was between 1230 and 1330 – everything stopped for it. After lunch and a beer in the Mess, flying resumed. Operationally pilots would amass 180 to 200 hours a year in accordance with the Fighter Command Training Syllabus. Special commitments such as the annual air firing camp and participation in air displays provided a welcome variation to the routine. With only one forty minute flight a day pilots were hard pressed to occupy themselves otherwise, although there were many routine station and squadron tasks to be carried out – kit inspections, pay parades *et al*. However, despite this apparently leisurely existence there was a determination from the top that 74 was to be the best of RAF squadrons and this filtered down from Sqn Ldr Brookes to all his men. Inter squadron rivalry was, as it always was and always will be, intense – a rivalry which was not restricted to the inter 54-65-74 Squadron air to air exercises but which spilled over too onto the sports field and into the Mess! Squadron loyalty was of paramount importance and has always been a notable feature of 74. Obviously not everybody liked everybody else and there were always the tensions that exist when a body of men work together in close co-existence, but at the end of the day it was to 74 that allegiance was universally owed. A good CO made all the difference and Brookes and his successor Sammy Sampson were certainly that. They ensured that 74 was at the top of the Fighter Command tree.

Munich was a landmark for all RAF squadrons in the sense that life livened up somewhat with additional training and some adjustments to Mess practices – dining nights were sidelined for example. More time was devoted to formation flying, inter flight interceptions and Fighter Command tactics, the latter being standard forms of attack which when the war started proved to be quite inappropriate. And yet it was still, by comparison with what was to come later, very much a gentle life in the service – and at times a tedious one. If there were no aircraft to fly – and with the well used Gauntlets with which 74 were by now equipped often unserviceable this was frequently the case – a game of cards was the next option. It was in many ways a recipe for idleness.

How did the RAF find itself in the immediate aftermath of Munich? In short – potentially in trouble! Germany's equipment strength, on paper at least, far outweighed that of the RAF and if nothing else Chamberlain's 'peace in our time' prompted a great acceleration of the plans to have in place the numbers of RAF squadrons and aircraft proposed in the expansion schemes. Various sets of conflicting figures have been produced to illustrate the comparative strengths (or weaknesses) of the German and British air forces but one on which several historians agree is that the Luftwaffe possessed 1,669 *serviceable* aircraft including 580 or so bombers on August 1st 1938 compared with a total of 1,642 with the RAF – a vast improvement on the total three years earlier when 74 returned from Malta. But whilst numbers might have been comparable it was a case of quality as opposed to quantity and as such the RAF would certainly not have had a particularly easy time of it were the Luftwaffe to launch bombing raids on Britain. One partially equipped and untrained Spitfire squadron (No. 19), five then troublesome Hurricane squadrons (they couldn't fire their guns above 15,000ft) and twenty biplane fighter squadrons (including the obsolescent Fury and Demon) with which Fighter Command was equipped would have been no match for admittedly the only two German types that could in 1938 have reached Britain's shores – the Do17 and He111.

– o O o –

This was the world into which new Tiger Cub John Freeborn was thrust when in October 1938 he reported to Hornchurch, commanded at the time by Gp Capt Walkington. Virtually the first person he met when he arrived at 10 o'clock on a Sunday evening was 65 Squadron's Bob Tuck who shared a few beers and then showed John around the station's buildings and then the airfield. Over the next few days it seemed to John, as a fresh faced pilot officer on a squadron for the first time, that everybody seemed so old. Of course they weren't actually old – they just looked to be so to the young and still impressionable Freeborn. It was good to have Tuck's calming influence by him. This was the RAF proper – where he found a very different regime from that of the training establishments to which he had hitherto been used.

Whether John was subjected to the ordeal of the oxometer in his early days is not on record. The oxometer was used to measure the height of bullshit and was a little hand held brass contraption consisting of a small container for paraffin and wick and an impeller on to which a jet of air was directed, blown through a short pipe and mouthpiece, causing the impeller to spin. The wick was lit, and holding the contraption close to the face the idea was to blow out the flame by spinning the impeller. The harder one blew, the faster it span. Many new pilots to the Squadron were inducted in this way and it usually took place before an audience of fellow pilots – and anyone else who happened to be nearby! In truth all that happened was that the flame was deflected by the airflow towards the initiate, generating a thick black oily smoke which deposited itself on one half of the face unbeknownst to the blower who was receiving bags of encouragement and being urged to blow even harder to make the impeller spin even faster… until eventually the penny dropped! In later times John himself was i/c such proceedings!

The day following his arrival John was introduced to the senior officers – the Squadron Adjutant – Sammy Hoare – first of all. John remembers Sammy well – they used to be regular adversaries at snooker. But they ended up in different Flights and after a while their paths didn't cross that often – particularly after war broke out when they were deployed to different parts of the airfield and sometimes different airfields. Under the increasingly austere regime that filtered into the Squadron the fragmentation of personnel became quite marked in a way it may now be a little difficult to comprehend. The truth is that Flights were in effect autonomous units and whilst the Mess still afforded the opportunities for the Squadron's officers to fraternise, elsewhere it was not necessarily the case and it would not be unusual for new pilots assigned to A Flight not to know their counterparts in B other than in passing. The same applied to ground crew and air crew. An aircraft's rigger and mechanic would know their own pilot: they would scarcely know any of the others.

Sqn Ldr George Sampson, known to all as Sammy, was the Tigers' CO when John arrived. Sammy was an Australian and although very strict was highly respected. He certainly cracked the whip and at those times everyone had to toe the line! As John came to appreciate, strong leadership and discipline when properly exercised was essential to the effective operation of a squadron. Barely five years later when he was given command of his own squadron, John remembered this lesson learned with Sammy Sampson and ran a tight ship with his air and ground crews smartly turned out on the premise that a tidy man had a tidy mind and this would be reflected in that man's performance. Recalling a particular instance on 602 Squadron which John would later join as a supernumerary Squadron Leader, Bill Loud was a Sergeant Pilot who was also a 'scruffy sod' but who responded to orders to smarten himself up which spilled over in turn into an immediate improvement in his job. He went on to

Sgt Pilot Bill Loud, a butcher's boy from Poole, who went on to be commissioned and win the DSO and DFC. This is a John Topham portrait from Bill Loud's 602 Squadron days

shoot down a lot of Germans when flying top cover on bomber escort work. For some, sloppiness in attitude led to the aircraft they were flying mastering them: a positive attitude in matters on the ground was reflected in positive handling of the aircraft they were flying. There is little doubt in John's mind that the two are inextricably linked.

Sammy Sampson had a soft side to him too and indeed was like a father to John to the extent that in the months ahead he pacified the indignant parents of more than one girl who had taken a shine to the personable young Freeborn! Sampson didn't fly a lot but did spend much time in the Control Room to practice his considerable skills in this respect. When Sammy Sampson left 74 he went to Fighter Command Control as indeed did Charlie Meares, Commander of C Flight – the Administration and Aircraft Serviceability Flight – another clever and competent man who was, like his CO, also an excellent Controller.

Having met Sampson, John was next taken to B Flight's offices where he found the Flight Commander Paddy Treacy and the other pilots. B Flight proved to be a good Flight although John quickly began to have reservations about Treacy himself. In the pre war RAF much of the training was done by the Flight Commanders who worked with the Squadron Training Officer. As an individual, Irishman Treacy was often an unkind and most unhelpful character as far as the new boys were concerned. It quickly became evident that another Irishman on the Squadron, Vincent 'Paddy' Byrne, had the measure of Treacy and regularly baited him – something the latter had difficulty coping with. It transpired that Treacy and Byrne had been at the same Dublin school and animosity had raised its head there. Neither attempted reconciliation and the feuding continued. This ill feeling and his inability to deal with the new boys aside, Treacy was a good Flight Commander and a brave and determined pilot. Whilst John didn't like him as a man he respected him as a fine RAF officer with all the right attributes demanded of officers in those days. It was Paddy who persuaded John to apply for his Short Service Commission. But that didn't stop John applying for a transfer to A Flight so as to escape his influence.

A Flight Commander was the soon to be famous South African Sailor Malan. John's first impression was that he was a pleasant fellow who as a married man was always broke and thus frequently borrowing money: if there was a reluctance to lend it was taken! Sailor was later universally recognised as being a clever individual and a top class pilot although John still feels he was a better one. Sailor was older than the average pilot at the time – he was in his late 20s – and a very aggressive flier, always going to the edge and making everyone else do it too. But as with Treacy, whilst a good Flight Commander, he was lacking in patience and was not good at encouraging the younger, newer pilots. John and Sailor struck up a friendship which lasted until Barking Creek – of which more later.

Given the reluctance of Treacy and Malan to deal sympathetically with the new boys on the Squadron it was a blessing that 74 had a Training/Safety Officer of the calibre of Ernie Mayne. Ernie was excellent in this role – a man of his experience on any squadron was an irreplaceable asset and an inspiration in the role model sense to the youngsters. He was unfailingly helpful and became a great friend to John and was popular, full of fun and enjoyed life to the full. Ernie was a very good Sergeant Pilot who had started his military career as a bugle boy on HMS *Hood* when she underwent her sea trials during the First World War. By the time John arrived on 74 Ernie had already logged an immense number of flying hours – probably more than the rest of the Squadron put together. However, whilst to many he may have been a remarkable man, he was treated unjustly by those who decided such things in that he was never decorated or rewarded for his considerable efforts as a Tiger although later in his career he was given the Air Force Cross. He was one of the few Sergeant Pilots (in fact only one of four in the RAF) to fly right through their career – normally for an NCO it was four years in the air then back to your trade which in Ernie's case was an LAC Fitter. He ended his non commissioned career as a Warrant Officer (First Class) – the 'First Class' earning him an extra 2d a week! – and was then commissioned and posted to an air firing unit at Sutton Bridge and was ultimately promoted to Sqn Ldr to take command of that unit. Ernie Mayne's log book, showing 2,000 hours flying in fighter aircraft, can still be seen at Manston

74 was blessed with other good Sergeant Pilots too – Peter Chesters and Tony Mould amongst them. There has been some debate of late about the role these non commissioned pilots played in the war and the way in which they were treated by the officers. The truth is that most of them were in fact ultimately commissioned – if they were good enough, and most of them were, why not? Those that weren't were by and large the lazy ones who didn't want the additional responsibilities and who invariably seemed to have a chip on their shoulders. They shirked the chance to be commissioned because they were simply not prepared to make the effort. Thus they were seen by others as being incompetent. It is not surprising that these individuals were sidelined by their commissioned colleagues: by contrast those who were prepared to be a part of the team that any squadron must be were treated accordingly. Although there has always been the distinction posed by the existence of Officers and Sergeants Messes that didn't stop the camaraderie between the two if individuals desired it. There were many Sergeant Pilots who were the salt of the earth – fine men and very capable pilots too.

– o O o –

The ground crew were in the main a dedicated set of men as well. A true competitive spirit existed on the ground as it did in the air and a fitter or rigger would consider an aeroplane to be 'his': if, when the fighting started, one of 'his' pilots shot an enemy aircraft down it was as much a victory for the ground crewman as the pilot. There was a great pride in ensuring the aircraft was in tip top condition – although of course it had to be for it was the Flight Sergeant's career and reputation on the line if an aircraft was signed off with a fault. Pilots soon learned that they could have absolute trust in their groundcrew and their aeroplanes. However, despite all this, contact between pilot and fitter was largely restricted to dispersal. As Derek Morris recalls:

The relationship between AC1 Armourers and officer pilots was not close! To me, pilots were those individuals who spent much off time in the crew room or in a Spit hidden under a flying helmet! The only ones I remember talking to were Malan and Treacy.

Groundcrew, without whom no squadron could ever survive and operate. With Flt Sgt Llewellyn on the right is an unidentified colleague. Llewellyn was a metal rigger on B Flight

12

Whenever I stuck my head around the crew room door to invite a pilot (as per regulations) to check the harmonisation before taking the Spit down off its jacks they always sent the newest Sergeant pilot! However I do know that 74 had better pilots than 65 Squadron judging by the number of Spits on their noses during landing. One time I recall 65 put one over every day for six days and at the same time we had just one bent.

And Colin Hales adds:

At that time of course never did the pilots mix with ground staff at a local to have a beer and a chat. The nearest we got was dispersal bays – and even that did not happen often.

There was as recognisable a hierarchy on the ground as there was in the air and Warrant Officers and Flight Sergeants ruled their domain in a frequently autocratic fashion! There were also of course strictly adhered to systems and procedures, designed to protect everyone from poor workmanship and lack of professionalism in the job done. Thus aircraft had to be signed for prior to each take off. This centred around the Form 700 and its purpose was to ensure that all work had been carried out, inspections had been correctly completed and the aircraft was fit to fly. Working through the strata of rank, the first signing was by the tradesmen who had done the work, then moved to the corporal who had supervised the work, the sergeant who was responsible for the work and finally the pilot who flew the machine. The Form 700 has become enshrined in RAF law. Not so the Administration Book which pre-war was signed by the pilot each time he flew and then countersigned by the pilot's Flight Commander. This practice ceased when hostilities started and the time for such niceties was no longer available as the alarm to scramble was urgently sounded.

– o O o –

There were one or two on the Squadron who seemed to be dogged by tragedy. Norman Pooler was a jolly, good looking Pilot Officer who appeared at the end of a party one night in a somewhat subdued mood carrying a revolver. After chatting for a while with those present he insisted on saying goodbye to everyone. But such was his very apparent depressed state of mind he was escorted to his room and settled for the night. The following day he didn't appear and after a search his body was found lying in the Mess garden. He had shot himself through the head with a Colt 45. The Squadron was not represented at his funeral which at the family's request was a private one although they did later ask that his ashes be scattered over the airfield. A fine rugby player, he had also been a capable and popular man. Sadly the Court of Enquiry, headed by 65 Squadron's CO Sqn Ldr Cooke and with John as part of it, convened to establish the reasons for his suicide and discovered that he had contracted syphilis. Having been cured he contracted it again and was not able to cope with the consequences. This had not been John's first Court of Enquiry. He had previously sat with Sqn Ldr Cooke after a Gauntlet pilot had beaten up his girlfriend's house, crashed into a tree and broken his legs and thighs. This had been in John's first few months on the Squadron and he sees it as Sampson's way of starting off his training in the administrative side of an officer's general duties. Cooke was a very helpful and supportive man to work with too and quickly put the young Freeborn at his ease. Having seen an example of John's handwriting he volunteered to take over and keep the notes himself – in the interests of being able to read them when it came to compiling his report!

At the time of John's arrival at Hornchurch 74 were still equipped with Gauntlets, a beautiful old aeroplane which by now had had their original silver finish replaced with camouflage. In April 1937 74 had lost its Demons and re-equipped with this product of the Gloster factory, the last squadron of fourteen to do so. Whilst a distinct improvement over the Demon it nevertheless lagged behind the later Gloster product, the Gladiator, which 54 were by now operating (and flaunting) from the adjacent hangar. The Gauntlet had better electrics than the Demon and certainly a better radio, the TR9, although this was still a somewhat primitive piece of kit. But overall the aircraft was not as reliable as the Hawker type it replaced and crews longed for the day when it would be replaced with, they presumed, Gladiators. Gauntlets in their day were the fastest of the RAF's fighters with a top speed of 230mph and to John in his early days as a Tiger there was nothing more exhilarating than the Battle Flight climb to 30,000ft which was executed once a week as a Squadron. But by the time he arrived they were in a poor state mechanically and rigging wise and were continuously being patched up. The Mercury 6S engine was troublesome. An abiding memory is the air bottle which injected air into the cylinders to start it – a work of art in itself! Indeed many of the Gauntlet's systems were air operated but leaking pipes presented a challenge to those who serviced the aeroplane. In truth, unserviceability and an increasingly despondent ground crew was a constant problem. Yet oddly, given their unreliability, if a Gauntlet were available it could be used to fly home at weekends with every chance that it would break again and be unavailable for Squadron duty on the Monday morning! John, living at Leeds, became used to flying into Yeadon regularly. It counted as a training exercise.

Soon after John's arrival Malan, Treacy, Heywood, Flinders and Hawkins of A Flight qualified for the finals of the Sassoon Trophy for Fighter Attack and indeed they went on to win with 74 beating units which were flying the Gladiator or even the new Hurricane. In fact 74 had now won the trophy three times on the trot thereby winning it outright – a wonderful piece of silver which took pride of place in the Mess during Guest Nights. The competition was the only one in the RAF which called for team-work as opposed to individual performance and this meant in turn a tough time for the ground crews as the demand for serviceable aircraft was a constant one. John was entrusted with the Sassoon Trophy ferry pilot's job. If a participating aircraft became unserviceable John would fly in to Upper Heyford (from where the Sassoon Flight was operating) with a replacement and then return with the unserviceable machine back to Hornchurch.

Of the Sassoon Trophy pilots Gordon Heywood was a great help to John in his early days on the Squadron. Indeed the likes of Heywood and Mainwaring treated the youngsters as they would a younger brother – Gordon in particular kept an eye on them all in matters of protocol. It didn't take John long to realise that most of those on 74 were proud of the Squadron, its tradition and its history. Neither did it take many weeks for him to realise that he liked the life and liked most of the people. The transition from training to an operational squadron was often difficult – coming from a training airfield to a front line station with a big Mess was in itself initially daunting – and was almost like stepping from make believe into a real world which at the age of 18 was not an easy transformation. To begin with even John, who had rebelled against authority from an early age, was a little frightened by the military version but in the main he quickly learned that that authority was a kindly one. He also quickly realised that promotion had to be earned. And Flight Lieutenants were addressed as 'sir'…

– o O o –

Apart from learning how to fly and fight at Sywell and Montrose, John and his fellow pupils had been well schooled in the ways of protocol in the Royal Air Force – everything from how to correctly complete a cheque to what to do in the presence of the Marshal of the Royal Air Force – and this training very quickly stood him in good stead for much of what he had learned was soon put into practice.

It was expected that within six weeks of arriving at Hornchurch a new pilot would have presented himself to all the married officers on the station from the rank of Flight Lieutenant upwards to partake of a sherry and share in a little general conversation. If you didn't do this you were considered a bounder! First port of call was traditionally the Station Commander and it was with more than a little apprehension that the young Freeborn donnned suit and Tiger tie (he still has this original tie which is special to all serving members of 74 Squadron, maroon for aircrew and blue for groundcrew, in his collection) and knocked timidly at Gp Capt Walkington's door and presented his card. He needn't have worried. The Group Captain and his wife were both charming people and made John feel very welcome and this kindly attitude helped enormously as he worked his way down the list of those on whom he had to call.

All commissioned officers needed a calling card. On first arriving John had left two – one on the visitors board in the Officer's Mess announcing the arrival of Acting Pilot Officer John Freeborn for the benefit of the Station Commander and the other in the 74 Squadron box announcing his arrival for the benefit of the Commanding Officer and officers of the Squadron.

John had also been taught how to conduct himself at Mess functions and dinners where, upon entry, you found the senior officer present and bowed smartly to him. The Squadron dined formally in the Mess as a unit on at least four nights in the week. On special nights ladies were invited into the Mess for Dinner and you were expected to escort them in. Normally ladies were restricted to the Ladies Room and they relished the occasional opportunity to join their husbands for a formal evening. These were splendid affairs – officers in dinner jacket and bow tie, ladies in their elegant evening wear, the Squadron silver dominating the top table with the magnificent, recently won Sassoon Trophy as the centrepiece. It was all very splendid and as in so many other institutions the length and breadth of Great Britain, the Royal Air Force was very good at carrying on the proud traditions that already distinguished this youngest of the military services. As John sat and looked around him on his first formal Dinner his heart swelled with pride. He was very sure that he was exactly where he wanted to be.

Chapter 3
Preparation for War?

It was at the turn of the year that Eden Webster first recalls seeing John Freeborn at the colour hoisting parade.

Without doubt he was the youngest looking officer on parade, so young in fact with his rosy cheeked, fresh faced school boyish appearance that I, still eighteen myself and some way to go before my nineteenth birthday, mentally questioned his right to be there and whether he actually needed to shave! He and Norman Pooler were the youngest looking pilots on the Squadron at that time.

Young he may have looked, but following in the footsteps of Sammy Hoare and Paddy Byrne, John was made Squadron Adjutant which in effect meant he was the equivalent to a Company Secretary. He couldn't pretend he enjoyed the responsibilities of the job particularly when it came to dealing with Monday morning defaulters and other disciplinary matters which usually involved those considerably older than himself. Unable initially to steer a middle course when it came to dishing out punishment – either too lenient or, when pulled up by Sampson, too harsh – John soon adjusted and in a while came to enjoy what he was doing, enjoying its perks and more importantly earning the respect of the Flight Sergeant i/c Administration for his approach to it. One of the perks was that the Squadron Adjutant avoided being rostered as Duty Pilot – which was not minded at all as you were on duty for 24 hours at a stretch, basically weather watching. As if to compensate the job of Orderly Officer was *not* avoided and as this involved regular patrols of the camp in company with the Duty Sergeant during the night this was certainly minded! Apart from the gathering war clouds, there were other security issues to contend with at this time of which the IRA threat was one. On John's first Sunday evening at Hornchurch, the station had been in a state of some excitement as a young girl's body had been found outside the camp's barbed wire perimeter. In the event her murder had nothing to do with RAF personnel. Neither was it proved to be the work of the IRA.

The first big event of 1939 was the arrival of the Squadron's first Spitfire on February 13th, delivered by former Tiger CO 'Brookie' Brookes. 19 Squadron at Duxford had been the types' first recipient in August 1938: 74 were the second. Flying from Eastleigh Brookes was met by Malan and Treacy in their Gauntlets and escorted to Hornchurch where all of a sudden the formerly cocky 54 and 65 Squadrons with their up to the minute Gladiators realised they were about to be upstaged by 74. Things were looking up!

The Spitfire I was fitted with a Merlin II engine rated at 1,060hp driving a two bladed fixed pitch wooden propeller. Armament was eight Browning .303 machine guns. By the time war broke out 306 Mk Is had been delivered and first blood was down to one of John's future squadrons, 602 who, with 693, engaged Luftwaffe bombers off the Scottish coast with each shooting one down. By mid 1940 nineteen squadrons had them despite large numbers being lost during Dunkirk. Spitfires coming off the production lines had been improved, most noticeably by the incorporation of a three bladed, variable pitch, constant speed prop. At the

17

Hornchurch, February 1939 – at the time the first Spitfire I arrived on the Squadron. There are too many to name in total in this evocative photograph but it is worth running along the seated rank from left to right: Sgt Leader (Rigger), Cpl Bennett (Fitter), unidentified, Flt Sgt Farmer (i/c Orderly Room and Admin), Flt Sgt Denley (i/c Sqn Workshops), W.O. Elcock (A Flt 'Chiefy') – then A Flight pilots Hoare, Temple-Harris, Heywood, Meares, Rowland, and Fl Off Malan (Acting A Flight Commander) with his dog Peter. Sqn Ldr Sampson with the Sassoon Trophy. Fl Off Treacy (B Flight Commander) then B Flight pilots Byrne, Mainwaring, Measures, Pooler, Freeborn, unidentified, Fl Sgt Mayne, Flt Sgt Etheridge (B Flt 'Chiefy'), Sgt Llewellyn (Rigger) and Sgt Whitaker (Fitter)
[Photo: Eden Webster]

Standing proudly in front of a new Spitfire I at Hornchurch are left to right: Llewellyn, Stephen, Mungo Park, Draper, Stevenson, Cobden, A Smith, Young, Mayne, Hastings. Seated middle rank - Malan, White and Measures. Seated front rank - Mould, Dowding, Freeborn

The Fitters and Riggers at Hornchurch. The pilots with them are (left to right) Temple Harris, Measures, Malan, Freeborn, unidentified, Dowding, Mould

same time the inadequacies of the machine gun were apparent and a few Mk Is were built with Hispano-Suiza cannon instead and designated MkIbs.

But we have moved ahead. Conversion by 74's pilots took place over the next few weeks as more aircraft arrived and it presented no particular problems other than getting used to this radically new piece of kit. The conversion process took but a few minutes, in John's case with Paddy Treacy leaning into the cockpit and saying: 'There's the undercarriage lever. You lift it up – don't touch it now! – you lift it up and then pump. Those are the flaps. Your trim is here. Now get off. Don't stay on the ground too long because these things overheat.'

There were no pilot's notes. John had never flown a monoplane before – not even a Magister – before he got his hands on a Spitfire! The first thing he had to do was taxi it – the Gauntlet was easy because you could see where you were going: with this new beast there was a long nose in the way! Once he had mastered the art of weaving, an art that had to be learned very quickly, John found himself thinking of all the things Paddy had told him. Where's the pump for the undercarriage? Is the radiator open? How much throttle do I give it?

The aircraft was nose heavy – the complete opposite to the Gauntlet. Taking off from the grass of Hornchurch I treated things very gently! Off I went between the hangars at 180mph, faster than I had ever been in my life before! I took off and climbed away. Once at altitude I settled down and found the Spitfire to be a lovely aeroplane. You became wholly part of it – rather like slipping on your overalls. As for landing you approached at 90mph. I checked undercarriage down, flaps down (speed reduced to about 75mph when this was done) and landed comfortably and easily at around 60mph. Stalling speed incidentally was 62mph.

It all came together very quickly with no real problems for John or indeed for the majority of the other pilots. Within three sorties he found himself confident enough to engage in a mock dog fight with Bob Tuck in his Gauntlet. After landing Bob phoned John – 'You were shot down Freeborn!' 'Never! I've got you on the camera gun. *You* were shot down! 'At this stage there was no camera gun fitted although the mounting was there. It was only around the time of Dunkirk that the cameras started to appear. Anyway, for the moment the threat was enough for Bob to shut up!

There were inevitably incidents with the new type, one of which concerned Paddy Treacy himself who, upon completion of a demonstration flight for a party of visiting Army officers, failed to pump the wheels fully down into the locked position when he came in to land. The landing itself was fine. It was the sight of the Spitfire slowly sinking to the ground as the undercarriage retracted into the wings that caught the eye! At the beginning of a sortie in those early days the retraction of the undercarriage after take off led to some unusually erratic airborne manoeuvres as well for it had to be pumped up (and down) by hand. It took fifteen minutes to complete the cycle and pilots at this stage felt that they really did need three hands. For a while a little more space was left between aircraft on formation take offs but it was not long before Malan and Sampson insisted that proper formation should be kept. 74 became adept at perfect formations on both take off and landing as demonstrated on a visit to France for the Bastille Day celebrations as will be recounted shortly.

Accompanying the Spitfires to the Squadron was a Rolls Royce engineer who helped sort out the many, but perhaps not unexpected, teething troubles with the Merlin engine. In the early days there was a *ten* hour inspection and plug change (twenty four of them), the latter not an easy job even with the special tools supplied. When starting up, if the mixture was a little bit rich flames would stream from the manifold – so flame traps were fitted. And Spits were always prone to overheating, particularly when on the ground as Paddy Treacy had warned John. The undercarriage leg blanked off the radiator. The problems hadn't been completely sorted by the war's outbreak although they had improved. The engine's reliability was put to the test during the Dunkirk episode when John flew his aircraft for a full seventy hours before there was the opportunity for servicing and maintenance. Incidentally the Merlin used a dry sump system which meant prodigious amounts of oil were burnt – four gallons to every tankful of fuel.

As time went by, modifications were made to the aircraft at squadron level. Eden Webster was very much involved with these as he remembers:

We were carrying out the armour plating and bullet proof windscreen mods. I showed John what we were having to do to the original windscreen to accommodate the rather clumsy casting containing the new bullet proof glass panel without damaging the perspex and then properly securing the whole assembly. We also had to lower the upper fuel tank to fit the enveloping ricochet cowling and fit the main armour plate component to the fireproof bulkheads. John and his fellow pilots took a great interest in these modifications which must have been reassuring for them.

It is worth recording that John has never felt that the Spitfire could be compared directly with the then far more numerous Hurricane – in his opinion an awful aeroplane in terms of ergonomics compared with the Supermarine aircraft in which all that was needed seemed to be at hand for the pilot. Having said that the Hurricane was well loved by those who did fly it – until they got their hands on a Spitfire!

Moving forward briefly, after the Spitfire I came the II and IIb. The V was the first clipped wing version and John recalls going down to Eastleigh to collect an early example – a II with the wing tips literally cut off and formers inserted in their place. John was given the parts that had been removed – and a bill for £100! This wouldn't have been a Spitfire V proper as they arrived on the Squadron after John had left, but was probably an experimental or prototype version of a II.

A very young Pilot Officer John Freeborn at the age of 18 at the time he crossed the Channel to celebrate Bastille Day with the French Air Force in July 1939

```
                                    Appendix 'A' to Air Ministry
                                    letter C.1476/39/D.D.S.D.
                                    dated July, 5th, 1939.
                                    -------------------------------

              PROFORMA - CARTE D'IDENTITE.
              ------------------------------------

     1. Name and rank of officer
        or airman in full.              PILOT OFFICER  JOHN CONNELL
        (Surname in BLOCK capitals
        and official number in
        case of airmen.).               FREEBORN

     2. Station, Squadron or
        Headquarters.                   No. 74 (F) SQUADRON

     3. Date of Birth.                  1 - 12 - 1919

     4. Colour of hair.                 LT. BROWN

     5. Colour of eyes.                 BLUE

     6. Height.                         5 feet 6 inches.


                       Signature of officer or airman. John O. Freeborn. P/O.

                       Signature of responsible officer. G.V.Sampson


                       Station, Squadron or
                       Headquarters Stamp.      [ORDERLY ROOM
                                                 10 JUL 1939
                                                 No 74 (F) SQUADRON]

     Date. 10th JULY, 1939.


                       PHOTOGRAPH.
                       -----------
```

An identity card was issued to all those who travelled to France to help celebrate Bastille Day in July 1939. John's signature is above that of Sammy Sampson. Today John is in great demand when it comes to signing prints of paintings featuring 74 Squadron, the Battle of Britain and his Spitfire ZP-C. His signature has barely changed: the only difference is he can rattle off several hundred in a couple of hours!

Preparation for War?

– o O o –

The Squadron deployment to Le Bourget to celebrate the Fall of the Bastille in July 1939 just prior to the Home Defence Exercises for that year was a memorable occasion which, when first announced, had caused considerable anticipation. It was certainly viewed as an honour to be chosen to participate. John had had an inkling of 74's involvement with this in advance when maps for Northern France were received for secure keeping in the Squadron's map cabinet – as Adjutant he was responsible for the recording and safe keeping of all maps and when these arrived he was told to divulge their existence to no-one. The Tigers, the only Spitfire squadron to attend, flew from Hornchurch and took off and landed as a squadron – typical of the standards demanded by Sampson and his Flight Commanders who decreed that wingtips would be overlapping or they would want to know the reasons why not! Twelve aircraft in four vics of three were ranged across the grass: the leader got airborne relatively slowly, not getting above half power (2-3lbs boost) thus giving the rest of the formation plenty of scope – for when in formation you have to juggle the throttle constantly to keep in place.

It must have been an inspiring sight when they arrived at, and later when they departed from, Le Bourget – and German observers (present under the Lufthansa banner) would undoubtedly have been impressed. After landing the pilots lined up to be presented to a French general who when he got to John, patted him on the cheek and said to Sampson 'you have brought your mascot then'. Sampson was livid. The French couldn't believe that one so young as John could be active in a front line squadron and the incident served to sum up the different approach each side of the Channel – which broadly speaking was that the British were serious about their air force, the French in those days were not. They had some pretty awful equipment to fly and then only Captains, or pilots over thirty years of age, could fly fighters. In itself this fact perhaps helps explain the attitudes of the two air forces.

74 were in Paris for a fortnight. Amongst the formalities was an official reception at the British Embassy to which the Squadron was invited but which turned out to be a rather dry affair in more than one sense. John attended this in borrowed garb – a set of tails procured for him by Paddy Byrne from who knows where but which was probably a waiter's outfit and so old that it had very worn fabric buttons. Attempts to quench thirsts proved fruitless and nearly cost John a beating for Mainwaring sent him behind curtains which formed a backcloth to the stage on which a military band was playing and where he had seen crates stacked up. A beefy guardsman caught John in the act – the beer belonged to the band! John scarpered. Enough was enough and a number of Tigers escaped into Montmartre and enjoyed a cracking good night on the town. Anybody seeing penguins escaping from the British Embassy over ten foot high iron railings must have wondered just what was going on!

The commander of the British contingent in Paris was Air-Vice Marshal Playfair although 74 didn't consider him to be an aptly named officer when he sent them home for enjoying themselves too much! They were determined to return with souvenirs though and, worried about customs at Hornchurch, somebody came up with the bright idea of using the Spitfire's parachute flare tubes as a hiding place for a bottle or two of champagne – a perfect ploy it seemed when the Squadron landed and was questioned and only perfunctorily searched by Customs. All was well until somebody pulled the flare release lever on one of the aircraft and a bottle crashed to the ground. Levers on all the Spitfires were pulled in short order – and the prospect of a celebratory evening with real French champagne quickly disappeared! Other squadrons learned from 74's mistake and when they returned from trips to Europe with flare tubes filled with things other than flares they would land at

Manston first to unload before flying on to Hornchurch for the Customs' check!

Further contact with the French was had during the Home Defence Exercises held in August of that year. In their antiquated aircraft they came across and 'bombed' London and 74 and fellow fighter squadrons intercepted them over the Thames Estuary and frightened them to death! John remembers coming down through a tight bomber formation and scattering them in all directions. How they avoided collisions he cannot think to this day. Only by hanging on their props could the fighters slow down enough to get some camera gun film of their intercepts. There is little wonder that the French were so ineffectual when they were confronted by Bf109s when the war started.

– o O o –

What everybody expected to happen, happened. What was the feeling on the Squadron when war broke out? Initial apathy earlier in the year brought about by a rather arrogant feeling that the RAF were simply too good and Germany wouldn't dare take them on was replaced on September 3rd 1939 by panic! The Mess was vacated immediately and personnel slept in tents and trailer caravans by the aircraft. Everyone was involved in the filling of sandbags and the creation of blast proof dispersals for the Spitfires. For many new recruits, their induction into the RAF took the form of sandbag filling although the larger part of this contingent was provided by the army's newer recruits. John himself got away with it – as Squadron Adjutant he was deemed to have too much paperwork and administration to deal with (along with the CO) in the wake of developments.

Despite all these preparations for war little immediately happened however. There was a Squadron scramble on the 4th when 74 were ordered to intercept an enemy raid approaching the coast from Holland. Nothing was seen and the Tigers later learned that the aircraft were in fact the survivors of the first RAF raid on the Kiel Canal. But then on the 6th came one of those incidents that for ever cast their shadow over the individuals involved and leads to endless theorising as to why it should have happened in the first place. At the heart of 74's particular controversy was John Freeborn.

Chapter 4
The Battle of Barking Creek

On September 6th 1939 Red Section of A Flight led by Malan was scrambled at around 0700. At ground level fog reduced visibility to twenty yards but overhead a clear blue early autumn sky could be seen. Yellow Section, led by Paddy Byrne with John Freeborn as his No 2 and Sgt 'Polly' Flinders as No 3, was climbing and catching Red Section up after their take off had been delayed because of problems with Byrne's aircraft. No sooner had the two Sections joined when Malan's call of 'Tally Ho! Number one attack – Go!' came over the radio. Looking round, Byrne and Freeborn saw two aircraft and dived into the attack.

Tragedy then struck. Harrup and Rose in Hurricanes of 56 Sqn, which had been scrambled from North Weald to intercept the same enemy formation that 74 had been sent up to catch, were shot down. Malan, immediately recognising that a mistake was about to be made, had tried to call Yellow Section off. He insisted afterwards that he had shouted 'Friendly Aircraft – Break-away!' over the radio. But the call wasn't heard if he did. The fact is that no such call was made. Neither Freeborn, Byrne nor Flinders heard it. Hawkins, in Malan's Red Section, maintained that he did – but that was because he had been told to say so. It's a regrettable truth that Sailor moved quickly to cover his mistake – and his back. 56 Squadron's Harrup was killed. Rose survived.

The pilot's order book stated categorically that, at that stage of the war, no single engined aircraft was to be attacked. But John and Paddy simply, if erroneously, assumed that Malan had identified them as the enemy. After all a very clear instruction to attack was given. Neither pilot could see identification markings such as roundels or codes themselves but they were approaching from the rear. Now, sixty years later, John admits that it wasn't an inability to identify the aircraft that was a problem for him – he should have realised, for the profile of a Hurricane was obvious even from the rear quarter. It was the excitement of war just declared and the resultant adrenalin surge that led them to attack without making a visual check. The attitude amongst the pilots on the Squadron at the time was certainly aggressive, even Gung Ho – an attitude fostered by Sampson, Malan and Treacy – and furthermore there was absolutely no reason to question Malan's call. Whatever John's eye saw, it just didn't register. Neither did it register with either pilot what they had done until they landed and were placed under close arrest. There could have been a second tragedy for immediately after the shoot down John lost sight of Paddy Byrne – then saw a Blenheim (again he didn't immediately recognise it as such) which was saved from John's guns by Flinders positioning himself between it and John and by calling John off.

Back at Hornchurch the two pilots were ordered to stay in their room in the Mess and not venture outside it. Malan had already landed and disappeared to leave Freeborn and Byrne to face the music although Sampson did later debrief Malan very carefully. There was no escaping the fact that a court martial would have to be convened and held at HQ Fighter Command. Sammy Sampson proved the calibre of his leadership by giving all the help he could and indeed arranged for a prisoner's friend for the two airmen. It was John's complete faith in Sampson that led him to never really doubt the outcome.

Prior to the proceedings John's arrest was commuted from close to open to enable him to seek out Sir Patrick Hastings, probably the most brilliant KC of his day. As his No 2 Hastings had the CO of 600 Sqn at Biggin Hill, Roger Bushell – another very well respected barrister. Hastings and Bushell defended both John and Paddy Byrne although the latter had slipped into fatalistic mode and did little to help himself. The prosecutor was an RAF lawyer. The Judge Advocate, Sterling, whose job was in reality clerk to the court and whose real expertise was in legal law, would not have been John's first choice were it down to him. There were four officers on the tribunal – an Air Vice Marshal, an Air Commodore and two Group Captains.

The hearing at Bentley Priory on October 17th 1939 lasted a half day. When it came to John's turn Roger Bushell's whispered 'don't worry: you're clear: it's all over' proved to be prophetic. For that was the verdict – complete exoneration. The Court Martial Register simply states against both P/O J C Freeborn and F/O V G L D Byrne's names 'Acquitted' under the enigmatic heading 'Misc 39(1)(B)'. Papers for the hearing have yet to be released for scrutiny but it was undoubtedly the brilliance of Hastings and Bushell which won the day. Hastings, John recalls with some pleasure, told Malan (who appeared for the *prosecution*) that he was a bare faced liar! Other witnesses were the downed airman Tommy Rose of 56 Squadron and Hawkins, Malan's No 2 in Red Section. Flinders was not called.

Much has since been written about this infamous incident by people who have not been privy to all the facts or who have chosen to put their own interpretation on facts as they have understood them. Emphasis has been placed on poor IFF procedures – but there was *no* operational IFF at the time – or a breakdown in 11 Group's system of control – and certainly many of the Controllers were inexperienced reservists. 56 Squadron were scrambled but some maintain this was done without reference to the Controller. Others cite poor equipment and procedures that led to a Controller wrongly identifying incoming Blenheims as enemy aircraft in the first place – an identification which led to the call for 74 Squadron (and others) to scramble. Whatever the facts here, and there is no doubt that the Tigers were in the air expecting to see enemy aircraft, the three salient points are that, firstly, all those involved in the air and on the ground were almost supersensitive to the situation with the war being just two days old: secondly, Malan definitely gave the order to attack and his alleged subsequent order to break off was not heard by Freeborn and Byrne: and thirdly, not enough care was given to identification. That is the situation as it was and which led to the tragic conclusion to the Battle of Barking Creek.

To broaden the scenario, Sammy Hoare painted a picture of the situation at the RDF Station at Canewdon which this author quoted in his book *Tigers*:

It is reasonable to assume that a degree of confusion would have arisen and that a conclusion was erroneously drawn that something big was about to happen. More squadrons would have been brought to readiness including those in adjacent sectors. Other RDF Stations would have been alerted as would the Observer Corps and AA batteries, all of which would have resulted in a flood of information being fed to the Controller. More Sections or Flights were ordered off to intercept and identify those already airborne, each in turn appearing as unidentified plots on the table as the result of the technical problems that were being encountered at the time. The picture was now one of aircraft being directed and redirected all over the sky, chasing each other and presumably sometimes themselves… The fact was that no one could have reported and positively identified an enemy aircraft as of course there were none anywhere in the vicinity. Who eventually ordered a halt to the situation two hours later is not known.

This, stresses John, is mere conjecture and assumption. Nobody knows the full story. Nothing has been officially published and certainly the court martial evidence has yet to be released – the hearing was held *in camera*. It is only now that

John has chosen to break silence. It was a Squadron Leader at North Weald who scrambled that Wing at his own volition. One incoming Blenheim had been picked up on radar (possibly the one John had failed to identify immediately after he had shot down the Hurricane) and the Observer Corps had also reported it, but by the time verbal reports to Fighter Command had been relayed this one aircraft had been transmuted into a squadron! Fighter Command ordered A Flight of 74 Squadron to scramble – B Flight were never so instructed as some accounts maintain. What happened in the air is as detailed above. Immediately the awful truth was realised John and Paddy were placed under close arrest when they landed and so was Group Captain Lucking, Officer Commanding North Weald. This was as a direct result of Keith Park's instruction who immediately saw the implications of the blunder in terms of morale within the RAF, public confidence in the RAF and probably his own career. It was only after a few days, when clearer heads prevailed, that John and Paddy Byrne's close arrest was reduced to open arrest and Lucking was reinstated (and shortly afterwards promoted).

Wing Commander `Bunny` Currant was a witness to the Battle of Barking Creek. He was one of the 56 Squadron pilots scrambled on that fateful day as his log book testifies. Messrs Freeborn and Currant met for the first time in 2001
[Photo: D R Cook]

– o O o –

Barking Creek was for John a watershed in his relationship with Sailor Malan. He felt betrayed by the fact that Malan had appeared for the prosecution and not the defence. Sailor's one major failing was that he was not prepared to be blamed for anything – ever. When the chips were down and in spite of his being in control of the attack, of having identified the Hurricanes as enemy aircraft and having called the Tally Ho, it was, it seemed to John, subsequently a case of Malan watching his own back and if not being specifically untruthful when he gave evidence at the court martial, certainly choosing to forget some salient points relating to those few tragic minutes. It is hardly surprising that there was a very significant cooling off of the Malan-Freeborn friendship.

Despite the disquiet it all caused, operational life on the Squadron after the court martial continued pretty much as normal. There was certainly no difficulty with other Squadron members from John's point of view but with Malan it became a case of only speaking when necessary and then conversations were cursory. Between arrest and the court martial not a word was exchanged between the two. John simply rode it out and got on with the job for Malan, despite his propensity for being blameless, was a fine pilot and Flight Commander and John respected him for that. Unfortunately Sailor never really forgave John for Barking Creek and the outcome of the court martial which was perhaps why, when he assumed command of the Tigers, he never recommended John for further medals or bars beyond his DFC awarded on 13th August 1940 and which was recommended by Laurie

White: and the bar to his DFC awarded on 25th February 1941, (the day incidentally that Malan was promoted to Squadron Leader) which was recommended by Mungo Park. Ultimately of course medal recommendation was the purview of the Station Commander, although he in turn took the recommendation of squadron COs and other senior officers.

Malan had his own yardstick which governed his recommendations – six aircraft confirmed as shot down for a DFC, twelve for a bar to a DFC, eighteen for a DSO. John's eventual tally was thirteen and a half kills and twelve probables but a DSO should have been a real possibility for him for after all this was a medal awarded for bravery in the air, not for the number of kills. And in any event Malan's system was a purely arbitrary one. But Malan rarely recommended other men in his squadron either: it seemed to John that he had to be the one who earned the glory or, now and again, one of his closest associates. Malan always claimed for absolutely everything, dubious or not, and with the more susceptible members of the Squadron on his side he employed almost strong arm tactics to persuade those that mattered to back his claims.

What of Paddy Byrne? John's assessment of him is that here was an example of a man who simply didn't do the job he was asked to do properly. Invariably such men ended up being shot down or as POWs and indeed he was flying with Byrne eight months later when he *was* shot down and captured. John has never been able to understand his attitude after Barking Creek. When they were placed under close arrest – a very serious state of affairs indeed – Byrne was relaxed to the extent that he was heard to comment that if they were found guilty they could always join the Air Transport Auxiliary – it was better pay anyway! The scruffy and irresponsible Temple Harris had already transferred there from 74 and was sending back messages as to how preferable it was. Byrne didn't seem to accept, or at the very least be concerned about, the potentially career breaking situation they were in.

In synopsis, post Barking Creek we find that there was unfortunate personal friction developing amongst a section of the aircrew of 74 for reasons which have become clear as recounted above. Professionally, though, the job continued to be done and done exceedingly well as the statistics testify and this is of course to the credit of those involved and their responsible attitude. The turn of events, from John's point of view, led to his determination to show that he could equal or better anything that Sailor could do. One area in which John felt he definitely had the edge over Malan was, perhaps surprisingly, his skill as a pilot. John could regularly outfly him and there is no doubt that he was very good with a natural ability to handle aeroplanes. The reason for this, John has always believed, was because he took time to listen to Ernie Mayne and act upon his advice of…

'… *get into the air – and practice, practice, practice. The pilot controls the aircraft – not the aircraft the pilot. Fly until it's all second nature to you.*'

At the beginning of the war the Squadron was involved in escorting convoys from Dover to Calais and as an occasional treat for the seamen on the ships below Freeborn and Malan would indulge in a spell of impromptu aerobatics. Try as he might, Malan could never shake Freeborn off – the latter matching him move for move, wing tips overlapping. After one such exhibition, the pair of them (with Hawkins for company) returned to Rochford, very low on fuel. John's Merlin cut out first but he had enough height to glide back to the airfield. He touched down, ran the length of the strip and taxied, dead engined, into dispersal – judging it all so perfectly that he stopped exactly where he wanted (and needed) to. He was delighted to see that Malan and Hawkins had tried a similar trick but had both come a cropper – one in a bunker, the other on his nose!

– o O o –

As the shock waves of Barking Creek rippled through the Squadron, it had to be remembered of course that there was a war on and distractions could not interfere with duty. In truth though a sense of anti-climax was soon to filter through because very little seemed to be happening. This was the time of the Phoney War and 74 settled into a routine of training and convoy patrols to protect reinforcements going across the Channel. But what was the situation at this time between C in C Fighter Command, Air Chief Marshal Sir Hugh Dowding and the Air Staff? How prepared was the RAF for what was, presumably, to come? Had the expansion programme already delivered what was required of it? Or was the Phoney War a welcome breathing space to allow the continuing build up of resources?

It is well known that in these initial months there was considerable disagreement as to what the RAF's strategy was to be although it is outside the purview of this reminiscence by one of its Fighter Command pilots to consider more than the arguments as it may have affected him. There is little doubt that since 74 had returned to England from Malta Fighter Command had undergone a transformation. The expansion schemes, although often hesitant, were bearing fruit and although targets in terms of numbers of squadrons had yet to be met (at the outbreak of war there were 39 Fighter Command squadrons which included the Auxiliaries), production of aircraft were exceeding forecasts to the extent that there was a reserve of modern fighters. Added to this was the steadily expanding chain of RDF stations.

As for strategy, thinking regarding the deployment of these assets focussed initially on the establishment of four defence zones with squadrons switching between them according to where attacks materialised. Dowding saw this as unwieldy and was not happy that such switching could happen quickly enough to meet the threat. He therefore instituted the three Group structure, based on the premise that when attacks came they would predominantly be against London and that, therefore, was where the weight of air defence should be. Thus 11 Group in the south had twice as many squadrons as 12 Group across central England which in turn had more resources than 13 Group which was tasked with defence of the north of the country. But there were other considerations. What if Germany invaded the Low Countries and could operate from there against England? How many aircraft, bombers and fighters, would they base there? Dowding calculated that the 39 squadrons he had at his disposal were inadequate for the defensive task, 46 was the minimum he needed. And he could not take on any extra commitments without them – commitments such as the need to protect east coast convoys, strictly Coastal Command's responsibility but which at the time was a responsibility they were unable to fulfil: the need to provide two squadrons to protect the fleet in Scapa Flow – the Navy had no modern fighter defence force: the need to deploy a single squadron to protect the industrial centre of Belfast: and the need to provide at least four Hurricane squadrons to provide cover for the British Expeditionary Force on the Continent. Sir Hugh was rightly concerned – and yet the Air Staff was still holding to the belief that the bomber programme must be maintained for it was bombing that would win the war – their deterrent value as a reprisal force still held sway in the corridors of power. Dowding's idea that it was the fighter that would deter any attacks in force on Britain represented a conflict in doctrine at this stage of the war. Yet it was to the credit of the Air Staff that they did not seek his replacement – rather the reverse. They asked him to stay on as C in C Fighter Command for a year beyond his appointed time.

– o O o –

From October 1939 the Tigers flew from Manston or Rochford (Southend) – the Squadron first moved thirteen aircraft to the latter on October 22nd – airfields to which they deployed for approximately three week stints from Hornchurch before being replaced by another squadron. Indeed they paid five separate visits to Rochford over the subsequent nine months. No enemy aircraft were seen until November 20th when William Measures – known to all as Tinky for some long forgotten reason – shot down a reconnaissance He111 over the Thames Estuary. 74 was ecstatic at this first success of the war but Measures paid a price for being the victor by bursting his eardrums in the process! He also rather upset Sailor who wanted to be the first!

The following day three Tigers force landed in France having found themselves short of fuel. One of these was Paddy Treacy and on his return to Hornchurch the next day he carefully removed three bottles of champagne from his aircraft's flare tube. The lesson of the post-Bastille Day return four months earlier had not been forgotten! Over the next few months tensions relaxed and Hornchurch even returned to something of its pre-war routines. Crews moved out of their tents by dispersal and moved back to the Messes and crew rooms. At Rochford they used the Flying Club buildings – although it is sad to record that both club and private aircraft had simply been broken up before finally being dumped at Newmarket when Southend Airport, as Rochford previously was, had been requisitioned by the Air Ministry. Operational life became even more mundane and a new mood became evident – one of either hoping for a diplomatic solution to the situation so everyone could stand down and go home: or hoping for some military initiative that would allow them to be the fighter pilots they had trained to be. It was not until the New Year, January 11th in fact, that 74 made its next interception off the East Coast. The aircraft proved to be Blenheims at 10,000ft. On February 13th 74 scored Rochford's first success by damaging an He111 over the Thames Estuary.

Perhaps the most significant event of this period was the departure in February of Sammy Sampson to his Fighter Controller's job and the arrival of Sqn Ldr F L White who came with a great reputation which sadly didn't transform itself into good qualities as a Squadron Commander and his appointment was quickly viewed by all on 74 to have been a regrettable one. Laurie White was a thoroughly nice fellow, but he didn't like the war very much: neither did he do much to lessen Malan's propensity for getting his own way and it was generally felt that White was apprehensive of Malan's apparent authority over most of the Squadron. The effect of this approach was to allow Sailor, still a Pilot Officer at this stage, to effectively run the Squadron which, it must be acknowledged, he did as a very tight ship.

Laurie White had started in the RAF as a boy entrant and at Cranwell won the Sword of Honour. His great strength was gunnery. He was a natural and was the leading air firer in all competitions. Many pilots could never hit target drogues: for others 20-30 rounds was the norm: for 'Droguer' White it was regularly up to 80% of rounds on target. However, there was a real difference between a drogue and the real thing: there were no target drones in those days but there was a next best thing. It was by accident that somebody discovered that firing at the shadow of an aircraft flying over water gave realistic training. Use of the gunsight was side stepped and pilots learned to point the aircraft itself at the target which increased the chances of success. Use of a camera gun later became a pre-requisite too as it enabled the debriefing of a pilots' performance – something which John was to insist upon when he later took command of a squadron himself.

Laurie White rarely flew with 74, preferring instead to wait at Hornchurch for his pilots to return. On one of the few trips he did make he shared a Henschel 126 with Tinky Measures over Calais on May 23rd but then had to force land with an engine problem. White called up John, who was also in the air at the time, and told him to inform his wife that he was in France, that he was OK, and he would not be over the Channel for too long! John, who was still the Squadron Adjutant, did so. After intervention by the Hornchurch Station Commander – by now Gp Capt 'Daddy' Bouchier – White was rescued by Flt Lt Leathart of 54 Sqn in a Miles Master (Leathart was to be awarded the DSO for his exploits) whilst Al Deere and Johnny Allan engaged Bf109s overhead and thus prevented the Tiger's boss from coming to any harm. Quite a day!

Chapter 5
Dunkirk

Paddy Treacy was shot down twice around the time of Dunkirk. The first time was on May 24th when he baled out of a burning aircraft but survived to get back to England. Three days later he was shot down again, being posted as missing over Lumbres. He managed to evade capture and find an escape route home after a quite extraordinary series of events which John recalls as including a frequent diving into ditches, finding a rowing boat and attempting to row across the Channel, a German seaplane landing alongside him and his capture, his subsequent escape again and the stealing by this tireless man of a tyreless bicycle on which he eventually got as far as Marseilles. From here the Irish consulate got him to Gibraltar and thence back to Dublin and England. He was awarded the DSO in the light of his exploits. Paddy Treacy was later killed when CO of 242 Squadron in a collision with a fellow squadron member on take off. When he disappeared from Tiger Squadron John almost inexplicably found that he missed the often bullying but equally helpful Irishman.

On 74 Treacy was not immediately officially replaced as B Flight Commander and John, as a Pilot Officer, assumed the responsibility on a *de facto* basis. There were actually supernumeraries on the Squadron at this time but they were not considered as replacements for Treacy. John revelled in this new responsibility – for responsibility has never been something he has been afraid to accept. At twenty years of age and to be in a position to lead a fighter squadron was a quite remarkable achievement, but not an unusual one when exigencies of war so often dictated that it should be so.

The Squadron records show that before and after Dunkirk 74 became a very active outfit which suddenly found itself in the thick of things. The German invasion of Norway had marked the end of the Phoney War in May 1940 and within very short order Luxembourg, Holland and Belgium fell. At the same time the Battle of France, and the severe mauling of the aircraft supporting the British Expeditionary Force, was heading towards a climax. Reinforcements were sent to the latter theatre as it was realised that only fighter aircraft could achieve the necessary air superiority that would protect the forces on the ground. Ten Hurricane squadrons were deployed by May 10th, the day all RAF leave was stopped. But Sir Hugh Dowding refused, despite intense pressure, to release any of his remaining Hurricane and Spitfire squadrons, 74 included, to France. To do so, he argued, would have seriously jeopardised Britain's own defence. The War Cabinet under the leadership of the new Prime Minister, Churchill, for the moment agreed but within a few days, as the Germans relentlessly rolled forward, more Hurricanes were ordered across the Channel. In the event they couldn't be accommodated – there were insufficient airfields remaining – and the final six Hurricane squadrons in Fighter Command operated from airfields in Kent in support of the beleaguered British and French armies. By May 21st all RAF assets had been withdrawn back to England. As far as AOC 11 Group, Air Vice Marshal Keith Park, was concerned, this meant that he was able to concentrate all his resources on the job in hand, the covering of the withdrawal from Dunkirk. By the end of the evacuation every

Fighter Command squadron except three in Scotland had been involved in one way or another. And despite the assertion of many soldiers on the beaches of France withstanding constant attack by the Luftwaffe and German artillery that they hadn't seen the Royal Air Force, the record shows differently. Fighter Command lost almost 100 aircraft (of which 42 were Spitfires) during the 2,739 sorties that had been flown directly in support of Operation Dynamo. 338,000 soldiers were successfully brought back across the Channel.

As far as the Tigers were concerned, pre-Dunkirk standing convoy patrols had been flown over the Thames and offensive patrols flown from Ostend down to Calais looking for enemy aircraft. Many of these patrols were flown out of contact with Controllers in England as the TR9D radios with which the Spits were fitted were not good – they had a very poor reception/transmission range. It then became very apparent that the BEF and allied soldiers were being pushed relentlessly back to the coast and suddenly Fighter Command were generating 300 sorties a day, often at extreme range, in an effort to stop the Luftwaffe from attacking the retreating men. As the army spilled over onto the beaches, the Tigers were patrolling the skies overhead, providing top cover against bombers. It proved to be dangerous work and 74 lost men and aircraft doing it. In the main though they were not involved in attacks on the approaching

John Freeborn stands proudly on the wing of 'his' Spitfire ZP-C at Manston

At Rochford during the time of the Dunkirk evacuation Left to right Bertie Aubert (sitting), Don Cobden (standing), Paddy Treacy (standing) Laurie White (sitting), Ernie Mayne (standing behind White), Flt Sgt Llewellyn, Mungo Park (standing), Derek Dowding (sitting foreground), Tinky Measures (sitting behind Dowding), John Freeborn and Tony Mould (standing) and Sammy Hoare (lounging!)

German army – at this stage that was left to the units still operating from French soil – although on one occasion Sailor Malan was persuaded to do so: they soon learned that flying at 2,000ft over Panzers was a bad move and John recalls hearing enemy cannon shells whooshing over his canopy as he climbed for all he was worth to get out of danger.

It was not a happy time. Flying over Dunkirk and the surrounding area was a sorry, sad experience and only too graphically showed the extent of the retreat and the scale of the impending evacuation. Thousands of men were crowding onto the beach exposed to enemy gunfire: covering destroyers offshore were being targeted by the Luftwaffe. On an early evening patrol on May 21st Malan and Aubert despatched a Ju88 and He111 each: Measures got a probable He111: and John claimed a probable Ju88 as well, his first German of the war and of which he simply says it was 'bloody good'. John learned to respect the Ju88 as the days passed. In the right hands it could give a Spitfire a run for its money. If you got on its tail it would extend flaps and air brakes and virtually stop in the air and you would simply sail past, unable to do anything about it. Once past, the 88 could turn and make its getaway.

On the following day's first dawn sortie John shared another Junkers with Sailor and Tony Mould. On the 23rd Paddy Byrne was reported missing and, after sharing his Henschel with Measures, Laurie White came to grief as already recounted. The 24th was a particularly active day. Malan shared in the destruction of an He111 with Brian Draper, H M Stephen, Tinky Measures and Don Cobden – the German didn't really stand a chance against such a concerted attack! H M Stephen featured again with a shared Hs126 with John Mungo Park and Paddy Treacy. Bill Skinner got a Ju88 and Derek Dowding a Do17 and shared another with Treacy (after which the Irishman disappeared for the first time) with both of them also claiming a probable Ju88.

– o O o –

There are several names here for which it is worth pausing and considering John's recollections of them. Brian Draper was a lady's man, a real lady killer. John could probably identify quite readily with him for John himself wasn't averse to flirtations with the opposite sex which unsurprisingly goes for a good number of his colleagues too! Amongst many amorous adventures he recalls from this period were those involving Billie who was in the ticket booth at the cinema in Romford. Don Cobden, an accomplished All Black rugby player with twenty eight caps for his country, also pursued her (as did Bertie Aubert briefly). John and Don would go to the cinema as a duo and she would come and join them after her ticket selling duties had been concluded. However relationships came to an abrupt end when she contracted scarlet fever and John and Don had no option but to declare that they had been in 'contact' with her. As a result they were immediately quarantined for three weeks so as not to infect the camp. They didn't contract the disease – but the preventative treatment was most unpleasant!

Young Derek Dowding had arrived from Cranwell fairly early on in the course of the war and with one eye on his habit of untidy dressing was quickly popularly nicknamed 'scruffy' Dowding in deference to his famous father's 'stuffy' Dowding. Was it his talking to Sir Hugh about Laurie White that prompted the latter's moving on for Malan to take over in August? Derek was a nice chap – but he simply couldn't care less, perhaps once again a legacy of his father's high standing and Derek's act of rebellion? John recalls him arriving back on the Squadron one night, drunk as a billy goat, and driving his Riley Imp straight into a Spitfire which didn't please Sir Hugh at all – so much so that he wasn't on the Squadron for much longer afterwards and was sent off to Transport Command. But whilst with 74 he was a great source of information for, despite everything, there were times when he did actually seem to get on with his dad. It was through young Derek for example that they a little later learnt of Sir Hugh's constant threat of sacking by Churchill during the time of the Battle of Britain – a fact not always appreciated in accounts of that period. This source of information could however have come to an unexpected and bloody end – John nearly shot Derek with a Smith and Wesson which he had got hold of and which went off accidentally, the bullet passing through a door panel and window and whistling past a bemused Dowding Jnr. who happened to be in the vicinity at the time!

John has a great fondness for Sir Hugh, who had been C in C Fighter Command since 1936. He may have been 'stuffy' as his nickname implies, but he thought highly of all his men and did all he could to make life easier for them which in turn endeared him to them and earned their respect. There was, for example, an occasion when John landed a Spitfire with the undercarriage retracted. This was whilst he was practising emergency landings at Hornchurch. He was at 4,000ft over the aerodrome and closed the throttle which immediately set off the warning horn in the cockpit – which became annoying so John switched it off! He executed a series of S turns and positioned himself for a perfect landing but having forgotten in the meantime about his undercarriage. After the incident a Court of Enquiry was convened (John attended quite a few of these during his career!) – and he was ordered to appear before Keith Park in company with Sammy Sampson. He received a severe reprimand and was fined £5. Sir Hugh had to confirm the finding – which he did, but paid the £5 himself as he was aware that a Pilot Officer on his pay couldn't afford to do so! Incidentally, it emerged afterwards that the wheels-up landing could have been avoided for it was watched from the ground by a Sqn Ldr Donaldson who John was to come across again in the States (by which time he had been promoted). Donaldson was at Hornchurch on the day of John's incident and watched him approach with his wheels firmly in the up position. Donaldson could have waved him round or alerted him to his dilemma. Instead he chose to leave things be 'just,' as he explained to a reception he was attending in the USA, 'to see what happened.' This amused and impressed nobody.

Following the Court of Enquiry John received a letter from the Air Ministry recording their displeasure at the incident. John had this framed in a toilet seat and hung on his quarter's wall. An AOC's inspection of Hornchurch followed shortly afterwards – and the framed letter was discovered and noted. This prompted a second letter recording further displeasure at the way in which the first had been treated – this too was framed in a loo seat! Both trophies were lost when John was on detachment to Manston and his room was used by visiting aircrew.

11 Group's AOC AVM Keith Park was an easy going and typical New Zealander, an up front man, one of the boys – a fact which did not stop him from imposing sentence when sentence was due as John had found out. Most people got on very well with him as he had a knack of taking notice of what pilots had to say. Only Douglas Bader seemed incapable of working with him – and that was probably because he couldn't always get his own way. Bader's nickname when he was CO of 242 Squadron was Dogsbody, taken from his initials 'DB'. If you were in Bader's squadron you found yourself under a hard and unrelenting taskmaster of single minded purpose. A little later in 1940 when 74 was pulled from the Battle of Britain for rest at Wittering and then moved to Coltishall, Bader contacted Malan about participating in his Big Wing – a flawed concept which in many people's opinion (Keith Park included) should never have happened. But happen it did. Actually the idea came from Leigh Mallory, AOC 12 Group, but such was Bader's enthusiasm for it that he has often been mistakenly quoted as its originator. 74

flew down from Coltishall to Duxford to make up the complement of two Spitfire squadrons alongside three Hurricane squadrons. One factor which had been overlooked was that you couldn't get a Big Wing of five squadrons of aircraft off the ground very quickly. You could rarely start a Spit on anything but a trolley-ack for internal battery power was not enough. And there weren't enough trolley-acks to go round. So the first wave of aircraft would go off and burn precious fuel as they flew in circles waiting for the rendezvous with the next wave. On one particular day that John recalls the five squadrons did eventually get off to intercept an incoming raid but Bader took the Wing the wrong way! John came across a lone Do215 and shot it down (as will be described in the next chapter). This was the only aircraft destroyed by any of the five squadrons. The Big Wing was unwieldy. You couldn't keep it together. Attacking with relatively small formations of aircraft was the preferred option.

John Mungo Park had joined the RAF from the Fleet Air Arm in 1939. He was a Liverpudlian and a charming man, a real gentleman and very gregarious. In the air he was an average pilot and an average shot who flew many sorties with H M Stephen as his No 2 or vice versa. He had rarely led the Squadron until he was made Commanding Officer in March 1941 when Malan was posted to command the Biggin Hill Wing and in truth he made a good, fair CO who led from the front. He was sorely missed when shot down and killed. There is no apparent animosity when John Freeborn speaks of John Mungo Park today but he does question his promotion as the Tiger's CO. The fact that he was not experienced in leading the Squadron into battle meant that he had no first hand knowledge to fall back on which surely should have been a pre-requisite or at the very least useful. As much a gentleman as Mungo Park was, as nice a person as he was, and as keen as he was, in John's opinion he was not really the ideal choice for command. John had lashings of such experience – he had regularly led 74 yet was not considered for promotion to command. Why? Because of Sailor who ensured that John was blocked at every turn both in terms of medals and promotion. There is nothing in the records to suggest that this was the case but if the promotion had gone his way John freely admits that he would not necessarily have found the responsibility an easy one to bear, even as a man who relished responsibility.

There may have been no hint of animosity between Freeborn and Mungo Park but there is evidence of much between Freeborn and Harborn Mackay Stephen who John views as having been too close to Malan. This being the case, they were possibly in cahoots when it came to victories claimed. Listening to Stephen, John says, the Germans were lined up waiting to fight. Not so! One minute the sky was empty – the next they were there – then it was empty again. The truth was you didn't engage if you didn't want to. Those who claim they were in continuous dog fights are not being truthful – it simply didn't happen like that.

There is considerable evidence, however, that H M Stephen was not John's greatest fan either. There was certainly no love lost between them. Before his death in late 2001, H M did concede that Freeborn made a real go of the often difficult conditions in which the Squadron were expected to work, live and sleep. But his major memory is of John exclaiming over the RT 'there is only one good German – a dead one!' as he apparently prepared to gun a Luftwaffe pilot hanging in his parachute. A blazing row ensued with Stephen defending the right of a German pilot to be given the chance of life. 'We were there,' he says 'to shoot Germans in aircraft, not after they had baled out.' 'I was there', counters John,' to give them a damn good scare. If they were hanging in their 'chute then we would either fly by them as closely as possible or give them a burst of machine gun fire across the top of the canopy. To gun them in the harness was not something any of us were liable to do.' Incidentally, British and German parachutes were easily distinguishable with the shroud lines of the former leading directly to the shoulder harness and to a single line leading to the harness in the latter.

– o O o –

The Tigers were cock-a-hoop as the 24th drew to a close given their successes of the day, although that success was tempered by the loss of Bertie Aubert. Bertie had been posted as missing on the 21st after his successful action against a Ju88 and He111 but returned to Hornchurch, having force landed near Calais, only to take off again within a few hours on a patrol south of Dunkirk and be shot down. Bertie was something of an enigma to several on the Squadron. John, for instance, always thought there was a spy amongst them – and Bertie Aubert, an American from San Diego who had enlisted in the RAF via Canada, was the candidate. He always seemed to stick up for Hitler and came over as being very pro the Nazis. Shortly after his loss at Dunkirk under circumstances which were not entirely clear the Germans were reported as flying a Spitfire – and popular opinion was that it was Bertie Aubert's.

The fact that John's log books were lost during the war means that there is sometimes inevitably conflict between official records, unofficial records and John's memory. On 24th May he got a probable Bf109 according to the official line. John is sure he got a pair of Bf109s and a Ju88 on that day but concedes that he could be wrong despite the sometimes inaccurate reporting that went on at the time, reporting on which Air Ministry records depended. There was no contact with the enemy on the 25th but on the 26th, the day that Operation Dynamo, the evacuation of the British Expeditionary Force from Dunkirk was inaugurated, H M Stephen, Ernie Mayne and Don Cobden shared an Hs126. On the 27th Sailor got a Bf109 and damaged a Do215, Ernie Mayne and Paddy Treacy got a Bf109 each and Bill Skinner a Do17. Paddy Treacy and H M Stephen shared a Do17 as did Tinky Measures and Peter St John. Peter Stevenson got a probable Bf109 and Don Cobden a probable Do17. Sailor shared a damaged Do17 with Derek Dowding.

As for John Freeborn on this very active day, he got a confirmed and a probable Bf109. The confirmed kill followed John finding it 'knocking hell out of a Spitfire'. John got on his tail and the German pulled the usual trick of pushing the stick right forward – which the Spitfire couldn't emulate because of its carburation. Instead John half rolled and went through cloud after him, emerging with the 109 right in front (and with a vivid impression even 60 years after of a farmer ploughing a field below him). He gave it two or three short bursts.

He was smoking and not doing very well at all. I got alongside him and looked at the German pilot thinking it's a bloody shame but you are going to be dead in a minute. He went down, hitting a telegraph pole and then crashing through a farmhouse, demolishing it, the whole aircraft emerging from the other side.

John felt no personal animosity towards the German – he was simply a professional doing his job. But he was terribly saddened by the deaths of anybody in the house itself. They wouldn't have stood a chance. As the years have passed it is these incidents that have caused John considerable remorse – the civilian casualties as opposed to the military.

On the same day John's records show an He111 as destroyed by him – but this is not confirmed elsewhere. What did happen at the end of that day though was the whole Squadron being withdrawn from Hornchurch and being sent up to Leconfield to recuperate – ground crew making the journey by Bristol Bombay. It was a great relief to them all not to not be in the thick of the fighting, not to see the harrowing scenes of defeat below them: to have no worry, no upset – just getting on with day to day training activities. Over a period of six days they had scored nineteen confirmed victories and ten probables set against four of their own pilots missing – Aubert, Hoare, Byrne and Treacy. Sailor was awarded the DFC.

Whilst at Leconfield 74 received a letter from Hugh Dowding – as indeed did all Fighter Command squadrons. Addressed to his 'Fighter Boys' it read:

I don't send out many complimentary letters and signals but I felt that I must take this occasion, when the intense fighting in Northern France is for the time being over, to tell you how proud I am of you and the way in which you have fought since the Blitzkrieg started. I wish I could have spent my time visiting you and hearing your account of the fighting but I have occupied myself working for you in other ways. I want you to know that my thoughts are always with you and that it is you and your fighting spirit which will crush the morale of the German Air Force and preserve our country through the trials which yet lie ahead.

After Dunkirk John was sent to testify at a Court of Enquiry (at Adastral House) to give his view as to what had happened there. Why had the army had to evacuate? What had gone wrong on the ground? What was the perspective of events from the air? John recalls this as a very interesting if intimidating experience (would he be blamed for the failures at Dunkirk?!), enduring long and serious sessions with severe looking gentlemen. He was not alone of course. Many other witnesses were called and the Navy and Army held similar enquiries of their own. The ultimate objective was to present a report to government and highlight the salutary lessons that might be learned from what was actually a humiliating experience turned to triumph by dint of the successful evacuation.

John by now had been officially promoted to Flight Commander (as a Pilot Officer) and it was in this capacity that he and the Tigers returned to Hornchurch on June 6th. Dunkirk having fallen they were back on to convoy and reconnaissance patrols with no contact with the enemy until the 10th when Ben Draper damaged a Bf109 and Do17. At Hornchurch they were operating from dispersal huts, on alert for twelve hours at a stretch at fifteen minutes readiness, reduced to just five as the days passed by and tensions heightened still further.

– o O o –

It was around this time that several Tigers volunteered to have a go at some night time interceptions. A flare path was laid out (using paraffin filled goose neck flares) with a trailer mounted Chance light at one end of the landing strip. Sailor and John alternately were in charge of the night flying programme and maintained contact with aircraft by means of a portable aircraft radio and battery, communicating with a flying helmet and Aldis lamp. John never had a contact at night in the air – not like Malan who was immediately successful on the night of the 18th/19th June with two He111s downed on his first sortie, thus becoming the first single seat aircraft pilot of the Second World War to destroy an enemy machine at night, not to mention the first to get a double kill in one night. Others, however, were not so successful and after their first attempts had many reservations about the whole business until the war entered the Battle of Britain phase and as angry young men who saw their capital city under increasing threat of damage and destruction they were more prepared and motivated to take the fight to the enemy day and night. Aircraft operated in total silence – there was no radio/radar vectoring – and pilots had to find their quarry themselves. The only clue they would have would be information given before take off that bandits were to be found in such and such a sector. On the night Sailor got his pair of He111s, Germans were flying around the Thames estuary and were relatively easy prey for any fighters that could be vectored on to them. Malan got the information as to where they were, saw his chance and took off. John wanted to go but was not allowed to: his immediate responsibilities were on the ground.

At this time 74 were getting through a prodigious amount of flying. There was no let up. After night patrols the Squadron would be in the air again at first light for the northern France reconnaissance flights from Lille to Bethune to the Channel, looking for evidence of the build up of aircraft on the occupied airfields or of invasion barges in the ports. Recces were inexplicably held at regular times which was a great advertisement for the Luftwaffe fighters! After the recces, offensive patrols continued to be flown but with little success other than for Ben Draper who had damaged a Bf109 and He111 on the 10th June, two probable He111s for Tinky Measures and Derek Dowding on the 6th July, another He111 shared by the same pair with Bill Skinner on the 8th and on the afternoon of the same day, Tony Mould forcing a 109 to land at Eltham and Peter Stevenson shooting another down over the sea.

People in the air and on the ground were again getting very tired and increasingly stressed too. It was not a good time. And then the Battle of Britain started.

Ben Draper, H M Stephen and Sailor Malan. Peter, Sailor's dog, always uncannily ran to the right aircraft to greet his master when the Squadron landed

Chapter 6
The Battle of Britain

Fighter Command emerged from the Battle of France in a seriously depleted condition having lost 453 Spitfires and Hurricanes. But there were now to be a few weeks grace (as the Luftwaffe itself prepared for the next phase of the German advance and invasion of Britain) to enable some of the damage to be repaired. Statistics relating to July 7th, just three days before the Battle of Britain is deemed to have started, show that Fighter Command could muster 52 squadrons with 644 aircraft and 1,259 pilots available to fly them. Then of course there were the ground crews to ensure they did fly: the staff at Command HQ at Bentley Priory, Groups, Sectors and Stations: operators of the growing and vital radar chain: and those who worked in the Maintenance Units. It was from Bentley Priory that the RAF's involvement in the Battle of Britain was to be controlled.

Although re-equipment had been encouraging, aeroplanes and pilots were still both scarce resources in terms of what Fighter Command might be called upon to do. 74 lost a lot of people during this time. The old hands survived but many new hands didn't despite being encouraged to avoid combat if it were reasonable to do so without compromise. John saw many new faces coming and going on the Squadron during the summer of 1940. Some were only around for a few days – young men from public schools, from working class backgrounds, from nice homes and caring families. Their deaths all seemed so unnecessary.

Much nonsense has been written as to how fighter pilots conducted themselves when they were not fighting. The common perception is that they flocked to the bar, quaffed many a pint and all stood around a piano singing the popular songs of the day before they wrecked it! This was patently not the case. Of course there were good parties and very often, when a colleague was lost, it was a traditional thing to honour him at the bar. But on a Pilot Officer's pay of 14/2d a day (or £1/0/9d as a Flight Lieutenant) it simply couldn't be afforded every evening. Even more to the point, pilots were generally so tired at the end of the day that they headed straight for bed. Being on standby from first light until it got dark – and of course in the summer that could be from 4.00am to 9.30pm – meant a long, exhausting and stressful shift, particularly if you had been scrambled, very often more than once during a day.

John's usual mount in the air was ZP-C although no particular aircraft was officially assigned to individual pilots. And if Dunkirk hadn't thrown the quality of their aircraft as compared with the Luftwaffe into perspective for these young, boyish fighter pilots, wise and experienced beyond their years, the Battle of Britain did. By this time 74 were re-equipping with the Spitfire IIa.

We've already seen John's views on the Hurricane – he was certainly thankful that 74 were not equipped with the type and jokes 'I think I'd have deserted if we had!' The Hurricane was of course a great aeroplane and four out of five victories during the Battle were scored by them (because there were many more of them in the air) but Spitfires were more organised – the cockpit was logically neat and tidy as opposed to the Hawker design. It had its own very memorable smell too – very much like that of a new car of the day and cellulose based. It was far from unpleasant and never really left the Spitfire however often it may have been used and however hard it had been flown. It was added to each time the Spitfire fired its guns for when armourers had completed their rearming, a dope patch was fixed over the gun ports and this too was cellulose based. One smell that is equally memorable but in a different sense is that of German bullets. They smelled like excrement when they hit although to this day John has never discovered what caused it. Conversely when the Spitfires guns were fired there was no associated smell – no cordite, no burning. Interestingly too, when firing there was no really discernible increase in noise, partly due to the tight fitting helmet with sculpted recesses for the pilot's ears. Not that the Spit was a particularly noisy aeroplane in the first place. But there was a noticeable increase in vibration. And what always intrigued John was that in certain light conditions on the Spitfire Vs he could actually see the cannon shells leaving the gun's muzzle! Tracer was not used as it didn't fly true, the flight path decaying fairly rapidly. De Wilde ammunition with its explosive tips sparked the target when it hit and was thus an accurate firing guide.

Spitfires did have their shortcomings. They were relatively short legged. Carrying 87 gallons of fuel and with a lot of power on all the time when flying sorties during the Battle, endurance could be measured in half hours. And if early examples had had cannon rather than machine guns they could have achieved much more – the difference between .303 bullets and 20mm shells was decisive. Initial problems with installing cannon in Spits centred around the wing shape which had to be modified to house the ammunition drum which held just 120 rounds. This could be interpreted as a case of under-arming until it is realised that just one shell could destroy an enemy aircraft if accurately fired. But 74 never had cannon armed Spits at this stage of the war. To illustrate the point about the machine gun v cannon issue, John recalls a Do215 which he caught over London. He shot at it with his machine gun armed Spitfire from all quarters all the way to Ashford. He could see the strikes on the Dornier and the crew had probably been killed, or seriously injured, at an early stage in John's attack – but it just wouldn't go down until the coast was reached. Cannon would have despatched it at the first pass. Eight guns and lightweight ammunition didn't do the job, even for John who always had his guns synchronised at 100 yards – which was pretty close. 200 yards was the norm. But whatever the armament issues, in those early days of machine guns pilots were quietly confident of the fact they would work smoothly and well – a tribute both to the design and to the fitter armourers who looked after them

In the Spitfire pilots always knew they had one advantage over Bf109s – at least up to around 30,000ft. The turning circle was tighter and they could thus turn inside the Messerschmitt – the wing loading on the British design being considerably lower and even more so as far as the Fw190 was concerned. Clipped wings such as on the Spitfire V were also an advantage, endowing the aircraft as they did with a better roll rate thereby enhancing its agility – although that was about the only advantage that version had over the Merlin 12 engined Spitfire IIa which was a far better machine and, of all the marks he flew, was certainly John's favourite. Speed as between the Spitfire and Messerschmitt was neck and neck. The latter had the advantage at height because of its injection rather than carburettered engine. And at this stage of the war as we have just seen, the German aircraft's cannon as against the machine guns of the Spitfire could be telling. However the 109 was very difficult to pull out of a dive and there are instances recorded of British pilots getting onto the tail of a German and following him right down, pulling out at the last minute and leaving the Messerschmitt to crash. Al Deere recorded at least one such kill.

– o O o –

From the German perspective the new phase of the air war signalled a change in tactics from convoy attack to airfield attack to the bombing of London: the latter

John Freeborn gets in on the act with a dog! Taken at Manston with Roger Boulding to his left and Sqn Ldr Wood to Boulding's left. Wood was a well liked supernumerary who flew with the Tigers for some weeks

in particular made John and his colleagues very angry and even more determined men. 74 increasingly flew regularly at night on patrol over the capital – not as a squadron but individually. Flying from Hornchurch, Rochford or Manston, on the approach to London a pair of searchlights would be lit and aircraft were given fifteen minutes to get through the portals of this illuminated gateway at 12,000ft at a prearranged time. Once through they were on their own with five minutes to attack and get out. Aircraft were by now equipped with IFF but that did not always mean AA fire didn't assume you were the enemy once in the Inner Artillery Zone. On one occasion John recalls he went through the gateway, climbed to 20,000ft with his IFF on but was hit by a full barrage of flak. His aircraft was peppered but he made it back to base and got his aircraft down safely. Within minutes he was airborne again in a second Spitfire and passed through the 'gate'. London was being bombed to hell – but in terms of enemy aircraft John saw 'not a bloody thing'. As he was letting down to land back at Hornchurch he suddenly saw sparks passing the cockpit from rear to front and it took a few seconds to realise they were going in the wrong direction

John Freeborn concentrates on his cards at Manston's dispersal whilst fellow Tigers, fully kitted up, prefer to relax as they await the next scramble

to be sparks! It was a marauding Ju88: John was attempting to land during the course of an intruder attack on the airfield. Mercifully the '88 missed John but sadly got a Beaufighter that was also attempting to land. John cleared the area and returned after a while once he could be sure the German had gone. Evidently it had only just done so for this time jittery personnel on top of the watch office opened fire and for the second time in one night peppered John's aircraft. Almost against the odds, this time he landed safely.

Aside from these moments of excitement both at the hands of the enemy and friendly forces there were also peaceful occasions when time could be taken to view the beauty of the world and John recalls some wonderfully clear, moonlit nights when he patrolled the south coast and could seemingly see for ever. He will always remember the times when he could see his home airfield from many, many miles out despite the blackout regime – there was no lunar blackout! – and the long slow approaches that he made when the instruction to land came. Not that such nights were always without incident. Operating uneventfully out of Rochford on a very cold one (on the Ashford – Bradwell Bay patrol line), as John prepared for a return to base he felt a jarring bump. There was no impairment of his controls and he saw nothing around him. It was only when he was on the ground that a hole in his wing was discovered and feathers embedded in his radiator cowling. It was probably a goose.

– o O o –

But it was only on the rare occasion that relaxation in the air could be afforded. The pages of history tell us that Battle of Britain started on July 10th for this is the date from which the Luftwaffe concentrated their daytime operations against British ports and convoys in the Channel and North Sea. Operating from Manston (flying in from Hornchurch in the mornings and returning in the evenings) to give them more time over the sea, the Tigers flew constant convoy patrols, their brief being to prevent attacks on shipping. These were quite harrowing in the sense that the sight of ships that had been sunk or damaged by magnetic mines became too commonplace for any pilots' liking. Magnetic mines were unpredictable things. Three or four ships could pass over one safely then the next could detonate it. At low tide on the sands around the Thames Estuary the skeletal shapes of funnels and masts were stark reminders of their effectiveness. As the war progressed convoys came to be routed around the north of Scotland, through the Pentland Firth into the Atlantic, rather than try and squeeze them through the vulnerable constriction of the Channel. They would meet up with other vessels from Southampton, the Clyde and Mersey to form States bound convoys. But there still had to be London bound traffic and the area around the North Foreland in particular was one in which all protective squadron patrols had to be particularly alert.

At Manston, the Tigers really were in the front line as Luftwaffe attacks increased and they were always amongst the first of the squadrons to be scrambled. Sometimes this would amount to just three aircraft depending upon serviceability or the fact that other aircraft were already deployed. John remembers such occasions vividly and recalls the daunting prospect of facing up to large enemy formations with so few aircraft as being 'rather intimidating'. Of course things did improve and the RAF was able to put up more Spitfires and Hurricanes. In the face of this mounting opposition the Germans pressed on but gradually the RAF's terrier like methods began to pay off but only at the cost of a considerable number of lives.

Manston was an airfield which John remembers with some affection. This large grass expanse was heavily populated with hares, attracted there no doubt by the vibration generated by running Merlins. That summer of 1940 was by and large an

The Tigers at Manston during the summer of 1940. From left to right are Kirk, Franklin, Richardson, unidentified, unidentified, Baker with the dog by him, unidentified immediately behind, Boulding, Szczesny, Malan, unidentified, Mungo Park, Draper, unidentified, St. John, Skinner, Hilken and Chesters. Some John remembers so clearly: others, who probably passed through the Squadron in a matter of days or weeks, he cannot put names to

idyllic one weatherwise (except for a short period during the middle of July), all the very best an English summer could offer. There is a familiar image of skies of brilliant blue, of glorious dawns and fiery sunsets – the sort of weather that had no right to be given the danger the country faced, danger that in people's minds should have provoked rain and storm. But instead in the weeks ahead as the crystal clear conditions prevailed the counties of Kent and Sussex were given grandstand views of the battle that was to rage overhead, a perverse beauty and symmetry of vapour trails against the flawless blue. The cinema has conjured up pictures for us of fighter pilots sitting in the warm sun at dispersal waiting for the alarm, reading, playing cards, chatting, smoking, dozing… then the incessant and urgent clang of the warning triangle. Suddenly the lounging pilots would be galvanised into action – chairs would be tipped over, coffee spilt, newspapers abandoned as they leaped up and raced for their waiting aircraft. And it was like that – exactly like that! Every time a Spitfire landed it was immediately prepared for the next sortie – refuelled and rearmed, cockpit prepared, helmet on stick, parachute in place, straps thrown over the cockpit side, oxygen tube connected, radio lead plugged in. The scrambled pilot clambered up onto the wing and slipped into his seat. He was followed by his fitter who would throw the straps into position and fasten them. The fitters were first class and without them the scramble would never have been executed so smoothly – two minutes from warning to take off. The only potential snags would be if an aircraft had landed in an unserviceable state and you were allocated someone else's. No one on 74 relished the prospect of jumping into the long-legged Don Cobden's usual mount – it took what seemed an

Manston during the first phase of the Battle of Britain, Summer 1940. The formidable firepower (l to r) of Willie Nelson, Piers Kelly, Peter Stevenson, Don Cobden, Dennis Smith, 'Sailor' Malan, John Mungo Park, John Freeborn, Douglas Hastings, Thomas Kirk, Ernie Mayne and Bill Skinner who between them accounted for 104 enemy aircraft shot down

An A Flight accident which John cannot recall!

inordinate amount of time to readjust the seat!

There would be plenty of scrambles in the weeks ahead – starting on the morning of the 10th July when a formation of eight of 74's Spitfires encountered a huge enemy armada – twenty Do17s, forty Bf109s and forty Bf110s. Coming up against these numbers of enemy aircraft became the norm but in John's case didn't particularly fill him with dread.

Once we entered the fray we were on our own. We concentrated on the German we were after and as such we were our own masters. In a one to one situation I was confident that I could always come out on top, added to which was the thought that I could fight without endangering anybody else's life – my number two for example who would be in the sky somewhere looking after himself – and so on. One thing that did astound us all was the fact that despite losses, the Luftwaffe could continually send such numbers of aircraft against us.

Despite being so hopelessly outnumbered on this occasion 74 dived into the attack and in the frenetic, whirling series of dog fights that ensued Mungo Park was credited with the first victory for the Squadron during this phase of the war when he watched a Do17 he had attacked turn lazily onto its back and dive into the sea. In the same engagement Tinky Measures damaged a Bf110 and Do17 and saw two enemy aircraft collide. Peter St

Manston July 1940. H M Stephen

Summer 1940 Manston. A spot of bother! Fitters clamber over a listing Spitfire whilst Mungo Park (looking right), Malan and Dowding (both backs to camera) debate the incident

The cowling is off ZP-T with its offending twin wing-up behind

Damage at the front end!

John damaged a 109 and Peter Stevenson two 110s. Ben Draper inflicted damage on a Do17.

During the next sortie, by a formation of six A Flight Tigers, John Freeborn made his mark. A single photo-recce Do17 and thirty escorting Bf109s were sighted over North Foreland paying attention to a convoy emerging from the Thames Estuary prior to sailing down the Channel. 74 caught the Germans at 20,000ft and thus had a good height advantage but were a little late in getting after them having first concentrated on the Do17 which in the end got away. John shot the leading 109 down into the sea.

I was so close I could see everything on this Messerschmitt and could very clearly see the man in it. I fired from fifty yards and it seemed to go sideways in the sky – then he turned over on his back and dropped out of the sky.

Another 109 then appeared on his tail with John's No 2, Tony Mold, behind him in turn.

At that height we could outmanoeuvre the Germans in their 109s easily. I began a stall turn to get me onto his rear quarter so that I could shoot the bugger down.

John saw guns flame and then his own top tank rupture.

It was Tony. Whilst having a go at the 109 he was having a go at me as well! But it was the tank I was worried about – fortunately it was full for if it hadn't been the vapour would have exploded. As it was I turned everything off that I possibly could. The thought of fire frightened the hell out of me.

John had turned across Tony's line of fire just as the latter opened up. He limped back – just – to Manston with his aircraft riddled with bullet holes. Sitting on the aerodrome waiting to be picked up and to have his aircraft towed away he saw

Manston during the Battle of Britain. Sailor Malan with `his` Spitfire ZP-A

Summer 1940 - Manston. Front left Alan Ricalton next to John Mungo Park and Bill Skinner in the back seat

another Spitfire coming in to land.

It was so full of holes it shouldn't have been flying. He did a bullshit turn in to land, side slipped his height off and got it onto the ground. But as he did so it literally started to fall apart!

Tony and John later had many a good laugh about that incident although John still remembers his fear – indeed the fear of all fighter pilots – that he would catch fire. To more than even the score on the day though Peter Stevenson had got another 109 and four more had been damaged. But the recce Do17 had escaped and they all knew what that meant – a whacking great fight all the way down the Channel.

– o O o –

A period of bad weather followed and it was not until the 19th that 74 were in action again with Sailor and Peter Stevenson attacking a pair of 109s and claiming them as probables. On the 24th they had two abortive encounters with 109s at the extremity of their range and were forced to break off over the coast although John (in R6706), together with Don Cobden and Douglas Hastings, damaged a Dornier Do215. Taking off from Manston to patrol the Channel at twenty past five in the afternoon as part of A Flight, they were detailed to intercept a raid near Dover but as they approached found three 215s at sea level. The Dorniers saw the Spitfires and immediately turned for the French coast, opening fire from 2,000 yards with their rearward facing MG15 machine guns in the process in an attempt to scare the fighters off. Aircraft of Red and Yellow sections of A Flight nonetheless managed to close to 300 yards and opened fire themselves and damaged one of the Dorniers but felt it prudent to abandon the chase as the French coast was reached.

On the 28th action came fast and furious. The Squadron shot down five 109s and damaged five. But they lost one pilot, James Young, in the process and Tony Mould had to bale out of his damaged Spitfire. Controllers had put 74 into a beautiful position to intercept the Messerschmitts telling them to leave the bombers they were escorting to a Hurricane squadron which they were vectoring in. The problem was 'the rest of the German Air Force appeared to be up behind us!' as John recalls: under Malan's instructions he tried to draw them off. Young and Mould were flying as John's two and three but both were shot down in short order leaving John (in R6706 again) in the middle of thirty six 109s at 18,000ft. He shot one down but then the odds stared to tell and he was on the receiving end himself. He was chased right down to Brighton pier where he rolled and dived down towards it. At an indicated IAS of 360 knots the big ends of his engine went but he was flying at such a speed that he managed to glide back to Manston where he landed. The rudder had been hit and knocked into the main fin and was locked solid into the left rudder position. Once on the ground the aircraft ran on erratically – about which John could do nothing. A wing tip dug in and the Spitfire tipped over on to its nose, going into the vertical before falling back down on to its wheels and giving John the opportunity to make a hasty exit. He was bleeding from head to foot and he had Mungo Park's helmet on which had been well and truly christened. There was glass everywhere from the reflector sight which had taken a bullet. Goggles saved John's eyes but the rest of John's exposed body was peppered. Once in Sick Bay he was wiped down – and as dramatic as the blood had looked there was nothing apart from the abrasions caused by the glass. Within the hour, all thoughts of extended sick leave dashed, he was back in the air leading the Squadron.

The Tigers lost two more of their number off Folkestone at the end of the month – Sergeant 'Tiger Tim' Eley and Pilot Officer Harold Gunn – as the attrition that was to become inevitably associated with sustained operations set in. John had seen

Gunn, flying P9379, in trouble and had broken off an engagement with a 109 to help as his combat report tells:

I saw a large number of Bf109 A/C approaching the coast at 18,000 ft and I attacked them head on together with my section. The E/A broke and scattered into 9/10ths cloud, a number heading back out to sea. I gave chase and fired a long burst from 500 closing to 200 yards, causing the enemy to dive steeply. I scored direct hits as I could see my ammunition hitting home from such a close range. I had seen P/O Gunn being attacked by two E/A seconds before and decided to help him so left the enemy trailing smoke about 12 miles s.w. of Folkestone and heading towards the French coast.

Dispersal hut at Manston, Summer 1940. In the doorway are John Freeborn, Brian Draper and Walter Franklin on the step with John Mungo Park and Peter St John in front

Unfortunately this was to no avail as Harold Gunn was killed and came down in the sea. His body was recovered by a German E Boat and taken back to Belgium where he was buried.

For July overall 74's tally board read thirty enemy aircraft confirmed as destroyed and nineteen probables. In the process they had lost seven of their number but as is the way in the ups and downs of war, on the reverse side of the coin there was great pleasure on the Squadron as a DFC for John and a bar to his DFC for Sailor was announced on July 31st.

Manston Summer 1940

The *Yorkshire Post* quickly got hold of the story of the DFC and issued a rather stirring editorial:

When older heads were perturbed about the trend of events in 1938, seeking some means of averting what we all dreaded, a Headingley boy left the Leeds Grammar School and went into the RAF… He has been awarded the DFC. Seven Nazi warplanes have fallen to his skill and daring… He is a typical young Englishman, obviously not warlike, with no crack-brained conception about the grandeur of a Blitzkrieg. Yet this young man belongs to a great company of others who like him possess the stuff, the initiative, that will smash their regimented opponents. It is not beside the point that this particular one bears the name of Freeborn. So are they all free born – and they know and cherish the fact. We have not reared them for battle but for a full life, whatever their class or creed, and we must see to it that they get their ample share in the moulding of a cleaner, less money-grubbing homeland.

– o O o –

On August 8th Sailor Malan was made the Tigers' Commanding Officer. The reserve that had built up between him and John Freeborn after Barking Creek was still present but as the days of the Battle wore on it seemed there was no time or place for this. Having brushed aside their differences, John concentrated on the job in hand. Tactics were talked at length by everybody on the Squadron. Sailor himself was a great tactician and although in the main he preferred to evolve and implement them without consultation with others he did sometimes seek confirmation as to their practicality – and that was usually with John, a tacit acknowledgement of the latter's skill and understanding of this important facet of fighting. Under Sailor they learned various approaches. From the outset the three aircraft vic formation with a 'weaver' behind to protect it from enemy attack was abandoned in favour of flying in fours – the Finger Four. The big disadvantage of flying in vic is that you can't watch the other pilots' tails – hence the need for the weaver. With four aircraft you had in effect two pairs of aircraft, two No.1s and two No.2s, with the latter keeping an eye out for the former. Undoubtedly a good idea on paper, it came to be unworkable in the cut and thrust of combat. All too soon you could lose your No. 2 – or vice versa. As John constantly reminds us – once you had begun to mix it with a gaggle of enemy aircraft you could look round and in seconds find all your colleagues had disappeared – not having been shot down but having moved very quickly to another part of the sky.

Another variation on tactics on which Messrs Freeborn and Malan worked was to fly in pairs – usually line astern but sometimes side by side according to the situation. It was found that aircraft flying in this manner would have a greater chance of staying together in the same airspace. But the definitive formation was to fly three pairs of aircraft in vic with a copycat formation behind – twelve aircraft all able to see each other and pairs of aircraft within the vic able to look after each other.

There was also 74's well known *Ten of My Rules for Air Fighting* around this time – starting with 'wait until you see the whites of his eyes' and concluding with 'go in quickly – punch hard – get out!' Whilst Malan gave his name to these rules they were in fact an amalgam of ideas formed by the Squadron as a whole. But for the first ten days of August there was no opportunity to put them into practice for there was no contact with the Luftwaffe although that was not for want of trying. This was the beginning of the so-called second phase of the Battle of Britain – the German offensive against coastal airfields and radar stations. 74 were still flying from Hornchurch and Manston, sometimes achieving seventy aircraft sorties a day. It was not until the 11th that they hit the jackpot with an incredible day during which they flew as a Squadron into battle four times between dawn and 1400 hrs and destroyed twenty three enemy aircraft, one probable and fourteen damaged.

AIR MINISTRY (Dept.OA)
KING CHARLES STREET
WHITEHALL S.W.1

31st July, 1940.

Dear Freeborn,

My very best congratulations on the award of the Distinguished Flying Cross.

Yours sincerely,

Pilot Officer J.C. Freeborn, D.F.C.,
  No.74 Squadron,
    Royal Air Force,
      Manston, Kent.

Pilot Officer J.C. Freeborn, D.F.C.,
  No.74 Squadron,
    Royal Air Force,
      Manston, Kent.

CHIEF OF THE AIR STAFF

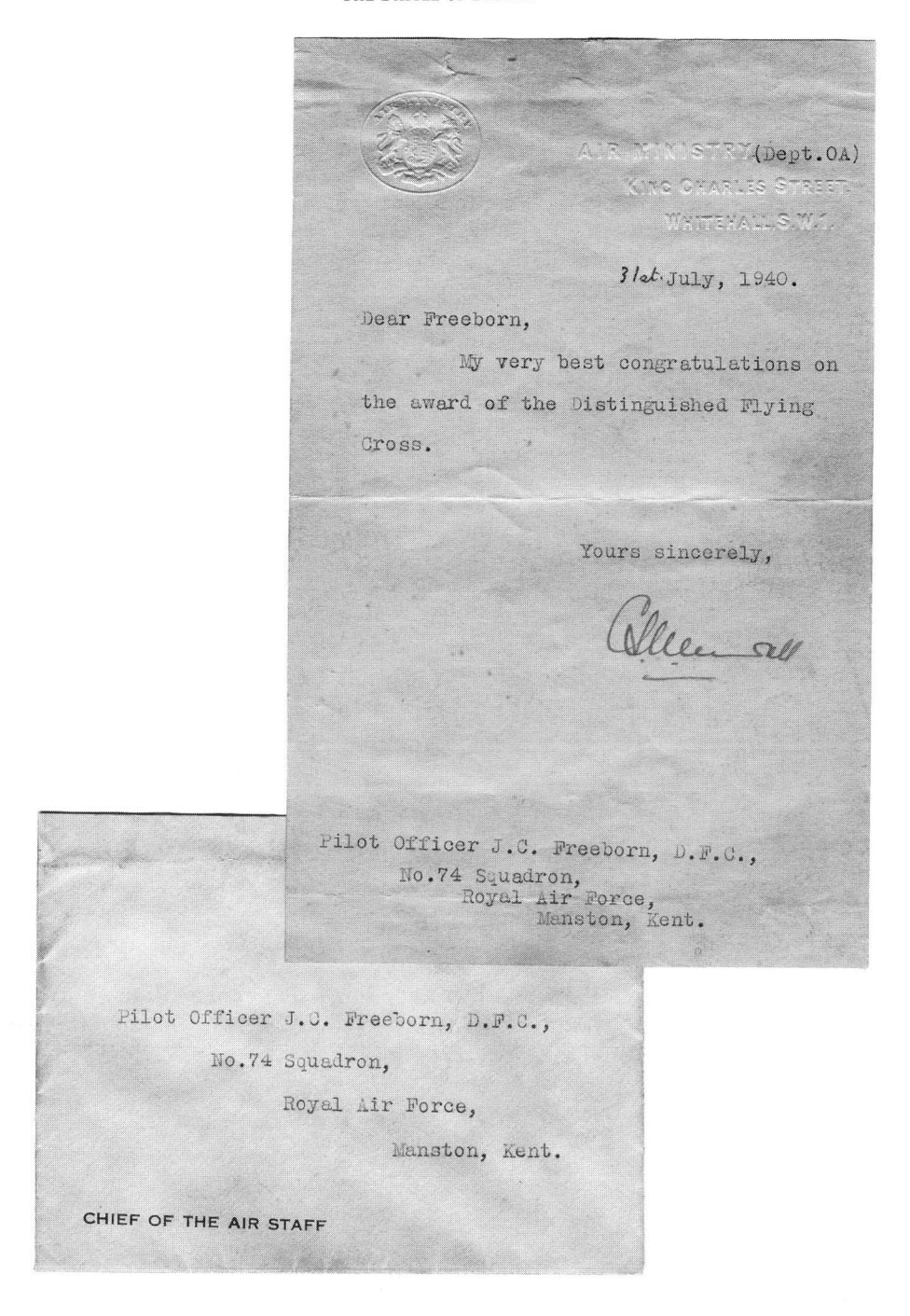

Congratulations from the Chief of the Air Staff on John`s DFC

This caused quite a stir. A telegram was received from the Chief of the Air Staff which simply said

...a magnificent days fighting 74...This is the way to keep the measure of the Boche. Mannock started it and you keep it up.

Churchill was aware of what had been achieved as well. In the evening of the day itself he arrived at Hornchurch to personally offer his congratulations to air and ground crew alike.

The first sortie had launched at dawn when eighteen Bf109s were caught at 20,000ft flying towards Dover. Eight were destroyed in the ensuing tussle and four damaged. Amongst those who scored was Peter Stevenson who watched his victim plunge vertically into the sea from 15,000ft. Peter then saw a further formation of 109s 2,000ft below him and manoeuvred to come up behind them from out of the sun but was himself caught as he dived towards them by further 109s coming out of the sun at him! It was his turn now to be trapped in a vertical dive as his Spitfire was peppered with cannon fire. He forced the hood back and the slip-stream tore him out of the cockpit. He pulled the ripcord having fortunately escaped relatively unscathed and came down in the Channel where he struggled for a while to release the parachute harness. He then spent ninety minutes in the heavy swell and by the time a Motor Torpedo Boat arrived he was pretty well exhausted. To attract attention he fired his revolver. Expending the first magazine without success – the MTB actually left the area – he frantically tried again when it returned and this time they saw him. Firing his second magazine off he managed to hit the launch! John recalls Peter very well as a bit of a ditherer but a lovely fellow. His father was Air Commodore Stevenson, Director of Operations for 11 Group.

John Freeborn in R6840 destroyed a 109 during the second sortie of the day on which twelve Spits took off mid morning to intercept enemy aircraft approaching Dover and engaged the Germans over mid Channel. He was with the third sortie too in the same aircraft – in fact he was leading the formation – when towards noon he and ten others having taken off to patrol a convoy to the east of Clacton climbed to 32,000ft with Ronnie Adams controlling. Ronnie was an actor in peace time and, John maintains, he thought he was still acting whilst controlling! (There were several instances of inopportune or inappropriate instruction over the radio – and not just by Ronnie Adams. 'Call me when you are out of range' was one of many classic directives issued!). On this occasion Ronnie had the Squadron at the wrong height and above 10/10ths cloud when he called bandits. John was unable to see them as they were below cloud so he had little option other than dive through.

The Squadron emerged in the centre of a formation of forty 110s east of Harwich. In the ensuing melee John destroyed two of the Messerschmitts. Others fell to Stephen, Mungo Park, Nelson, Tom Kirk, Skinner and the veteran and ever popular Ernie Mayne. The loss of Don Cobden and Dennis Smith on this sortie were 74's first (and only) casualties of this extraordinary day – and John has always had a nagging doubt as to whether the loss of at least one of these was not down to collision. To come blind out of cloud into a formation was undoubtedly an extremely risky and danger ridden experience.

The combat report that John filed for this action reads as follows:

Two of our A/C went down immediately. I made a sharp turn and got directly onto an E/A which I gave a short burst of 2/3secs and E/A turned and went down. I did not follow as many E/A were engaged and I had noted another of our a/c damaged. I was again attacked from astern by a 110... and I took decisive action coming up under him and sending a long burst into his tailplane. E/A fell as T/p broke up, falling in a spiral. I watched him go down to 5,000ft before breaking off due to being short of petrol and ammunition. I then returned to Hornchurch.

This was to be Ernie Mayne's last operational flight for he blacked out during the course of the fight and his Spitfire had fallen 20,000ft before he came to. The rapid drop had burst both his eardrums and he was grounded. The role of Training Officer which Ernie had filled in the pre-war years was one which had ceased to be officially held once the fighting started although training did, of course, continue – albeit on a more informal as and when basis. So no appointment was to be made to replace Ernie and instead Douglas 'Parrot' Hastings – he just wouldn't stop talking! – decided that it was a role he could unofficially fulfil himself. Sadly it didn't last long for Frank Buckland, a new pilot on the Squadron, flew right through Douglas when they were practising formation flying. This was in October when 74 had been temporarily withdrawn to Coltishall.

August 11th hadn't finished yet. By now thoroughly exhausted 74 took off for their fourth and final engagement in the early afternoon. The previous sorties had taken their toll on aircraft as well as men and only eight Spitfires were available to patrol Hawkinge and Margate at 15,000ft. Ten Ju87s were sighted passing through cloud at 6,000ft with twenty Bf109s above them at 10,000ft. Once again the Tigers roared into the attack, leaving the Ju87s and concentrating on the 109s and once again they got the better of their adversaries with four destroyed (one by John) and one damaged (this was John's too).

This had been the busiest day the Squadron was to have during the Battle and it seemed to the pilots that the Germans were relentlessly pushing everything they had towards England. It was the day that, if they were going to succeed in breaking the RAF, this would be it. Most pilots in most squadrons did come to think the unthinkable – the possibility of defeat – and many had a contingency plan of their own as to what they would do if the Battle was lost. John was no exception and he had determined that if it came to it he would fly up to the Orkneys, then Shetland, then the Faeroes and finally Iceland to escape, refuelling as best he could on the way. It is idle speculation to wonder whether, if he had had to put this plan into effect, he would have succeeded

There was some respite for the Tigers on the 12th – the day was spent in patching up their aircraft and in pilots recuperating back at Hornchurch. It was also the day that Manston was hit hard by the enemy and which 74 avoided by the skin of their teeth, 54 Squadron having flown in from Hornchurch to replace them. Do17s wreaked extensive damage. August 13th was *Adler Tag*, the day on which the Luftwaffe was to be finally victorious. Instead they lost forty five aircraft against the RAF's thirteen. It proved to be the day when the German High Command began to doubt their chances of invasion success and Goering's claims of victory in the air seemed nothing more than hollow words. Indeed within a month Operation Sealion was postponed by Hitler. It was a day on which once again 74 scored well – four Do17s and two Do215s destroyed: four Do17s and two Do215s claimed as probables: one Do17 damaged. Douglas Hastings' Do17 was the first to be shot down on this historic day and another fell to John (in R6840). The Tigers had been ordered to patrol Manston in the early morning and had been vectored onto an incoming raid of forty aircraft in four sections line astern which they saw at 3,000 feet, just below cloud base, off Whitstable. They surprised the enemy and in the words of the ORB 'a grand dogfight ensued.' But they lost aircraft as well – although on this occasion no pilots. Piers Kelly (in R6759) was hit by return fire from one of the Dorniers and his coolant tank was punctured. He force landed safely. Henryk Szczesny (in K9871) found he couldn't lower his undercarriage when he came in to land and belly landed at West Malling but was unhurt. His Polish colleague Brzezina baled out of N3091 after being hit. He too landed, safe and unhurt.

– o O o –

Such had been the pace of battle that 74 were now withdrawn from the front line to rest and recuperate at Wittering with the Spitfires diverting in after their final sortie of the day on the 14th and the groundcrew and equipment flying up in lumbering old Heyfords on the following day. Only a handful were left behind to work on a few unserviceable aircraft. It constituted a considerable logistical effort but finally all personnel and aircraft did make it to Wittering – and not before time. John and many of his colleagues had had enough and desperately needed some relief. But having been on such a high over the previous days, to find themselves suddenly languishing away from the action perversely proved to be a downer as far as morale was concerned!

There is a certain paradox here for in common with many of his colleagues John had come to thoroughly dislike the job he was doing. To cope with it individuals needed to simply get their heads down and get on with it – hence the rather guilty feeling that they shouldn't be languishing whilst other units were still in the thick of things – and try and push the fear to one side. Everyone was very afraid and those who try and tell you otherwise are not being truthful. Fear manifested itself in many ways ranging from physical sickness as the scramble was called to an introspection which left individuals very much with their own thoughts. There were always officers on a squadron who could tell when an individual had had enough of front line operations – usually the Intelligence officer or Medical Officer. On one of his later squadrons, 118, John had an excellent MO, Pettigrew, who was exceptionally good at recognising the symptoms and he would arrange for a posting to a second line unit, an OTU for instance. There was one particular pilot on 118 who had simply reached the end of his tether and when the time came for a sortie he would refuse to go – very often getting to the take off strip before his nerve failed him. In this case, he was posted out and seconded to the Fleet Air Arm with whom he flew Sea Hurricanes for a while, being catapulted off merchantmen on convoy to intercept Focke Wolf Condors which might be sniffing around. This posting was an odd choice for someone who could no longer be relied upon to operate from the relative security of a land based unit – and was no more successful for on his first launch he flew straight off to land in a southern Irish field.

Putting their cards on the table are Roger Boulding, Henry the Pole aka Sneezy aka Szczesny and John. H M Stephen tries hard to ignore the game whilst somebody else's dog gets a nose in on the left!

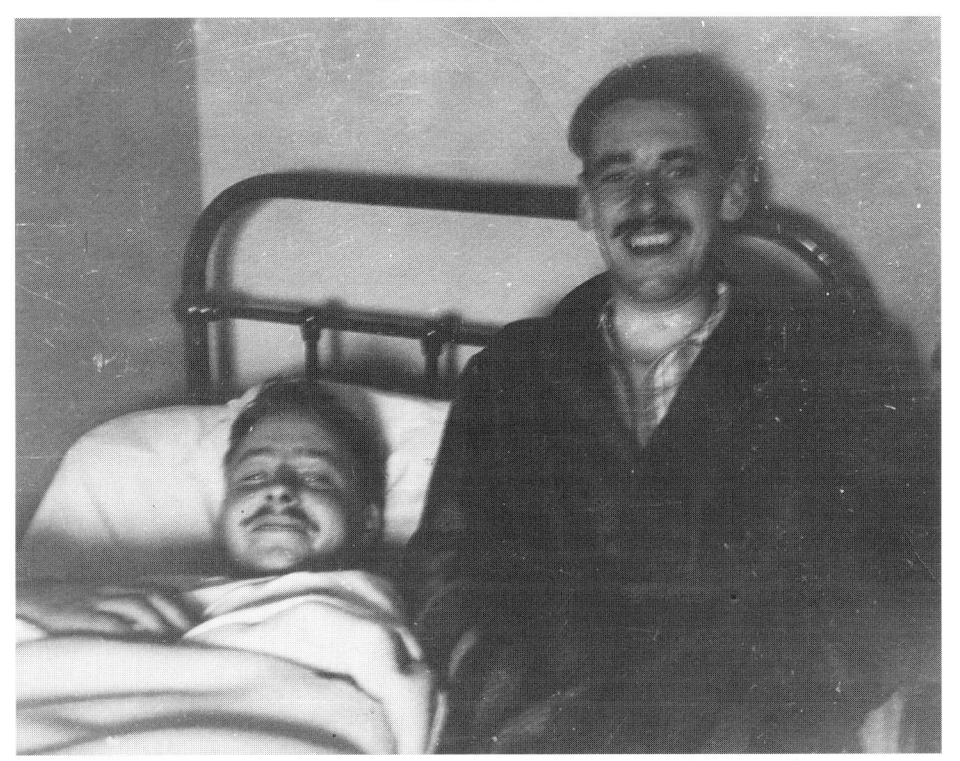

These chaps can afford to smile. They've just been pulled from the Battle of Britain and sent north to Wittering to rest. The two Johns - Freeborn and Mungo Park

The really courageous men were those who fought through their fear – and it strikes this writer that John Freeborn was one of those and this goes a long way to appreciating why he stayed with 74 for so long. He was one of those who got their heads down and coped with the fighting. He never asked for a posting for despite everything he needed to stay with his friends, friends with whom he did everything (legally or otherwise!) socially or operationally.

Team-work was the name of the game and was vital to a squadron's survival.

There was a job to do. We didn't necessarily like it – indeed there were many times when we were frightened out of our wits and hated it. But overall all we could do was make the best of it and make the best of the people around us. Some of us were more successful at doing this than others. After all it wasn't just us fighter pilots who won the war! It was everybody on the Squadron. It was called team-work and everybody had their part to play. Most played it successfully. A few opted out – not always by choice but for reasons of mental or physical stress.

Whilst at Wittering 74 missed two of the fiercest days fighting of the Battle of Britain – the 15th and 16th August – and this pleased no one. It is interesting to note that eight or nine of the pilots who went up to Wittering to rest were the same pilots as those who had been withdrawn to Leconfield after Dunkirk. Experience was certainly telling: many of the new boys hadn't survived for long. Others had though. The Poles Brzezina (soon dubbed Breezy by their new colleagues) and Szczesny (who inevitably became Sneezy) had arrived at the beginning of August. Breezy was a most affable fellow and an aggressive pilot – extrovert and friendly. Sneezy was the opposite. He was an 'old' captain (he was around 40 years of age when he arrived on 74) who had transferred from the cavalry to the Polish Air Force but who to John didn't outwardly display the same aggression as his countryman. He was a more thoughtful character although there is no doubt that the fires of revenge for all the Germans had done to his homeland burned very bright. John's parents were keen to keep in touch with Sneezy's parents and thereby offer some measure of support. This they managed to do until suddenly all contact with Poland ceased. It was later discovered that they had been gassed by the Germans.

New Zealander Wally Churches was another new arrival – a quiet, unassuming and thoroughly likeable man. There were several nationalities on 74 by now and there were marked differences between them – and between New Zealanders and Australians in particular. The former were somewhat quieter and simply got on

Every time Stanley Black put on a Black Varieties show at the London Palladium, the money raised went towards buying a Spitfire. Spitfire II P8388 Black Vanities (shown here) was one such. P8380 Black Velvet was another. The pilots are Bob Poulton, John, Sqn Ldr Wood with his dog, Butch Baker and Tony Mould

with the job although Bob Spurdle, whose father owned a newspaper back in his home country, was a rare case of a not-so-llikeable New Zealander. From elsewhere in the colonies, Don Thom was a Canadian high diver – not the most sensible of fellows by all accounts but dedicated to his job and a thoroughly nice guy.

Don Cobden was a quiet New Zealander who as an individual was not an aggressive fellow although his exploits in the air belied this. His loss on August 11th had been the loss of a popular man. John shared many moments on the ground and in the air with Don and memories of him bring to mind details of particular operations. With Don at 10,000 feet on one occasion they were jumped by a 109. John pulled up, Don pushed the stick forward and he made it safely and quickly back to Rochford. John by contrast found himself in a thunderhead and a combination of super cooled water droplets and electrical storm currents caused his prop tips to glow and sparkle and then fire to wrap itself around the wing's edges and ripple

The Australian, Bob Spurdle. At times it seemed that everyone on the Squadron had a canine friend! Bob and John rarely saw eye to eye – to the extent that Bob sought a transfer away from 74 as soon as it could be arranged...

down the fuselage side. Rain appeared to be going upwards instead of falling earthwards. A disorientating experience and although not inherently dangerous, quite frightening. Eventually though, after what seemed like for ever but was in reality only minutes, John cleared the thunderhead and let down over what he thought was the Channel but in the clear air below the clouds there was no land in sight. His compass was spinning uncontrollably but gradually settled down: confused by the storm he had wandered far off course and was, it transpired, over the southern North Sea. When his instruments became readable again he set course and made a landfall over Norfolk from where he had fuel remaining to get back into Rochford.

– o O o –

From Wittering 74 moved to Kirton in Lindsay where training continued and then on to Coltishall, all the while with eyes firmly fixed on what was happening further south as the Battle moved to phase three – attacks on inland airfields around London. John (newly promoted to Flight Lieutenant) and Malan had actually headed south from Kirton in Lindsay – but not to rejoin the fray. Instead they went to Buckingham Palace on September 3rd to receive their DFCs. John's citation read:

This officer has taken part in nearly all offensive patrols carried out by his Squadron since the commencement of the war including operations over the Low Countries and Dunkirk and more recently engagements over the Channel and South East of England. During this intensive period of air warfare he has destroyed four enemy aircraft. His high courage and excep-

tional abilities as a leader have materially contributed to the notable successes and high standard of efficiency maintained by his Squadron.

The trip to London turned out to be a bit of an adventure in itself. Flying down in the Squadron hack, a Master, they didn't leave Kirton until it was nearly dark with Sailor at the controls. A call had been made to Northolt, their destination, to put the airfield lights up at the projected arrival time: this Northolt failed to do and Sailor found himself dangerously around the edge of London's balloon barrage. In the blackout and in what they thought was the Beaconsfield area, Sailor slowly let the Master down and, as luck would have it, they were able to land on the fairway of a golf course. Along the edges of this fairway were posts to act as a glider landing deterrent, some of which the Master hit but fortunately at minimal damage to the aircraft. Alerted by engine noise, the local constabulary were soon on the scene but once John's and Sailor's *bona fides* were established, they were escorted to Northolt. The following morning, prior to the investiture, they were driven back to Beaconsfield to rescue their aircraft. Getting off the fairway was going to be a tricky business: even with the exceptional performance of the Master in getting out of tight corners, this was tight by anybody's standards! Powering up the engine to full revs whilst holding on the brakes, when these were released the aircraft leapt forward and into the air, just squeezing over trees at the fairway's end.

They were not late for the investiture, for which John's parents proudly came down. Sailor was quick to corner them and extol John's virtues, which given the strained relationship between the two John considered to be a bit rich. Also a bit rich was H M Stephen's request that John should drive back a car of his from London which when collected proved to be a battered old Opel. Not only was it battered but it was unreliable too and a succession of breakdowns saw John searching for accommodation in Grantham before finally making it back to Kirton the next day.

John with his mother Jean in Leeds shortly after receiving his DFC. The Investiture had been held on 3rd September 1940 and this photo was taken for the Yorkshire Post. *'It is not beside the point that this one bears the name Freeborn. So are they all'*

John regarded Coltishall, which the Squadron reached on 9th September, boring as a place! He was to pass through with 74 now but this impression was only heightened when, as we shall see, he returned there in 1942 to command 118 Squadron. It was isolated, with no transport to get anywhere despite Norwich being only a few miles away. It was also brand new having been opened in May and declared fully operational as part of Leigh Mallory's 12 Group on June 23rd – so 74 were one of its early incumbents. The Station Commander, Wg Cdr Beisiegal, was a stickler for what he considered to be the priorities of station life, such as not being allowed to bring cars on – bikes only to be used! The fact that cars continued to be brought and parked all the way round the outside of the perimeter fence was neither here nor there. Fuel could still be transferred over the fence anyway! Facilities on the station were rudimentary and things were only made bearable by the knowledge that they wouldn't be in Norfolk for long: they were sure to be sent back down south to rejoin the air battle within a matter of days although in the event this didn't happen as quickly as anticipated.

John proudly wears the Distinguished Flying Cross after the Investiture at Buckingham Palace

To make matters worse Douglas Bader was with 242 Squadron at Coltishall at the time and 74 briefly became a component of the flawed Big Wing concept. But at least the Tigers did have the opportunity to rejoin the fight and they enjoyed some success. On the 11th they flew down to Duxford where they teamed up with 19 and 611 Squadrons (74 flew as the rear squadron of the three having been briefed to leave the fighters to the other two and go for the bombers) and were detailed to intercept raids over the City of London, raids which became the whole focus of the Luftwaffe's effort until the end of the month. On this occasion, flying in three fours in section line astern, they intercepted a large rectangle of Ju88s. Malan gave the order for a head on attack but John, leading Yellow Section, could not comply because of interference from escorting 109s which had at this stage eluded 19 and 611. Yellow Section drew off the fighters but in the process lost the Ju88s and found themselves over south London where John in R6840 intercepted a Do17 (or a very similar 215 – the identity has not been resolved) and attacked it head on, hitting the German's port engine. Pulling round tightly he then executed stern and beam attacks in succession and the aircraft finally crash landed in a field near Dungeness and burst into flames. 74 returned home safely to Coltishall in the evening with this one enemy aircraft destroyed but with ten probables under their collective belts.

On the 14th they went after targets around the East Anglian coast, damaging a pair of Bf110s, claiming a Ju88 as a probable and damaging another, and John damaging an He111 as well. Leading Red Section in P7368 he had been detailed

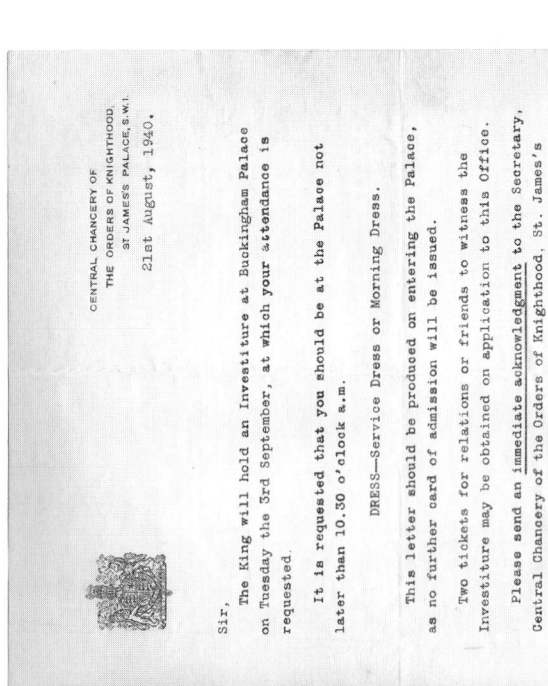

CENTRAL CHANCERY OF
THE ORDERS OF KNIGHTHOOD,
ST JAMES'S PALACE, S.W.1.

28th March 1941.

Sir,

The King will hold an Investiture at Buckingham Palace on Tuesday, the 8th April, 1941, at which your attendance is requested.

It is requested that you should be at the Palace not later than 10.15 o'clock a.m.

DRESS—Service Dress, Morning Dress or Civil Defence Uniform.

This letter should be produced on entering the Palace, as no further card of admission will be issued.

Two tickets for relations or friends to witness the Investiture may be obtained on application to this Office and you are requested to state your requirements on the form enclosed.

Please complete the enclosed form and return immediately to the Secretary, Central Chancery of the Orders of Knighthood, St. James's Palace, London, S.W.1.

I am, Sir,
Your obedient Servant,

Secretary.

Flight Lieutenant John C. Freeborn,
D.F.C., R.A.F.

CENTRAL CHANCERY OF
THE ORDERS OF KNIGHTHOOD,
ST JAMES'S PALACE, S.W.1.

21st August, 1940.

Sir,

The King will hold an Investiture at Buckingham Palace on Tuesday the 3rd September, at which your attendance is requested.

It is requested that you should be at the Palace not later than 10.30 o'clock a.m.

DRESS—Service Dress or Morning Dress.

This letter should be produced on entering the Palace, as no further card of admission will be issued.

Two tickets for relations or friends to witness the Investiture may be obtained on application to this Office.

Please send an immediate acknowledgment to the Secretary, Central Chancery of the Orders of Knighthood, St. James's Palace, London, S.W.1, on the enclosed card.

I am, Sir,
Your obedient Servant,

Secretary.

Pilot Officer John C. Freeborn,
D.F.C., R.A.F.

A Pilot Officer in August, a Flight Lieutenant in March. Young men grew up very quickly in all ways during the war. These are John's invitations for the Investiture at Buckingham Palace for his DFC and bar to the DFC

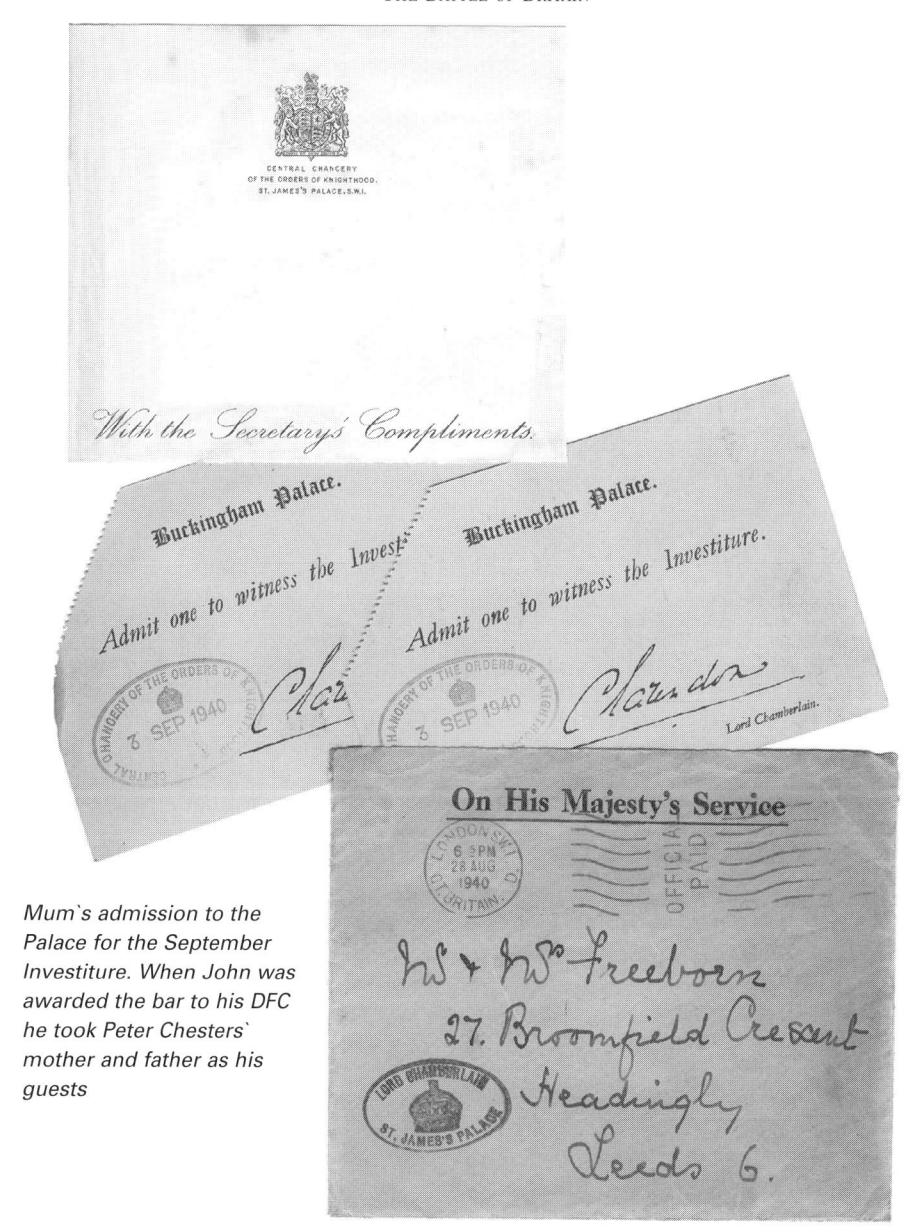

Mum's admission to the Palace for the September Investiture. When John was awarded the bar to his DFC he took Peter Chesters' mother and father as his guests

to intercept an enemy raid coming in towards Lowestoft mid afternoon. It was not long before John saw a German flying east at 11,000ft and set himself up for a good three second burst from his machine guns, opening fire at 250 yards and closing to 160. The He111, which he had now identified the enemy as, disappeared into cloud but John stayed around, betting on it re-emerging which it duly did and he attacked it once more, closing this time from 250 to just 50 yards. Once again cloud proved to be the German's saviour. Bob Spurdle was with John and he had seen John's fire hit the port engine and white vapour but had also attacked the German himself. As a result John and Bob claimed a shared aircraft destroyed.

But it was all very well skirmishing locally – the big battles continued to be fought in the skies over London and the southeast. September 15th came and went with no involvement by the Tigers but Malan kept up a stiff training regime knowing that it would only be a matter of time before the Squadron headed south again. In the meantime David Ayres was lost off Southwold whilst chasing an enemy aircraft: a Do17 which he damaged off Sheringham finally came down over Antwerp! John had a close call himself. It was on the day King George visited Coltishall – although John and his section were on readiness and were not able to be formally presented to HRH. As it happened a raid materialised and they were scrambled. An interception was made on a Bf110 which came out of the clouds and which was chased all over the sky as they tried to make a kill. Some pretty aggressive manoeuvering was called for and with the German jinking and corkscrewing in his attempts to shake the Tigers off, lines of sight criss crossed. John's aircraft was hit – not by the 110 but rather by one of his own section, Bob Spurdle. Bob was not a character whom John got on with and this incident only exacerbated the difficulties of the relationship – to such an extent that Bob pleaded with Malan for a posting out to get him out of John's way!

The final phase of the Battle of Britain was inaugurated, despite the postponement by Hitler of Operation Sealion, by continued incursions of Luftwaffe fighters and fighter bombers with the hope of luring the RAF into the air. As H M Stephen and Peter Stevenson each received news of an award of a DFC, 74 were at last given the opportunity of getting back into the thick of things and on October 15th they flew down from Coltishall to their new home – Biggin Hill.

Bob Spurdle

Chapter 7
From Defence to Offence

When 74 joined 92 Squadron at Biggin Hill, it had become the most heavily attacked station in Fighter Command with the damage caused by the Luftwaffe all too plain to see as the Tigers flew in. 74 were to be on the receiving end of some of these attacks during their tenure but by far the heaviest and most devastating had been over a three week period at the end of August, beginning of September. On Sunday August 18th the Luftwaffe attacked for an hour, cratering the runway and hitting the MT sheds as well as virtually destroying the golf course next door (which had not been their prime objective!). On the 30th, radar detected a hundred incoming aircraft and sixteen squadrons were scrambled to intercept them. Despite their efforts some Germans got through and dropped their bombs but such was the harassment they largely missed their intended target – but which sadly fell on adjacent villages. Biggin survived a second attack shortly after lunch although on this occasion half a dozen radar stations were put out of action. It was the raid at 1800 hours which did the damage when Ju88s carrying 1,000lb bombs managed to intrude without opposition. Robin Brooks in his story of Kent airfields during the conflict captures the horror of the moment:

The noise was indescribable as explosion after explosion rent the air. In the shelters the crump, crump of detonating bombs sounded as though they were coming through the roof. Some of the WAAFs and men began to pray out loud as the devastation continued. At ground level the power, gas and water mains were all severed with the main GPO telephone link damaged in three places, thus no link was possible with headquarters 11 Group. Two aircraft were destroyed in the hangar which received a direct hit but worst of all was the bomb which hit one of the shelters crammed full with airmen. As the roof and

John today with the charcoal drawing of him made by Cuthbert Orde on 17th October 1940
[Photo: D R Cook]

sides caved in 40 lost their lives. In a WAAF shelter a bomb which had landed nearby blew the door in and entombed the girls in dust and rubble. Choking and crying at the same time, many started pulling the bricks and mortar away in an attempt to get out...

Biggin's technical site was devastated – workshops, stores, the WAAF quarters and one of the hangars were reduced to rubble.

On August 31st the operations block received a direct hit. The station armoury was set ablaze along with many other buildings and four Spitfires. On the following day, a Sunday, burial services for all those killed in the previous weeks raids were held at the cemetery just outside the perimeter. But even now they were not to be laid to rest in peace for as the service started Biggin was attacked again. Bravely the padre continued with the service although civilians were sent to the shelters only to re-emerge when the attack had finished. This one just about finished the job – Biggin was by now so badly damaged it could sustain no more than one squadron. Virtually no buildings remained habitable. Services and communications were out of action and the operations room had to be moved off the airfield. The Station Commander, Gp Captain Grice, reasoned that, although wrecked, the fact that hangars were still standing would only encourage the Luftwaffe to come again. So he had them blown up. He was court martialled for doing so but was exonerated.

– oOo –

Six weeks later, accommodation at Biggin Hill was still in very short supply. Tiger groundcrew slept in a motley collection of wooden huts, or (for the lucky few) in old married quarters. Aircrew on the other hand were billeted in the country home of Warren Smithers MP. For food and entertainment the Tigers would frequent The Crown at nearby Knockholt where the pub's landlords, the Elliot family, more or less adopted the Squadron. Pheasant was favourite on the menu, locally poached and locally prepared! And the landlord's daughter took a real shine to the popular Wally Churches. She was devastated when he was killed six months later.

Biggin seemed to be a hive of activity – not only with the constant launching of aircraft to intercept incoming raids, but with the repairing of the damage that had been caused, and at times continued to be caused, by those incoming raids. The miracle was that Biggin – or parts of it at least, for the North Camp had hardly been touched at the time 74 arrived – was rising from the ashes of destruction! Everywhere the Tigers looked they could see maintenance gangs and heavy equipment. Bomb crater filling was an ongoing activity although the old practice of mass formation take offs in which 74 took such pride had to be abandoned – there was simply not the room to execute them without being obstructed by craters or indeed by

John at The Crown at Knockholt, the Tigers' favourite pub when they were at Biggin Hill in late 1940

unexploded bombs, their position marked by an airman with a red flag until such time as bomb disposal teams could deal with them. Maintenance of aircraft was carried out in the often flooded dispersals. All major repairs, including those which would normally be done on the home airfield, had to be sent to MUs. Many offices and sections were operating from requisitioned premises in nearby villages.

But John never liked Biggin – ' a loathsome place' he describes it as. It always seemed to epitomise tragedy to him, tragedy born of the effects of constant enemy attack during those frightful days and latterly tragedy at air shows which for no apparent reason has seemed to afflict Biggin with several display pilots losing their lives before crowds of onlookers amongst whose numbers has been John. But in its heyday the airfield was one of the most famous in the country – if not the world – because of the part it played during the Battle of Britain as a Sector Station for 11 Group. There was good reason for it becoming known as the Strongest Link – words subsequently featured in the station crest. At a more prosaic level, the station was also known as Biggin on the Bump by virtue of the undulating land on which it is built – a feature which has been put to good use over the years for display flying with aircraft seemingly appearing out of nowhere to launch themselves into the sky. Sadly the Bump has seen tragic accidents too...

John had a Talbot 90 at Biggin in which he used to run about, a car complete with a 40 gallon fuel drum in the back, plumbed into the car's fuel system. He was certainly never short of fuel! On one particular morning, when time had passed rather too quickly and John was late for duty, he was careering along narrow back roads when he came face to face, at speed, with a three wheeler. Such was his momentum, and with nowhere to go other than in a straight line, the three wheeler was knocked off the road. Its driver, a decorator by profession, emerged shaken and covered in paint! As he was late John bid a swift farewell and resumed his dash to Biggin. The next morning a policeman appeared and took a keen interest in the Talbot. It wasn't taxed – but there was no visible sign of damage which may have resulted from the previous day's incident. Rousting John out, the constable commented on the lack of tax and on the fact they were looking for a vehicle that had forced the local painter and decorator off the road. 'Is this your vehicle sir?'

'Good God no. I'm afraid its owner was shot down over the Channel yesterday!'

This appealed to the constable's sense of patriotic duty and indeed to his humanity. 'In which case sir I'm very sorry. We'll forget it.' Some years ago John was back at Biggin attending an airshow and signing prints and during his time in the area he visited a local museum, met the curator and in the course of their conversation the above story was related. John detected a hint of a knowing smile cross the curator's face and that evening, John was introduced to the decorator and the bobby at the local club! The story was retold a few times and everyone had a good laugh about it. It was a good way to lay the incident to rest!

– o O o –

Within a few days of their arrival 74 were in action, intercepting the Luftwaffe over Gravesend and Maidstone. On the 15th Peter St John and Willie Nelson got a Bf109 apiece. On the 17th Sailor, Ben Draper, Nelson and St John all scored (against 109s again) but Alan Ricalton was killed when he was shot down near Maidstone. Three days later the Tigers were in the air with 66 Sqn (the three intervening days having been spent on patrol but without contact) when they found thirty 109s over Maidstone. Mungo Park bagged one as did H M Stephen and Ben Draper (whose tally was steadily mounting). Two of the Squadron's Sergeant Pilots were downed though – Clive Hilken who survived and was soon back at Biggin: and Sgt Thomas Kirk in P7370 who sustained horrific injuries. He lived for some months however until finally succumbing in July 1941. On the 22nd, in the air with 92 Sqn this time, the Tigers lost Peter St John. This was a blow to John for Peter and he had been particularly close – as indeed had he and Peter Chesters of whom more later. St John was 'as daft as Chesters' – a phrase meant in a totally endearing way. Indeed both the Peters had a great knack of annoying everybody with their antics and both enjoyed life to the full. which is probably what attracted John to them in the first place. The sad thing about St John's loss was that he disappeared on patrol under circumstances that were not known: the later discovery of his wrecked aircraft showed him to have been shot down but exactly when and by whom was never discovered. Bob Spurdle was shot down as well but he survived. Some measure of retribution was paid by the Germans with Sailor and Mungo Park destroying a 109 apiece on the same day.

On the 27th an increasingly tired 74 took off again – the three Biggin squadrons were flying constant standing patrols. Thirty more 109s were found and Willie Nelson, now John's opposite number as A Flight Commander, put one down near Rochester: and Peter Chesters damaged one which subsequently force landed at Penshurst. With no more to do Peter landed beside him and personally took the German pilot prisoner after a heated debate in which the latter insisted that the only reason that he had come down was because he had run out of fuel, not because Chesters had forced him! Words led to fisticuffs and the need to be separated by the army when they arrived on the scene!

On the 29th, the day prior to the ending of the Battle of Britain as now determined by historians, more 109s felt the sharp edge of the Tiger's machine guns: John Mungo Park got two and Willie Nelson one. The Battle of Britain may have been won but trade was still to be had with Luftwaffe fighters continuing to escort bombers across the Channel, both genres of aircraft often still in huge numbers. Records show that November 1940 was again a busy month for 74 and they still encountered predominantly Bf109s – such as on the 2nd when they sighted sixty over the Isle of Sheppey and bagged four. Three days later Mungo Park learnt that he had been awarded the DFC (and H M Stephen a bar to his).

On the 7th 66 Squadron flew in to Biggin from West Malling to join 74 and 92 and their Boss, Sqn Ldr James Fisher, was totally perplexed by the gulf between the operating ethos of his new stablemates. Robin Brooks again:

On the one hand there was 74 Squadron, a strict disciplined unit under Sailor Malan who even insisted his pilots were in bed by 10 o'clock each night – and there was 92 Squadron! As opposite to 74 as you could ever get with their sophisticated outlook on life. Fast powerful cars, parties until dawn, special catering arrangements and an abundance of lovely females virtually living in the Mess...

On the 14th Mungo led 74 in Sailor's absence on leave and took on fifty Ju87s escorted by Bf109s with 66 Squadron. In the course of fifty minutes 74 destroyed fourteen Stukas and a single Bf109 as well as claiming probables and damage to others. This was akin to the Squadron's phenomenal success of August 11th and a resumé of the decimation of the German formation makes for exciting reading. The Tigers took the port flank and 66 the starboard. Mungo immediately got two Stukas: H M Stephen got another which he watched roll into the aircraft next to it – so that was two! A third burst into flames and dived into the sea. Ben Draper's first crashed onto the Kent shore by Dover Harbour: his second hit the sea. The escorting 109s were now recovering their wits and attempted to put up a fight but Draper quickly damaged one and it found cloud into which to scurry for protection. Wally Churches shot down another. Walter Franklin meanwhile was still having a go at the Stukas and despatched another into the Channel whilst John Glendinning set one on fire. Bob Spurdle watched an '87 roll over into a vertical dive – claimed as a probable – and damaged three others in quick succession. Bill

Skinner caught one at sea level and promptly destroyed it as well as claiming another as a probable. Laurence Freese shot two into the sea. Bill Armstrong was the one Tiger casualty of the day but although forced to bale out after his Spitfire was set on fire he got down safely near Worth and made his way back to Biggin. He hadn't done so badly though. He had one confirmed Stuka to his credit.

On the 15th, John Freeborn was back in action having been away on leave, or presumably so for he had been conspicuously absent from the combat reports of the previous couple of weeks, and having missed the exciting events of the previous day. (Was this the time he had volunteered for tram driving duties in Leeds at the time of a drivers' strike, a career which lasted just thirty seconds from the moment he left the tram depot in Swingate when he managed to derail his tramcar!) On this day twelve Tigers had left Biggin Hill at 1515 to patrol Maidstone at 20,000ft with 92 Squadron leading but had then been ordered to Littlehampton to intercept thirty plus enemy aircraft that had been detected there. Having reached their revised objective they patrolled the coast on a westerly course from where they could see vapour trails above them going north and towards which they climbed to intercept. The Tigers received a very rude awakening when twenty Bf109s bounced them from above, the enemy attacking in pairs and suddenly they were fighting for their lives once again. In the melee John (in P7542) fired at the leading 109 but saw no hits: he then turned his attention to No 3 of the formation at the same time as H M Stephen sent a burst of gun fire into it – but the 109 dived away as it contrived to escape. Not reckoning on the tenacity of the Tigers, Messrs Freeborn and Stephen stayed with it and closed enough to fire further bursts. The 109 was now mortally hit and crashed into the sea some miles off Brighton. John recalls this as being his first success with a Spitfire II, the mark which had been phased in from June: the last Spitifre I was not phased out until September.

Then came a period of November weather which precluded any flying – until the 27th when Peter Chesters baled out having been bounced by three 109s. Peter came down on the mudflats of Conyer Creek and was dragged to safety by a local Air Raid

Mungo Park in the cockpit and H M Stephen assisting at Biggin Hill. These two were responsible for that Station's 600th German shot down. But was it Mungo Park or Stephen who got it? The record books say Stephen: John is sure it was Mungo Park who was too much of a gentleman to deny H M's claim

Warden, Bob Hodges. On the 30th H M Stephen destroyed a 109 which just happened to be Biggin Hill's 600th downed German aircraft of the war and which earned him £35 in an organised lottery. That is the official version. John's recollection is somewhat different. H M had arranged for the Controllers to tip him off so that he could get off and claim the 600th – but when the call came Mungo was detailed to go with him and actually got the kill. According to John it was with Sailor's collusion that H M was credited with it: Mungo was too much of a gentleman to dispute the decision. When the pair landed the cameras were waiting and pictures appeared in the national press. Whichever version of events is accepted today, at the time more awards were handed out as a result and H M Stephen became the first Pilot Officer to be awarded the DSO – he had been recommended by Sholto Douglas (who had recently taken over from Dowding as C in C Fighter Command). Furthermore Sailor himself got a DSO, Bill Skinner a DFM and Ben Draper a DFC.

HQ 11 Group produced a listing for November of enemy casualties inflicted by squadrons within the Group and 74 topped the list with twenty six aircraft destroyed. December proved to be successful too. On the 1st Sailor and Sneezy shared a 109: on the 2nd these two got one apiece as did John Glendinning and Neil Morrison. The 5th was a good day for John (as it was for H M who claimed his twentieth victory) when he shot a 109 into the sea off Dungeness, damaged a second, sent a third into the sea ten miles off Boulogne and caught a fourth escaping back to France. The sequence of events went thus. At 1410 twelve aircraft took off from Biggin Hill in company with 92 Squadron and with John in P7366 leading the Tigers to once again patrol Maidstone at 15,000ft. This was subsequently altered to Dover at 25,000ft but with 10/10ths cloud at 17,000ft the order was found to be counterproductive and 74 were brought back down 13,500 ft where they immediately encountered fifteen Bf109s over Folkestone. It was at this crucial moment that John's radio packed up so he immediately signalled to Yellow One to take the lead before taking on the German formation's leader with a one second deflection shot from fifty yards. The German pushed his nose down but John stayed with him and was able to fire another couple of two second bursts which was enough to ensure the German's destruction. He dived straight into the sea fifteen miles off Dungeness. John immediately climbed back to height over Dungeness itself where he caught another 109, firing from the rear and damaging its cooling system. At this point a 92 Squadron Spitfire joined the scrap and finished the job which John had started. This 109 too ended up in the sea. But there seemed to be plenty left and within seconds John had another in his sights, firing a couple of bursts from above which damaged it. The 109 immediately high tailed it for the French coast but the German's card was marked – John was not about to let him get away and ten miles off Boulogne a further burst from his guns brought the 109 down. The sea claimed its third victim of the day. By this time those 109s still in the air were running low on fuel and all were trying to make the safety of France but still had to run the gauntlet of two squadrons of Spitfires with their tails up! John went for his fourth German and once again managed to close in for a stern attack, knocking bits off the aircraft's fuselage. He was saved by John's running out of ammunition and reluctantly having to break off. Still, it had been a highly successful few minutes – for a few minutes was all it had taken.

– o O o –

From the beginning of 1941 the emphasis for the RAF changed to offensive sweeps into France. Air Marshal Sholto Douglas became C in C Fighter Command on November 25th 1940 with the words of Lord Trenchard ringing in his ears – the time had come for Fighter Command to go onto the offensive. Any initial doubt about such a policy that Sholto Douglas may have initially had were soon dispelled, particularly with the enthusiastic embracing of such a doctrine by 11 Group's new AOC, Leigh Mallory. Thus began the fighter sweeps codenamed *Rhubarb*, the idea being to bring the Luftwaffe up to fight (74 were somewhat perturbed to be told that there were 3,000 enemy fighters opposing them in the Calais area but did rather suspect this was an exaggeration!) – but the fact is they didn't come up in any numbers, often not at all. However, although the Germans were not always to be found in the air, the Squadron did at times feel they were being controlled by the Luftwaffe from France rather than Bentley Priory or other Sector Stations and the suspicion was that the code which the RAF were using at that time for vectoring its aircraft had been broken.

74 and its sister squadrons flew formations of three across the Channel to look at the German airfields in northern France such as Abbeville or Lille: if that didn't provoke the Luftwaffe, a run down the coast would be made to see if there were signs of any invasion barges or other shipping: they also at times escorted bombers which attacked such concentrations. However, the whole strategy proved to be a largely wasteful exercise in terms of effectiveness and in casualties, for despite the German's predilection for staying on the ground, RAF pilots were still being lost to Anti Aircraft fire. The 80mm gun in particular was very accurate and was probably the best AA gun in the war. The British had learnt that the quickest way to escape AA fire was to put the aircraft into a dive: the gunners couldn't adjust the shell's fuses – for height of burst – quickly enough. Unfortunately not everybody paid heed to that lesson and losses still occurred. Of course first bursts sometimes got unsuspecting pilots but many, John included, became very adept at evading flak by diving although on at least one occasion he was caught by a first burst which punched a great hole in his wing and from which he was thankful to get down safely.

The Germans may not have reacted to the institution of *Rhubarbs*, but they did show more concern at the joint Fighter Command/Bomber Command operations codenamed *Circus*. Large numbers of fighters accompanying smaller numbers of bombers were deployed, once again the major objective being to lure the Luftwaffe into the air. In the first six months of 1941 they flew 2,700 sorties and lost 51 pilots. But the numbers of Germans claimed shot down during the same period was initially just 41 – and even this figure was subsequently revised downwards.

The New Year saw the beginning of significant changes to the Squadron's complement. H M Stephen was the first to go – to 59 OTU. Then in March Sailor was promoted to Wing Commander and took up his new role as Officer Commanding Flying, Biggin Hill Wing – so 74 would still be flying under his auspices. Nobody on the Squadron was unhappy that John Mungo Park was in turn promoted to command the Tigers – although a few perhaps felt that they could have laid claim to the job, John Freeborn included. Mungo was a popular figure – a determined fighter, good leader of men and somebody not averse to a little skulduggery when the occasion arose: he was quite good at blind eye turning! But as mooted previously he was not necessarily the right man for the job.

Of other established Tigers, John Freeborn learned on February 17th that he had been awarded a bar to his DFC. His tally at that time stood at twelve enemy aircraft destroyed and the Yorkshire press were quick to comment again:

Yorkshire may well be proud of the record of its sons in the RAF. The county leads all others in its quota of awards for gallantry in air action – leads, too, by a considerable margin. Courage is common to all Britons, but the dash, wit and imagination needed to be a successful air fighter are qualities not normally ascribed to Yorkshiremen. It just shows the folly of antiquated generalisations. We are supposed to be dour, slow thinking, cautious and tough but not resilient. Alas for our detractors! The brilliant record of our young men in their Spitfires and Hurricanes gives the lie to such notions. Now comes the announcement that young

Freeborn of Headingley has won a bar to his DFC...

Dour, slow thinking, cautious, tough but not resilient... hardly a description of John with that cheerful disposition of his that comes through in all the photos we see of him, a twinkle in his eye, cap set at a jaunty angle! Not resilient?

This officer has been continuously engaged on operations since the beginning of the war.

So reads the citation. Twelve confirmed victories plus damaged aircraft does not smack of lack of resilience. No wonder the *Yorkshire Evening News* was quick to leap to the defence of its young aces. The investiture was held on April 8th.

– o O o –

There were new Tigers to welcome on to the Squadron. One popular arrival around this time was another Pole, Jan Rogowski, who in common with many of his countrymen seemed fearless, even a little reckless and who, also in common with many of his countrymen, was one for the girls. But set against this there continued to be losses and Sgt Laurence Freese was killed force landing at Detling when he ran out of fuel. John shared a Do17 on the 5th February. With 74 flying fighter sweeps from Manston from February 20th (when weather allowed), Sailor and Sgt Alec Payne claimed a Bf109 apiece and Wally Churches and Neil Morrison shared a Bf110 shortly before the latter's disappearance. On 4th March John Freeborn shared another Do17, this time with Bob Poulton – they seemed to be his speciality at the time! Tony Bartley (later to marry the actress Deborah Kerr) arrived to take command of A Flight after Mungo's promotion. John Glendinning in P7506 was shot down over Ivychurch on March 17th: Wally Churches got another 109 on the 18th: Bob Spurdle and Sgt Dales shared a Ju88 on the 24th and damaged a Do215 on the 25th. Two days later Sqn Ldr Wood damaged a 109. Wood was a supernumerary on the Squadron, a quiet, unassuming Cranwell graduate who, it was rumoured, had been drafted in to be groomed to take over from Malan who had therefore been understandably wary of him. In the event of course the job had gone to Mungo Park. Into April, and on the 6th Bob Spurdle got a Bf110. On the 7th Jan Rogowski opened his account with a 109. So the story goes on – sorties, engagements, successes, losses, tragedy...

Operating from Manston at the same time as the Tigers was 101 Squadron which, with its Blenheims and under fighter escort, maintained regular patrols across the Channel in a continuing attempt to close the route through the Straits of Dover to German shipping – sorties codenamed *Channel Stop*. They also participated in attacks on convoys up and down the French, Belgian and Dutch coasts. Ship bombing was a low level affair for the Blenheims – a sea level approach and bouncing the bomb off the sea's surface into the target. That was the theory anyway. The Blenheims took a beating – both from on-board defensive fire and from 109s who quickly got themselves into position to intercept them. Such was the mauling that 101 were withdrawn – but they left behind one Blenheim at Manston which, once repaired, needed to be returned to West Raynham to join the rest of the squadron. Could 74 do it? Nothing if not adventurous, and always ready for a new experience, John volunteered. His choice of crew was not auspicious – Peter Chesters and Peter St John, the latter in the turret and simply along for the ride. Taking off proved to be no problem – but raising the undercarriage was. And how did you operate the engine cooling gills? It was a matter of trial and error, finding these things out as the flight progressed. Approaching their destination, John radioed ahead and warned ATC of the inexperienced crew bringing the Blenheim in. Next problem – how did you change the pitch on two-speed props? The levers to do so were at the back of the armour plate to the pilot's left and it was quite a stretch to get your arm round to reach them and change from coarse to fine. Getting the undercarriage down was no problem, just reverse the procedure for getting it up! Once done, landing was straightforward.

Delivery complete, John and the two Peters spent the night at West Raynham and the next morning were invited to fly a Mark II Wellington to which 101 were in the process of converting – this time with an experienced pilot on board to keep an eye on things. The Mark II was a great improvement over the I, but a pilot new to the type would be hard pressed to decide where the improvement, performance wise, lay. The Mark I must have been awful. The Mark II you had to hold on the brakes at the end of the runway, open the throttles fully and then release the brakes. Slowly, oh so slowly it seemed, the Wellington moved forward, waddling like a duck down the runway and not apparently getting much faster! Just as it seemed as though it would never lift off the aircraft bounced and almost leaped into the air, but not such a great leap after all for it barely cleared the boundary hedge! This, to a fighter pilot used to the performance of a single seater, was frightening. Whatever was it like with a full bomb load aboard? The truth was it had an abysmal rate of climb.

Then tragedy. On the 10th April Peter Chesters added to his tally with another Bf109. This Peter was another of John's bosom companions on 74. He had an element of eccentricity, even 'madness', about him. He came from a wealthy family of silk merchants who lived in Westcliffe and had spent time in Germany during the pre war years of Nazi repression. As a young impressionable man, what he saw had shocked him deeply and he developed a loathing for the German people as a result and this became his total motivation for fighting the aggressive war he did. A Sergeant in the Reserve before the war, as a flier Peter was both a good pilot and good shot. But he was subject to moments of carelessness, of disregard for his own well being, and one such moment was after this latest success in the air. He came back to Manston and roared across the aerodrome at low altitude, attempted a Victory Roll, stalled and ploughed in inverted. A horrified John Freeborn saw it happen – Peter was too slow and the roll developed into a flick roll from which there was no way in which he could recover at the sort of altitude he was flying. It is not speed that kills – it's lack of speed. There were some things the more experienced pilots just couldn't get through to the less experienced – and the need for speed in certain manoeuvres was one of them – although by this stage Peter Chesters should have counted as one of the more experienced pilots.

Another Tiger was lost a few days further on when the gentle Wally Churches disappeared. The loss of close colleagues and friends had a profound effect on those left behind. John always felt it very keenly. Still only twenty one years old it is perhaps too easy for us to forget that young men such as John were missing out on many of the pleasures of life, of the transition to adulthood, of the joys of forming relationships without the backdrop of war. They lost their youth very quickly and the reason so much is remembered so vividly sixty years after the event is that all that they went through served to focus the mind to such a extent that the memory has never left them.

Looking back, and despite what was to come over the remaining years of the war, 74 was John's surrogate family more than any of his later postings ever would be. And he needed that. He needed something that approached normality, as far as normality could ever be conceived in those hectic and frightening days. Which is why the three Peters – St John, Stevenson and Chesters – and Don Cobden as well, were so important to him. There were others too – and not necessarily of 74. Ron Courtenay from John's training days was by now on 111 Squadron not far away at North Weald and he would go and spend free weekends with his family whether Ron was there or not and was always made to feel so very welcome. As he was with the Chesters family. These genuine and warm people also more or less adopted the Squadron in the way that the Elliot's at Knockholt had and most of John's colleagues would gravitate to their splendid Southend home at one time or another. Most people – but not Sailor who was not invited. The married Sailor's pecuniary embarrassments left him out in the cold. He was unable to join in for lack of money with the card schools which were held at the Southend Palace – his IOUs became unacceptable. The fact that he was not included led to jealousy and further aggravated his standing with other Squadron members to the extent that he came to be left out of everything socially. An unfortunate and indeed unhappy position for all concerned.

For the most part these young pilots who spent so much time in each others' company were cocks of the walk. They responded very well to people's reaction as they sauntered into pubs, top buttons carelessly undone, cigarettes constantly to hand, boastful and braggardly, loud and full of *joie de vivre*. They enjoyed too the status that being a member of 74 Squadron conferred on them and wherever they were, be it Hornchurch, Southend or Biggin Hill, their entry would be marked by the playing of what became the Squadron's signature tune, Tiger Rag. They really did give the appearance of devil may care young heroes – which is precisely how many of them coped with the reality of their situation.

– o O o –

Gravesend overlooked the River Thames but at 250ft elevation it was usually above any river fog that formed. The Tigers moved in on May Day 1941. Aircrew were billeted in the rat infested Cobham Hall. Owned by Lord Darnley, the family had become impoverished having at the turn of the century been one of the richest in the country. Three successive deaths had dealt a mortal blow in terms of death duties. On the airfield itself they found a sadly deteriorating de Havilland Comet racer in the corner of a hangar. Gravesend had been the departure airfield for a number of record breaking flights and aeroplanes – Alex Henshaw's to Capetown and back in Percival Mew Gull G-AEXF in 1936 being one of them. Pre-war, after unsuccessful attempts to make Gravesend a commercially viable undertaking, the Air Ministry requisitioned it as a satellite of Biggin Hill. But once the necessary construction works had been completed and services installed it became more of a front line station and indeed during 1940 was regularly used by a succession of Fighter Command squadrons.

The move to Gravesend presaged a bad day for the Tigers on the 6th May when eleven Spitfires took off to escort three Blenheims and returned with three of their number missing – John Howard, Sgt Wilson and Arnott. Some retribution was granted the next day when three 109s were destroyed, probably destroyed and damaged respectively. On the 9th May John recalls Roger Boulding making a night contact when he was sent up and unwittingly found himself in formation with another aircraft – an He111. Roger throttled back and shot it down, his fire knocking the injector off the port engine – which was fortuitous as an He111 couldn't fly on just the starboard. The German came down not far from West Malling from which airfield the Tigers sometimes operated at night. The Squadron chased off to the crash site and liberated the Heinkel of various souvenirs including the dinghy and a bomb sight. More than anything else John wanted a 9mm Luger – why he cannot recall, but it was at the top of his shopping list. However, in the absence of that, he thought he would settle for the camera that Heinkels invariably carried. Returning to the wrecked aircraft by himself he began chiselling off the camera port when a very nervous Flight Sergeant from Farnborough suddenly materialised and demanded that John stop doing what he was doing immediately. 'Good God Sir! Don't you realise there may be an explosive charge beneath that panel!' No second thoughts had been given to this possibility. Neither had the danger of paddling the liberated

Gazing thoughtfully into an Emergency Water Tank at Gravesend in May 1941 are, left to right, Roger Boulding, Bob Poulton, a sergeant fitter, and Sqn Ldr Wood (who was a supernumerary on the Squadron at the time) with his Alsatian

Another Gravesend photo from May 1941. Seated at the front are Sqn Ldr Wood and John Mungo Park. Standing from left to right are Sgt Llewellyn, Peter Stevenson, John, the Squadron doctor, Tony Mould and Alan Ricalton. Seated on top of the vehicle is Bob Poulton

Gravesend May 1941

Above and Below:
Roger Boulding's and Sqn Ldr Wood's dogs

Above and Below:
Gravesend May 1941. Ops

dinghy around a local lake been considered – that too may have contained an explosive charge in its inflation mechanism. Farnborough relieved 74 of that too.

Gravesend was not without its lighter moments. Taking off from west to east took aircraft over the Assize courts with a regularity which upset the sitting judge to such an extent that he contacted the Station Commander and told him that flying would have to cease until the court sessions were over. There was a measured silence at the other end of the 'phone for a while before the carefully considered reply came: 'Why of course – we'll do all we can to minimise disturbing you. Mind you I'll have to ring the PM first to get his permission to cease operations.' Needless to say no more was heard from this particular Assize judge!

– o O o –

This is one of John's last recollections of his time with the Tigers for after three years (and just as they were re-equipping with Spitfire Vs), he was suddenly on the move away from the front line to rural Cheshire, Hawarden and 57 OTU where a whole new regime opened up for him. The powers that be had decided that John had been on the front line for far too long.

A little different from a Spitfire! A de Havilland Puss Moth. Dogs 3 - Tigers 3. Sitting proudly on the Puss Moth's wing is Ben, Mungo's dog. The human element is made up by Wood, Mungo Park and Freeborn. Woods' two dogs, Sam and Pat, hog the limelight in the front row!

Retrospectively, although John would again be in the thick of things later in the war albeit with squadrons employed in an essentially different role to that he had flown with 74, we can now appreciate that he had already shot down his last German of the war. That was on the 5th November when he had killed two and damaged one although another 'damaged' had been added to his tally on March 4th.

That is not to say that the rest of John's war was mundane – far from it. Several new horizons were to open for him.

Gravesend May 1941. John Freeborn brings ZP-C in to land

83

Gravesend May 1941. Bob Poulton stands in front of John's ZP-C. Note the code letter under the nose of the Spitfire

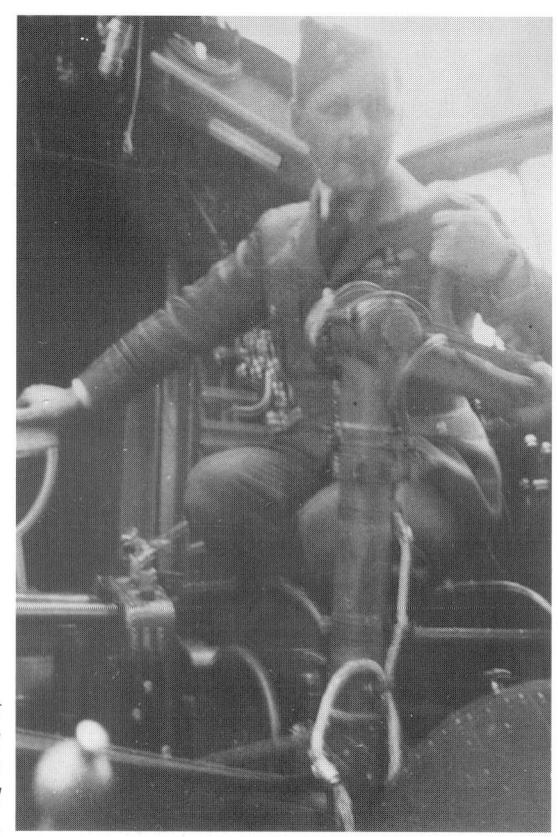

John in the He 111 which was shot down on 9th May near West Malling by Roger Boulding and from which the Tigers liberated the dinghy and various other bits and pieces...

Dispersal, May 1941

John with Bob Poulton, Gravesend May 1941, the emergency water tank behind them. How many actually ended up in the water? It certainly seemed to hold a certain fascination for them!

Plt Off Brian Draper ...
[Photo: 74(F) Tiger Squadron Association]

Sgt Pilot Clive Hilken
[Photo: 74(F) Tiger Squadron Association]

Fg Off Bill Nelson
[Photo: 74(F) Tiger Squadron Association]

Fg Off AJ Smith
[Photo: 74(F) Tiger Squadron Association]

Chapter 8
57 OTU

A posting to an Operational Training Unit in 1941 was essentially viewed as a posting granted to those who had been on constant alert during the Battle of Britain and its aftermath and who needed to rest away from the stresses and strains of intense operational flying. The truth, as John Freeborn quickly became aware, was that OTUs were also very busy places with flying, weather permitting, from first light to dusk. 57 OTU at Hawarden just to the south west of Chester was no exception and the particular brief here was to convert pilots who had completed their initial training in Canada to the Spitfire. This was no easy brief: some arrived at Hawarden not having flown for a year. As a result there was a terrible accident rate and it was invariably the mountains of North Wales which killed them. Warnings notwithstanding they proved to be a constant lure which was difficult to resist – perhaps because of, rather than despite, the area of flat lands between Chester and Manchester.

John quickly became used to the rookie pilots doing silly things – like getting lost. Regular landings would be made at airfields other than Hawarden when disorientation set in! In these instances a Master or Magister would be sent to collect the student pilot and his Spitfire would be flown back by an instructor. The lost pupil himself was never allowed to fly back. Another sheered off more than one pair of undercarriage legs. Making his approach he couldn't see past the Spit's nose as he came in to touch down and applied right rudder with all the resultant stresses of an off centre landing. John took him up in a Master to cure him of his predilection for doing so and after some perseverance just about succeeded. A system of fines and punishments was introduced for pilots' lesser misdemeanours, ranging from financial penalties (usually 2/-) to being made to walk around the perimeter track with parachute pack on to a term in the stocks outside the Flight Office! These proved to be very effective: all were painful in the pocket or physically and only the more obtuse student failed to be persuaded that he should be more careful in the future and make sure that when he switched off his engine he disengaged all the switches, or didn't leave his radio on when he exited the aircraft – and so on.

Not only were there stocks outside the Flight Office – but a pub sign as well! Inevitably this spent most of its time being hijacked and finding its way to obscure corners of the airfield before being returned on payment of a small ransom. Its presence was a gentle reminder to all those who had paid fines that the money collected was pooled and at the end of a course, when four or five pounds was in the kitty, it would be spent on all newly graduated pilots in the local hostelry! At the end of the day then it had been worth transgressing...

The aerodrome at Hawarden existed because of the decision to build a plant for the production of Vickers Wellingtons there. Work started on the factory in November 1937: the first Hawarden Wellington flew in August 1939 although initially test flying had to be carried out from the parent company's Weybridge airfield because the Cheshire airfield was already flooded! By the time production ended in October 1945 over 5,500 of the type had been rolled out of the Cheshire assembly plant's doors.

The busiest users of Hawarden however were Operational Training Units dedicated to the readying for war of fighter and fighter reconnaissance pilots – although with often only ten hours or so flying at OTUs before being sent to front line squadrons this could hardly be described as readying for war. There could, by official decree, be no failures at OTU and during John's time every new pilot he was allocated was passed. It had been a conscious decision to reduce the OTU training period to keep up with the demand for aircrew but this had an adverse reaction in that it only served to reduce efficiency on operations themselves and markedly increased wastage through accidents, particularly landing accidents on the return from operations. 1941 actually saw a surplus of aircrew – but for all the wrong reasons, primarily a shortage of aircraft due to production failures – but that is another story.

7 OTU was the first incumbent at Hawarden from June 1940. At the end of the year it was renumbered as No 57 OTU. At this stage Hawarden was still a very wet grass field with only one paved runway for Wellington testing (laid to alleviate the flooding problem). In the Spring of 1942 contractors moved in to remedy the situation on the rest of the airfield.

The OTU's record books are not replete with information about the day to day activity of the airfield. They do however confirm the intensity of the flying – 2,850 hours in the June that John arrived, 2,576 in July, a massive 4,357 hours in August, 2,776 in September, 2,758 in October and 2,532 hours in November. They also list the casualties and at the same time confirm the cosmopolitan nature of the OTUs – shortly after John arrived a Pilot Officer Cushion crashed into a hangar whilst taking off and was killed. In July six were lost, two Belgians, an American, two Canadians and an Australian: in August four, including an American and a South African. This was the month that Marshal of the Royal Air Force Viscount Trenchard visited the station: at the other end of the spectrum it played host to 1378 ATC Squadron from Mold. Indeed the ATC were frequent visitors. A practice defence exercise was held during September alongside the day to day activities. Just before John was posted away from the OTU six Spitfires were caught out by a sudden deterioration in the weather. Two pilots were killed; the rest mercifully survived. In the air sometimes something a little out of the ordinary would happen, such as the sighting of an enemy aircraft. This happened just the once to John when he was aloft with two students in formation. An He111 appeared suddenly and the three gave chase although if they had caught it it would have been to no effect as their aircraft were not armed. The 111 could have been part of an attacking force on Liverpool which was regularly targeted. Very often bombs missed their intended target and were dropped on surrounding moorland setting it on fire. In effect, this created a huge decoy and the burning moorland, wreathed in dense smoke, was often bombed in mistake for the city.

Course sizes varied. As John arrived, so did No 22 Course consisting of twenty four officers and twenty three sergeants. Concurrently six officers and twenty four sergeants from Course No 20 were posted to squadrons as operational pilots. Fledgling pilots didn't of course climb straight into a Spitfire cockpit. Arriving at Hawarden they had to start afresh on the Magister which was in itself quite a challenge as in Canada they had flown the Harvard, a very different beast from the British design. The Maggie, as it was affectionately known, was the RAF's first monoplane trainer which had been introduced in September 1937. Faster than contemporary biplane trainers with a top speed of 132mph it had a landing speed of only 42mph and proved to be an ideal training tool. Powered by a 130hp Gypsy Major engine, it had anti-spin strakes ahead of the tailplane and equipment included split flaps and a blind flying hood. In the main though, recalls John, pilots quickly showed their lack of confidence even on this docile aircraft although that was soon replaced by a growing awareness of their abilities in the hands of the experienced aircrew who were now instructing them. Once a check ride showed that a pupil could handle the aircraft safely he was sent off solo to do a series of circuits. Once this had been done to the instructor's satisfaction he progressed to the Spitfire and once safe handling had been established they were taught the rudiments of formation flying and low flying. A demanding schedule which was inadequately taught before being whisked away to the front line – at this stage of the war at any rate.

John was no stranger to teaching new pilots – he had had occasions on 74 to do just that, including the Hornchurch MO Sqn Ldr Lipman whom he took up in the station Magister. A familiarisation flight over Gravesend had included a demonstration (or rather an exhibition) of flying skills. This included some fairly unorthodox manoeuvres witnessed by a pair of Wing Commanders from Equipment Branch who were playing golf on the local course and who viewed with some displeasure John's attempts to 'attack' them! He was duly reported – but only after the pair had presented themselves, all sweetness and light, in the Mess that evening.

'A great display in the Magister this afternoon. Who was flying?'

John kept mum but some bright spark piped up: 'Freeborn sir. He was with Dr Lipman.'

'Well done Freeborn!' Drinks were bought and conviviality reigned. It was after the move to Hawarden that John was ordered to an interview with AOC Training Command at Worcester. He attended, was acquainted with the charge of dangerous flying levied by the devious Wing Commanders and was told to 'consider himself reprimanded'. John turned to leave the AOC's office. 'By the way, I don't really mean it. But it's got to go down on the record!'

Whilst at Worcester fog had descended and impatient of waiting for it to clear maps were produced and John considered means of getting back to Cheshire. If he took off east to west and picked up the River Severn and then the railway line heading north he calculated that could safely get to Chester. Although he hadn't counted on the fog persisting all the way north he made it by flying low and slow – no more than 60 knots he reckons – and at Chester station picked up the tracks of the North Western Railway which led him to the Vickers hangars at Hawarden where he was able to turn in and land safely. There is little doubt that his interest and knowledge of the railways helped in this venture although railway lines were regularly used as a navigational tool by everyone else as well.

John had been at Hawarden for some time when the powers that be suddenly decided to send him on an Instructor's Course at CFS Upavon. Here they flew Masters, two seat advanced trainers produced in great numbers (3,450 when production ceased in 1942) and used by all the Flying Training Schools and Advanced Training Units. The wooden Master Mk I had a Rolls Royce Kestrel engine with belly radiator and the main gears retracted backwards into the inverted gull wings, the wheels turning to lie flat. The instructor in the rear could crank his seat to a high position, tilting the roof of the canopy to form an external windscreen should he have to do a landing. Another lever down by his right hand (looking rather like a handbrake) allowed the rudder bar to be adjusted: and another to the left took the brakes away from the pupil. The Mk II was faster and was powered by a Bristol Mercury 870hp engine. The Mk III had the Twin Wasp Junior. John regards the Master as the finest purpose built training aircraft of that era – faster than the Hurricane and an aircraft in which an instructor could simulate many emergencies. At Upavon John was instructed in the art of instructing by Flt Sgt George Lillywhite, the initiator of IFR – Instrument Flight Rules – taught by the whole world today as one of the basic tenets of flying: thus John and his fellow pupils spent many hours in the Master's cockpit with the blind flying hood pulled over. They spent time in the Link trainer too, practising the same drill. George, one of the RAF's few long serving sergeant pilots who didn't return to their trade but just kept on flying (it will be recalled that Ernie Mayne was another), was a competent and dedicated man who was also quite a character, somewhat short sighted and who on one memorable occasion, so a probably (indeed hopefully) apocryphal story goes, taxied out to take off with a pupil without his glasses and mistook a crow coming down on the grass ahead of him for a landing Armstrong Whitworth Siskin!

John passed the course comfortably with his log book endorsed as 'average to exceptional' although in truth he found the whole thing a somewhat stuffy and serious affair. He was pleased to return to Hawarden so that he could get on with his job.

– o O o –

Of the five flights that made up 57 OTU, John commanded D Flight and recalls that 'Dirty' Watkins commanded C Flight and 'Ginger' Lacey commanded E Flight. James Lacey was not someone who courted friendship and preferred to be left alone. He was one of those whose actions spoke louder than words. Flying Hurricanes as a Sergeant Pilot throughout the first eighteen months of the war with 501 Squadron, his personal tally of victories started with a Bf109, Bf110 and three He111s prior to and during Dunkirk. From 10th July this tally mounted rapidly. He baled out twice after being hit by return fire but in both cases was back in the air in short order. On 23rd August he was awarded the DFM and a Bar was added on 26th November. In January 1941 he was commissioned. By the time he was posted to 57 OTU his total of enemy aircraft confirmed destroyed stood at twenty eight.

John had one other instructor pilot on the strength of his Flight, the former Gloucestershire cricketer Philip Mitchell. With just the two of them and with two courses running concurrently it was indeed hard work and at times, John felt, harder than flying in the Battle of Britain! There were two runways at Hawarden – one which was paved running east/west (which principally served Vickers) and the other a grass strip running south west/north east. The Vickers works were the cause of much congestion – around the airfield were dozens of parked Wellingtons awaiting delivery – and potential conflict in the air. Other residents were an MU and its attendant test pilots together with a unit of ferry pilots, No 3 Ferry Pilot's Pool. Amongst the new types being tested and evaluated at the time were the Blackburn Skua and Roc at which John looked askance, thanking God that he was in the RAF and not the Fleet Air Arm and being expected to fly such underpowered and overweight aircraft. Thus with the OTU, Vickers and the MU the scale of activity can be appreciated – landings and take offs every minute at busy periods. There was no flying control as such – a hut at the runway's end housed an LAC who fired a Very pistol if too many aircraft were gathering on approach, but a Very pistol that was sometimes ignored by the likes of Vickers' test pilot Mutt Summers as John recalls, an attitude engendered by the fact that everything and everybody at Hawarden appeared to be at a state of high priority. Summers was also predisposed to taxi straight out of the Vickers complex and irrespective of wind direction would take straight off from the Vickers runway. However, despite the lack of Air Traffic Control in the modern sense there were few accidents.

Mutt Summers was just one of several interesting members of the test pilot fraternity of those days that John met during the course of his RAF career, the next stage of which would involve him in similar activities as well. He recalls on more than one occasion the oddball, extrovert and fearless Mutt barrel rolling a Wellington! He also met those who would a few years later become fully fledged test pilots. Roly Beamont flew regularly with operational squadrons in between test flying and evaluation duties including those from Coltishall when John was later there: John Cunningham was 'top of the tree', a fine pilot: and Geoffrey de Havilland and John's paths crossed on one or two occasions during the wartime years.

To help ease congestion at Hawarden a new airfield was being built by McAlpines at Wrexham and once the runways were down and perimeter tracks laid C and D Flights moved across to operate from there during the day, returning to Hawarden some evenings, staying over on others. There was a golf club adjacent to the new airfield and aircrew made the clubhouse their own but the members soon had had enough of this rowdy intrusion and heaved a sigh of relief when the order went out to return to Hawarden *every* evening! There developed a sense of good natured and mischievous rivalry between the two Flight's commanders, Messrs Freeborn and Watkins – as with operational squadrons an OTU was a unit which demanded total discipline but which outside the training regime was one of friendly camaraderie. Taxying in after a sortie one day John spied Watkins sitting outside dispersal. As he swung his aircraft round to park he gunned the engine and raised a dust storm which liberally coated Watkins. Watkins promptly grabbed a rifle and by taking regular pot shots above John's head kept him pinned in his cockpit for forty minutes before relenting and letting him out. John's retribution came in the form of a Very flare let loose in a toilet cubicle inhabited by Watkins! A man can certainly run with his trousers round his ankles! This sounds very much like Freeborn and Watkins at war rather than a friendly rivalry!

After John left the OTU in December 1941, construction of a satellite to Hawarden was begun at Poulton which lay four miles to the west. By the time it was fully operational 57 OTU's successors, 41 OTU, moved in. Wrexham meanwhile no longer supported OTU flying and was host to 96 Squadron with its Defiants before its conversion to Beaufighters.

Whilst at Hawarden the local girls would become friendly enough to ask for a flight if the chance arose, including a little Jewish lass called Jessica who kept John supplied with the Craven As he smoked in those days – she even managed to get a supply down to him at Upavon when he was there! Where she got them from John never asked. Wrexham, with its lack of security, gave John the perfect opportunity. Here he was relatively out of authority's eye and on more than one occasion in a Magister he was able to meet the girls' requests. Some of them were confident. Others were rather more timid – but either way John took delight in putting the aeroplane through its paces even to the extent of inverted flying for the more brazen females! Others were quite content to stand and observe and at times there was quite a contingent of onlookers from Wrexham assembled to watch the flying, fortunately staying out of harm's way for there was no perimeter fence.

There were other antidotes to the hard work that Hawarden was as well, usually in the form of nights out in Chester, frequenting all the pubs and taunting the army. Last buses home ran at 9.30 – no good at all to instructors and pupils who wanted the nights to be long ones: invariably lifts back to camp were hitched on milk floats departing their depots in the early hours…

Chapter 9
The States

In December 1941 John was posted to Catterick in a supernumerary capacity to 145 Squadron – but he was only there for a week before he took some leave owing to him. On his return, he found that he had been posted to the USA as a Liaison Officer. John moved to a transit camp at Winsford where he waited for a passport and embarkation instructions. This gave him the opportunity to sneak off to Leeds to see his fiancée Rita. Rita had been engaged to John's cousin, but that relationship came to an end once she had seen a photo of John in the *Yorkshire Post* which she cut out and kept. The love affair began when John took a Master and a colleague down to Ringway (Manchester) where a pupil had landed a Spitfire with a problem and the aircraft needed collecting and flying back to Hawarden. John's return in the Spitfire was via Headingley where he put on something of an aerobatic display over his parents home – he was remembering stories he had read of World War One German aces who would be prone to aero-batting to entertain those on the ground! A low level pass over the rooftops of Headingley as a farewell gesture had people diving for cover – was this the Luftwaffe on a bombing run? John regularly announced his presence by beating up Rita's house and then landing at Yeadon when he came home for a weekend's leave. She always knew when he was about! But his unauthorised antics were inevitably brought to the attention of the AOC Training Command – John was on the carpet once again!

John eventually received joining instructions for his journey to the States – pack your tropical kit and get the train to Gourock! This was a bitterly cold and long journey and its discomforts were exacerbated by the need to sit on the train for hours once their destination had been reached whilst merchant sailors who had only recently docked after months away from home were being rounded up to be taken across to the USA to pick up and crew liberty ships in San Diego.

John sailed from Gourock in the 25,000 ton SS *Rangitiki* (74 was transiting to the Middle East on her sister ship the *Rangitata* at around the same time). It was not a good passage. In convoy with the *Louis Pasteur* (34,000 tons) and escorted by four British destroyers (relieved by four American ships at mid point so that the Royal Navy could divert into Iceland to refuel), the eight day crossing to Halifax was a rough one. Also aboard were German POWs – surly submariners who did what any self respecting prisoner of war would do which is to make life as difficult for their captors as possible. Amongst them was reputed to be Lieutenant Prien, responsible for the sinking of the *Royal Oak* in Scapa Flow. All the crew and many of the passengers were enlisted to keep watch as the convoy zig-zagged its way across the Atlantic – and whilst John may have been willing, he found it impossible to stay awake and alert when he was called to take his shift which earned him a prompt reprimand from the Captain! One redeeming feature about taking passage on the *Rangitiki* was the excellence of the food. It seemed the merchant navy were still in a position to look after themselves well in that department!

John arrived at Halifax without a passport, neither did he have movement orders – a familiar consequence of apparent ineptitude on behalf of those responsible for the RAF's administrative affairs which became a familiar feature to many in the service during the wartime years – but his ID papers were acceptable to the Americans in lieu after the British consulate stepped in. From Halifax – it seemed as if all the shipping of the North Atlantic was in harbour there when *Rangitiki* finally entered port – John took a train to St Johns (which given John's love of trains suited him very well as it gave him the opportunity of experiencing North American railroads) and then on to New York. (Here, for environmental reasons, steam trains were not allowed, only electric traction). New York was a revelation and being an RAF officer he was treated royally, especially by taxi drivers who would decline to accept fares. Next stop was Washington where John and Geoff Rothwell – who had a Bomber Command background and had come to the States with John and would a year later go home with him as well – reported to a Gp Capt Hogan, noted for his attempt at the Egypt to Australia non stop record in company with two other Wellesleys which ended ignominiously with Hogan running out of fuel, something which he was apparently regularly predisposed to do! After Hogan came an American two star general in whose presence John found it was a case of hats off before saluting – disconcerting to begin with but soon gotten used to. After this interview he was drafted to South Eastern Air Force Command having assumed the American rank of Major, with the job of British Liaison Officer to British pilots training in the States. It was not only American rank he received but American rates of pay and an American car too! American living standards were so very different from what he had been used to at home of course. He had access to Officers Clubs (they were the equivalent to the British Mess) and met several USAAF senior officers including Eisenhower who at the time was a Lt Col. The Americans were very friendly towards the British in their open and generous way and it became a common sight for John at the training camps to see American family cars lined up at weekends to take British students home with them. The young British pilots certainly had few quibbles at being so adopted!

John was impressed too by the often extreme patriotism of the Americans: they were not afraid to fly the flag as a country or as individuals – and once they had overcome the shock of Pearl Harbor they were even more determined to do so. In fact this extended to a devotion to the flag that in many ways surpassed the expected limits – such as the willingness to crew the B17s and B24s on murderous daylight bombing raids in the European Theatre of Operations simply because allegiance to Old Glory demanded it. Personal safety and an appreciation of the awful risks involved didn't seem to come in to it. John would later see the horrendous damage inflicted on these daylight bombers and their crews and the almost compulsive need for those who survived to go through it all again.

John also quickly became aware of a blatant money is no object approach when it came to getting things done. If the American military wanted something – they got it! Conversely, if they had finished with it there would be no attempt at salvage: and if something seriously broke, there would be no attempt to repair it, just replace it.

– o O o –

John's first bases of operation were Montgomery and Selmer in Alabama in the heart of the deep south, a small white community amongst a large one of blacks. He saw the despicable way in which the minority could treat the majority which somewhat tarnished his hitherto more than favourable view of the States.

At Selmer there was a huge training establishment. Three courses were running concurrently and they involved 600 men. The training aircraft was the Harvard – and there were seemingly hundreds of them. Great efforts were being made to train the Brits to get them to a level of competence which would see them in good stead when they joined an OTU in the UK. But there was a fundamental difference between the American and British training system which was reflected in the inadequacy of the finished product in the American case. Their ethos of instruction was basically one of 'I can fly, so you can too. Just watch me!' There were no professionally trained instructors as in the Royal Air Force. The *ab initio* course lasted three months and included some preliminary air firing instruction, where the student learned to use the aeroplane as a weapon once he had learned to fly it. From Selmer they would go to Eglin Field in the Florida forest lands which together with its six satellites was under the control of Wright Field, Dayton, Ohio. Facilities here were basic and as John became familiar with the system and the shortfalls he was able to suggest means of improvement. Continuing air firing was one area which demanded attention. John came up with the idea of using Link trainers on oval tracks in a huge sand pit, round which pilots would be pushed and from which they could fire (using a .22 rifle) at a drogue mounted in the centre, a system which once adopted immediately began to show results when the students became airborne and attempted the real thing. There were some problems with using the Link, one of which was sand in the giros which effectively nullified the trainer. No problem! Replace the trainer – and later, if necessary, replace it again.

But for John his role was largely a sedentary and administrative one: he soon tired of his liaison work and hankered after flying again. There was a brief interlude of interest when 20th Century Fox were contracted to make a training film: location shooting took place at Selmer and Eglin and John was able to follow progress closely. In the film was Tyrone Power with whom a lasting friendship was struck. Tyrone at this stage of his career was virtually penniless and the story goes he kept himself going physically by eating avocados that were growing under the window of his rooms. His fortunes were to change of course and he and John kept in touch with each other, looking each other up if they were in the same country at anytime – UK or USA. When Tyrone died of a heart attack in Madrid John felt his death keenly for they had become close friends.

It was typical of the States that all the big film studios would be involved in the production of training films unlike the RAF where invariably in-house photographers and service personnel were used on a shoe string budget and doing it all as part of their day to day jobs! It was through 20th Century Fox that John got an invitation to visit their Los Angeles studios if leave could be arranged. (This turned out not to be an easy task as his CO, Gp Capt Hogan, opposed it. There was a suspicion of pique here as he had not been invited himself!) Staying with an aunt and uncle in Pasadena (John's father's brother had had an fascinating career fighting in the Spanish-American war and then acting as Chief Engineer on the building of the Panama Canal) having travelled across the continental USA by the famous Sunset Limited train which seemingly stopped at every station between New Orleans and Los Angeles, a fascinating three weeks was enjoyed, hobnobbing with the stars of the day. It is a little appreciated fact that in its heyday there were more miles of permanent way in Britain than in America whose railroads were invariably single track. In the Sunset Limited's case this was certainly true. At the towns through which the line passed passing loops had been built and John and Geoff Rothwell – who spent the holiday with him – were intrigued to watch great double headed freight trains with prefabricated sections of Liberty ships aboard allowed through on their way to San Diego where all the components would be mated. This is the sort of thing the Americans were good at and where their organisational skills were best employed.

In LA, editors Hector Dodds and Barbara McLane were the passport to famous people. Henry Fonda was a charming and quiet introvert, very much in real life as he came over on film: Mae West was nothing like her screen image but was an unassuming woman living in a high rise apartment block: and, most memorably for John, Betty Grable with whom he contrived to spend three days and from whom he was pleased to escape. An empty headed woman if ever there was one!

Back in the real world, the training film was soon completed and it was a return to what was for John routine.

– o O o –

On his visits to Eglin he had encountered Major Bill Waller who was in charge of additional test flying of the new Republic P47 Thunderbolt. Wright Field was at the spearhead of this testing programme, as indeed it was of many others, and they farmed out some of the testing to Eglin to take the pressure off themselves. John was interested in what they were doing and in the knowledge that any aircraft the Americans produced could be potentially considered for RAF service he argued that there should be some British input into these initial testing phases, an argument he put to the Air Ministry. His ideas were accepted and John became one of the test pilot team at Elgin.

The P47 Thunderbolt would be built in larger numbers than any other American fighter. For its day it was huge and thereby attracted the popular nickname of The Jug – short for Juggernaut. It was big not only in size but in all up weight (initially over six tons but by 1945's later version well over nine!). From the Republic stable (a successor to Seversky Aircraft), chief designer Alex Kartveli had submitted the designs for a radically new machine to the United States Army Air Corps in June 1940, designs which were technically the most advanced then in existence. The engine installation – the 2,000hp R-2800 – was so complex that Kartveli had designed this first and then built the rest around it. The multiple exhausts for the engine were grouped into two massive pipes which glowed red hot at full power. The long landing gear shortened by nine inches on retrac-

John with Major Bill Waller at Duxford in 1943. John had met him during his tour in the States and when Bill brought a P47 Thunderbolt Group to the United Kingdom they met up again. Bill Waller was killed whilst escorting B17s over Germany

tion so that it could fit into normal wheel bays between the wing spars. Outboard of the undercarriage there were four 0.5" Browning guns in each wing together with their bulky (350 round) ammunition boxes. A four bladed 12ft 2ins Curtiss propeller absorbed the great power of the engine. The turbocharger was for aerodynamic reasons mounted under the rear fuselage instead of close to the engine. This together with a compressor which fed air to the engine via large ducts which incorporated intercoolers meant that internally the P47 was a mass of pipework which could only be incorporated in a deep fuselage. The design proved to be inherently very strong and could absorb much in the way of battle damage. The P47D was the definitive version of the type. In total over 15,500 of all marks were built. Conceived as an interceptor it found its true role as a ground attack aircraft.

John didn't like the P47. It was, he says, 'an evil machine' and as soon as he got into the cockpit he knew, because of the poor ergonomics, that he was into something bad. Everything was wrong about the aircraft – to him it was a very large thirsty engine in a scaled up Seversky P35 which itself was an aircraft which displayed nasty tendencies near the ground with wing tip and wing root stalling a characteristic. Water injection was in time added to give a boost in power and therefore performance but the fact that the P47 was so very heavy meant that it took a while to get up to speed – although once there it was amongst the fastest of aircraft around and when operational in Europe could outrun the Bf109 and FW190. There is no denying that the Thunderbolt was responsible for the deaths of many a good pilot until the problems were sorted out but, to their credit, Republic persevered and most of those problems were resolved. In the early stages the 56th Fighter Group, on Republic's Farmingdale factory doorstep, were given the job of evaluating the new fighter. Ground crew were won over, particularly in the engine department, for accessibility to the big Double Wasp was particularly good. Pilots were less convinced. The cockpit was unfamiliar with a mass of hydraulic lines, electrical cables and strange controls for the turbo-supercharger and other new systems. Added to this was the unimpressive climb performance. There was also the preconceived idea that a fighter should be a sleek needle nosed machine and here pilots had a hugely bulky and heavy radial fronted aircraft that simply didn't look as they expected it should. On the plus side, at altitude performance was much better and it handled well. But it acquired a reputation amongst RAF pilots that seemed hard to shake off: when John had returned to the UK and was at Coltishall with 118 Sqn his old friend Bill Waller came across with a squadron of P47s to Duxford. John went down and gave the Americans a scintillating demonstration in a Spitfire Vb. To reciprocate Bill brought a P47 to Coltishall and gave pilots there an opportunity to fly one. No one took him up on the offer. In retrospect, though, it must be acknowledged that the Thunderbolt was, despite its size and complex design, the first to have the capability of taking the fight to the enemy as an escort and a ground attack single seater.

John's out and out favourite aeroplane of the war was the P51 Mustang. One of a small number of aircraft that was conceived, developed, produced and put into wide scale use within the six years of war, its genesis was in April 1940 when the British Purchasing Commission negotiated with North American Aviation to design and build an advanced fighter for the RAF. The matter was urgent. German forces were in Denmark and Norway. They were likely to move westwards imminently. Britain was threatened. The country had to be defended and the home aircraft industry was struggling to provide enough aeroplanes for the job. The Americans were given 120 days to build a prototype. The rest, as they say, is history. Actually, the design wasn't completed from scratch for Raymond Rice and Ed Schmued had already had ideas down on paper before the British visit, ideas which they tailored to the British requirement. Thus they were able to meet the prototype deadline in airframe terms with an aircraft that looked absolutely right: unfortunately delays with the Allison V-1710-39 powerplant meant delays with the first flight which didn't take place until October 26th 1940: but subsequent testing proved the old adage about aeroplanes looking right and flying right. In May 1941 the first production aircraft came off the line. By November the RAF were evaluating the type as the initial examples of the 320 ordered were produced.

The Mustang, says John, was quite simply the best fighter aeroplane of the war. It looked elegant and was, in concept, simple – not a complicated design like the P47. Yet it carried a very significant punch. In the European theatre its main asset came to be its tremendous range which enabled it to escort bombers deep to the heart of Germany. Much thought had been given to the pilot – ergonomics were spot on, everything was where it should be. And this of course was crucial when it came to turning an aircraft into a fighting machine. Any experienced pilot could quickly see that with its laminar flow wing it was, at low levels, going to be fast and manoeuvrable with a low stalling speed. It was safe, sturdy and strong. The limitations of the Mustang I were at high level where the power output of that first engine installation fell off rapidly. But these problems were quickly addressed and as with all successful designs the Mustang went through a series of improvements and developments. Over 14,000 were eventually built world-wide, the majority serving with the USAAC, USAAF and USAF.

With the P38 Lightning John flew 1,000 mile legs at 40,000ft to test fuel economy and to suggest operating changes to increase efficiency. Eglin to Chicago to Milwaukee and back was a regular sortie. Allison engined but underpowered, it would have been a superb beast if Merlins had been fitted. As it was there were some problems with engine temperatures and the turbo blowers were not as good as they could have been. The higher the aircraft flew, the faster they ran. John had to watch the rpm for the engine was restricted to just under 3,000rpm and if he exceeded this he was forced to throttle back. But aerodynamically it was an excellent design. Over the vast distances of the Pacific, if a P38 needed an engine change and had to be ferried back to a main servicing base to do so the propellers could be removed and the aircraft towed back as if it were a glider so good was it! There is no denying that if the engines had been better, the P38 could have given the British Mosquito a genuine run for its money.

There were other types John got his hands on as well – types which he would encounter again the following year in the European theatre as escort to them on their forays into German occupied territory. The B17 for example – John flew what was probably one of the early production E model aircraft with the enlarged fin on a sortie which was one for the logbook rather than as a requirement for evaluation. This, he recalls, handled beautifully but couldn't compare with the experiences of crews flying the type, fully laden, in the war theatre. Actually the B17 is a classic case of an aircraft which enjoyed a measure of affection from its crews which was really out of all proportion to its performance and effectiveness as a fighting aircraft, heavy and very tough that it was. The Douglas A20 Havoc too was a delightful aircraft which, at the right height, could be aerobatted in fighter like style. This twin engined aircraft, designed by Ed Heinemann and Jack Northrop, was to become the USAAF's most numerous attack aircraft although it was initially built for foreign air forces. France, for example, ordered the type but after the fall of that country deliveries were diverted to the RAF who operated the aircraft as the Havoc and then as the anglicised Boston, primarily in the light bomber role at which it excelled. The Mitchell, another twin engined type, this time from the North American production line, was to John not as pleasing as the Boston – not that pleasing was a word on the minds of its designers: satisfying the whims of fighter pilots turned evaluators was not at the top of their list of priorities! 11,000 were ultimately produced and they served on every front. John flew either the C or the D model. Also regularly flown were versions of the North American AT-6 Harvard, mainly in its role as a liaison and communications aircraft.

One of the very few photographs that survive from John's time in the United States. This was taken at Selmer on John's arrival and he makes the acquaintance of one of the officers – name forgotten – who supervised the British students there

The Americans at Eglin and other test centres around the States were as keen to get their hands on British equipment as the British were American. The Brits in the States felt compelled to live up to the expectations of their cousins who believed that the British and British equipment was amongst the best available. And not just aircraft – but a whole range of kit from motor cycles to radios. So very often the Americans took the best of what they found and with their seemingly limitless (by British standards) financial resource, developed it and created even more technologically superior materiel which found its way back across the Atlantic – to the United Kingdom's advantage.

But there were certain things which the Americans didn't appreciate so much, particularly in the traditional sense. Tropical clothing and the wearing of shorts for instance, a facility which their military didn't have but which British forces in the heat and humidity of the world's warm places always wore. John always made a point of wearing his so as to reinforce the British tradition. And the kilt. At Selmer a Flt Lt MacTaggart was in charge of the drilling of new British student pilots and as a native of Scotland he always turned out in full RAF tropical gear, complete with the family tartan, and had his charges marching in the Guardsmen's way which was in complete contrast to the American soft shoe'd shuffle and relaxed style of drill. MacTaggart, as so many others had been and for ever will be, was inspired by the sight of a battalion of Guards in full uniform, kilts swinging to the marching step and the skirl of the pipes. Those who saw this defiant gesture at Dunkirk, for example, will always remember the pride, the essential Britishness that this represented. The Americans had no such tradition and to a certain extent they were in awe of it.

– o O o –

On the way back to the UK from the United States, John and Geoff Rothwell spent some days on the town in New York. The Diamond Horseshoe was a famous and expensive club in which they were entertained by staff of the RAF Benevolent Fund. John is second left, Geoff far right

After a year in the States the time came for John to leave. He had made many great friends there but he was homesick for Rita and despite the attractions of the New World he was not sorry when his posting came through. The trail home (in Geoff Rothwell's company again) began with a flight to Montgomery in Alabama where Gp Capt Hogan gave them a good send off. From Montgomery John went to New York where he reported to the Royal Air Force Benevolent Fund Centre. Here he found a staff dedicated to raising money for the Fund but at the same time managing to live the life of Reilly. This appealed to John who was promptly let in on the act and he had a high old time in the Big Apple. However, having the UK in his sights and wanting to be with family and loved ones he became impatient to be on his way, a desire satisfied with his and Geoff's receipt of a movement order sending them on to Boston and a berth on the *Queen Elizabeth*. This didn't actually turn out to be the luxury the orders suggested for it was soon found that overcrowded cabins were to be shared with numerous other bodies – a factor to which objections were raised. Ultimately this resulted in another movement order which sent the pair off to Halifax which for John represented the joining of a circle – in via Halifax, out via Halifax. Once again he found this Nova Scotian port to be drab, cold, wet and bedevilled by almost constant sleet. But it at least offered a means of getting back to England, a means confirmed with assignation to the Motor Vessel *Cavina* (an ex-Fyffes banana boat) on which the passage to the UK would be made. Pending sailing John and Geoff were booked in to a local hotel where to their delight they found Anna Neagle and Herbert Wilcox were staying – and what's more, the couple were waiting to board the same ship for England. Once again, in John's gregarious manner, he struck up a friendship with this famous couple. 'Dear Anna, what a lovely person she was,' he recalls. 'The awful reality that was Halifax was immeasurably brightened by her presence: Rothwell and I enjoyed our dining sessions with her and Herbert immensely.'

Outside the pleasure of dining in the local restaurants, the opportunity was taken to date a local nurse who was quite happy to return to John's hotel room. The hotel were less than happy that she did so and promptly ejected our man who thus found himself homeless. The Master of the *Cavina* took pity and allowed him on board for the few days prior to their departure. Indeed John was allowed to pick his own cabin – a nice outside berth with its own porthole. It so happened that when Anna boarded she was allocated a single cabin opposite to John much to Herbert Wilcox's dismay. He had to share with others and that didn't go down at all well: he also apparently distrusted John and took up an almost permanent vigil outside her door! Not that John had any designs in that direction. 'She was a lovely lady whom I respected and liked very much' – too much to have any thoughts of impropriety. She was a rather different proposition to Betty Grable!

With a full complement on board the *Cavina* set sail for the UK, on the Commodore's instructions at the head of one of several columns of ships. A large contingent of civil servants who had been working in Washington had taken the majority of the available berths on board. What a poor lot they were, suffering terribly from seasickness and not being particularly discrete about the fact. The truth was that the weather was awful and John benefited by being blessed with sea legs (Geoff Rothwell unfortunately wasn't!). The convoy in which they were sailing was a large one, sixty eight ships of all nationalities escorted by four corvettes, meagre protection indeed. There should have been a fleet auxiliary too but that vessel didn't show. An often unpleasant aspect of convoy operation was the need for the majority to regulate its speed to match that of the slowest ship, in this case a Russian coal burner with a top speed of just six knots. The result was an awfully uncomfortable voyage – a combination of slow speed, high seas, the vicious weather of winter in mid Atlantic, the *Cavina* lurching from trough to crest with the constant threat of U boats and with infrequent views of their protective corvettes scurrying around, or at least trying to, in the mountainous seas, shepherding their charges along but being very nearly swamped in the process. Rain, hail, sleet, snow – and the moaning and keening gale force winds. Sheer misery for the civil servants and those not born to be sailors. Within hours of encountering the constant storm the dining room emptied leaving John as virtually the sole patron for meals. The crew of the *Cavina* coped pretty well though. Captain Denning was a sailing master of the old school and under his protection were half a dozen young cadets with whose education he continued even in the foulest of weather. The captain and John struck up a rapport very quickly and from the first night the latter would present himself at the former's cabin door at 6 o'clock ready to share a drink.

The civil servants saw over indulgence in drink as a route to escape from the misery they were feeling: rum and beer were the preferred tipples: perhaps they were the only ones! But this predilection was also their downfall. Anna Neagle and Herbert Wilcox too proved to be very good sailors and they determined to put on a play as a diversion from the weather, the civil servant's plight being at the forefront of their minds when they conceived the idea. The two of them, with very limited resources, of both material and human kind, managed to stage *Queen Victoria*. Sadly the civil servant brigade were past caring about Queen Victoria and progressively became drunker and drunker. Captain Denning was appalled at their behaviour. The main offenders were locked up and were kept in the cells for the remainder of the voyage, ready to be charged with disorderly and offensive conduct when they reached a British port. John was not impressed. 'Poor buggers! That was harsh treatment for getting drunk. They were only trying to forget their misery and although it was disrespectful to the efforts of Anna and Herbert a little more leeway might have been given by Captain Denning.' However, remember he was of the 'old school'.

Seemingly countless days after setting sail from Halifax the convoy wearily approached Belfast where it broke up – some ships going into the Northern Irish port, others heading for Liverpool, the Clyde and Avonmouth. The *Cavina* berthed at the latter and the total complement of passengers was subjected to a rigorous Customs' search. Anna Neagle was not immune from this and much of the stuff she brought from Hollywood was confiscated after being fined for non disclosure! John got away with it: his trunk was packed full of cigarettes and tobacco but such had been the preoccupation by Customs officers with the actress that he was overlooked. From Avonmouth John and his possessions were sent to Uxbridge and thence on three weeks leave – but not before he had bumped into his old 74 Squadron mate Tony Mould in Aldwych when en route to the Air Ministry. Tony had actually been on a bus and John had caught sight of him and chased him down to the Strand! A few nights out in the capital allowed old times to be mulled over. Tony had recovered from the injuries sustained whilst with the Tigers and had gone on to transfer to a Mosquito night intruder squadron. Sadly he would be killed whilst on a mission in Europe.

During the three weeks of happy leave up north with the family he had not seen for twelve months, John married Rita. It was a marriage that would last 34 years but it ended sadly. After a long troubled period Rita finally had to be committed to a psychiatric unit from which she refused to be removed even to come home. There she died, leaving John to cope with life with his daughter Julia. John would later remarry and find happiness again with Peta whom he met when he moved to Spain in the early 80s but whom he also lost in early 2001.

– o O o –

The idyll of marriage and honeymoon didn't last long – although John's posting certainly turned out to be no hardship. Orders came to report to London's famous

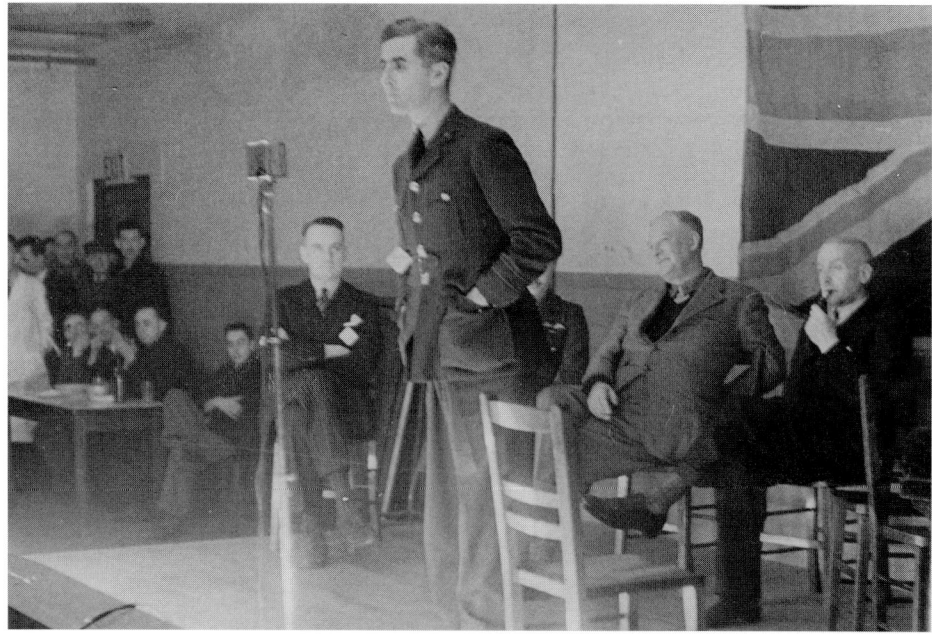

Taken at Morris Motors at Cowley whilst John was seconded to the Ministry of Supply on his return from the United States. Not only were the Forces involved but guest speakers too. Here Brooklands Bentley racing driver Tommy Wisdom takes to the floor

Morris Motors again - and John addresses his audience

Adelphi hotel. Here he found a Major Richard Turpin (who must have blessed his parents for their choice of Christian name!) who headed up a department dedicated to spreading the news of the war as it was to the people of Britain. This initiative was not a recruitment drive but rather an information exercise during which teams were sent to the factories of the country to address the work force. Generally the reception was friendly and interested. Only occasionally and for unfathomable reasons was it not. John was teamed up with a badly injured and disfigured Wellington bomber pilot, a Flt Lt Pooley who, despite his horrific facial injuries, was a cheerful soul. This short tour of duty was for both of them the 'bees knees' – for expenses appeared to be no problem. (Dick Turpin's favourite trick was to produce a thick wad of bank notes and peel off a more than generous amount for his teams when they left for their next assignment!) It was also a time for acquiring limitless numbers of railway travel warrants.

John was with the Ministry for around three months during which time he travelled the length and breadth of the country, sometimes with just Pooley, sometimes with invited speakers such as famous Brooklands Bentley racing driver Tommy Wisdom. From the Morris factory at Cowley to the shipyards of the Clyde they travelled, happily lecturing their audiences, enjoying the experience – and notching up a quite formidable expense account! Newly married John recalls a trip to Glasgow as the best. After the lecture he took himself off to a local dance hall. The story that followed was one of girls, the Royal Navy, finding themselves on a naval salvage vessel with a renegade and slightly potty captain who had no intention of letting them off as he sailed down the Clyde to the open sea in search of his latest salvage, the appearance of a pilot cutter at an opportune moment, a flying leap (girls and all) and a return to dry land. Good times indeed!

But of course it could never last. There came a call to report to RAF Exeter but once there nobody seemed to know what to do with him until out of the blue he was posted to Bolt Head on the north Cornish coast as Station Commander. This was situated atop a wild section of West Country coastline and was a grass airfield which acted as a diversionary airfield to Exeter and overlooked the bay where the Marines trained. The problem for John was that there was nothing there – no aircraft, very few people. In fact this gave a clue to its existence – for Bolt Head was purposely built as a rudimentary airfield with very few facilities and its proximity to the coast was to enable it to 'collect' the often short endurance fighters of the early war years. Short endurance was not such a problem when operating defensively but for aircraft on escort work this could be critical and they were grateful for the existence of this cliff top airfield and others like it!

Eventually things improved considerably with the arrival of 257 Squadron with its Typhoons but as soon as that happened and just when things looked as though they could have become rather more interesting, an erk ran up a Typhoon on engine test, forgetting to chock the wheels. Both man and machine disappeared over the cliff edge. Before anyone was able to argue that this failing was John's responsibility, he found himself on the move again, this time to Perranporth to join 602 (City of Glasgow) Squadron as a Squadron Leader supernumerary. It was December 1942 and life was about to take another new direction.

The States

Chapter 10
602 Squadron

602 (City of Glasgow) Squadron (*Cave Leonem Cruciatum*) had been the first of the famous Auxiliary squadrons to form on 15th September 1925. Initially equipped with the DH9a it converted to Fairey Fawns in 1927 and then Westland Wapitis in July 1929, the type which it took to Abbotsinch from Renfrew in January 1933. In common with other Auxiliary squadrons 602 went on to fly Hawker Harts and Hinds in the 1930s before in November 1938 becoming an army co-operation squadron with Hawker Hectors. This however was a short lived requirement and in short order 602 converted to the fighter role with Gloster Gauntlets in January 1939 shortly followed by the Spitfire – the first Auxiliary to do so and testimony to the reputation the squadron had carved out for itself in the fourteen years of its existence. At the outbreak of war it was fully operational on the new aircraft and moved to its war station at Grangemouth. It was quickly into the fray when in October it repulsed the first Luftwaffe attack on British soil in concert with 603 (City of Edinburgh) Squadron, two He111s being shot down in the process. 602 remained in Scotland until August of the following year when it moved down to the south coast and Westhampnett which was a Tangmere satellite station. Immediately flying defensive sorties a tired and hard worked squadron gave a very good account of itself, flying as part of 11 Group. It was rested at the end of 1940, returning to Prestwick to do so and in fact remained on the Clyde until July 1941 when it joined the Kenley Wing and re-equipped with Spitfire Vbs which it flew on offensive sweeps, bomber escort duties and *Rhubarbs*. Moving from

Sqn Ldr John Freeborn at Perranporth with 602 Squadron. This photo was taken by John Topham, the Squadron's Intelligence Officer who prior to joining the RAF had been a bobby and after the war became a very well known freelance photographer

109

one extreme to the other yet again, in July 1942 602 was moved to the Orkneys where it became a component of the Scapa Flow defence force flying airborne patrols with new high altitude Spitfire VIs. It was after the Squadron moved on yet another north to south posting – to Perranporth – that John joined them in March 1943. Perranporth had originally been opened as a satellite to Portreath and was situated on the exposed north Cornish coast, a bleak place when the weather was poor and which was not well like by those stationed there. 602 was one of a number of Spitfire squadrons that were based at Perranporth on escort and coastal defence work together with the patrol of the South Western Approaches.

Mike Beytagh was 602's Commanding Officer. He was a great character who nonetheless had had a bellyful of fighting having arrived at Perranporth from the desert and had been in a combat situation for far too long. As so often happened, for those in positions of responsibility, relief was not always forthcoming when it should have been and willing horses were continually flogged. When he did finally get away, Mike left the RAF and joined the Diplomatic Corps: it was whilst with them that he died in South Africa.

602 was flying anti shipping and *Circus* patrols with Spitfire Vs. It was also escorting bombers – sometimes heavies such as Lancasters and Halifaxes but more likely Mitchells and Venturas – on forays across the wider Channel to attack the German ships holed up in Brest and the U-boat pens. John was never comfortable with these raids – they were all over water with no margins for error or accident. 602 were the sole squadron committed to the escort role in that part of the theatre with only occa-

602 Squadron's Commanding Officer, Sqn Ldr Mike Beytagh

sional back up from other units if they were available. This was rare although when they did materialise they could be interesting forays: a Westland Whirlwind squadron made one appearance and after bombing had been completed and the bombers had been safely shepherded towards home, course was set for Perranporth – except for the CO of the Whirlwinds who insisted that *his* course was the correct one. 602 recovered safely to Perranporth: the Whirlwinds were never seen again – well, not at Perranporth anyway! Perhaps the Bishop of Truro had blessed their endeavour before departure as he had done a component of 602 before they set off some weeks earlier. Four Spitfires had been the subject of his prayers: sadly they were all shot down and the Bishop was quietly asked not to make a return visit.

John's first convoy patrol with 602 (he had been allocated to A Flight) was on

602 Sqn at Perranporth. John Freeborn and Mike Beytagh are flanked by other Squadron pilots

the 14th March (flying EP328) and it was an uneventful one. The same was true of the 15th. The same cannot be said of a raid escorting Mitchells to Dieppe which John led and on which the leading Mitchell, and thus the formation behind it, inexplicably lost height as it neared the target. The price was paid when this fully bombed up aircraft was hit by flak and exploded spectacularly, literally vaporising the Spitfire on its far side. John immediately pulled up and was far enough away to escape damage. The whole formation turned back. But as to why it had been losing height was a question which would not now be answered.

A week later Leigh Mallory, by now C in C Fighter Command, visited Perranporth and spoke individually to each member of the Squadron. This should have been an inspiration for John who, having met his Boss, was due to go to nearby St Agnes to take part in a Wings for Victory parade – and make a speech! John was wise to that though. A prerequisite of participation in these parades was to be dressed in best blue. John made sure he was in battledress and forage cap! No parade – and definitely no speech!

He quickly became part of the Squadron's social scene – in fact he was quite a valued member of the 'club'. He took on Fl Off Jimmy Yates (also known as Piltdown Prune!) in a friendly competition to take leading honours in the use of the gun and took advantage of Jimmy's absence on leave to beat and best his score. The targets, incidentally, were seagulls and crows, not 109s and 190s. Rabbits were on the agenda too and John went off in the company of Pl Off Strudwick to bag a few for the pot. 'The rabbits', note the diaries rather laconically, 'were never in any danger!' Most stations were equipped with an arsenal of single bore and double bore shotguns, the idea being that they would be used for clay pigeon shooting as a prime means of learning the art of deflection shooting for when in the air and engaging the enemy. They had better uses though, game shooting being just one them! They were a good deterrent too and a means of exacting retribution – Dirty Watkins had used one to good effect, you may recall, at Wrexham when he pinned John down

John's good friend Jimmy Yates on 602 Squadron. Jimmy was an explosives expert who had been a Captain in the army before joining the RAF as a Flight Lieutenant. This is another John Topham photograph

in his cockpit. Peter Chesters had also been forced to flee in the face of a gun toting Freeborn after speeding through a muddy puddle and drenching John's best blue. He grabbed a twelve bore, Peter swiftly retreated up a tree, John shot at him in the tree – and the MO spent a few hours pulling pellets from his anatomy!

Jimmy Yates, incidentally, had been a Captain in the Royal Engineers but later opted for a transfer to the RAF. As with so many of the people John befriended he had a very vibrant sense of humour and was one for practical jokes. But John, as always, gave as good as he got and, for example, took great delight in telegraphing ahead to Jimmy's parents that their son was on his way home on leave and was bringing his wife and baby to meet them – which would have been something of a shock for they had no idea that Jimmy was spoken for. He wasn't of course.....

John also befriended 602's Intelligence Officer, John Topham, who was to become a renowned photographer after the war. Both Johns were lovers of their food and they dreamed up a little ruse to ensure they got more than the exigencies of the time usually allowed them! Disappearing (with permission) from the Squadron for a couple of days at a time, they took to booking in to local farmhouse B&Bs just so as to enjoy a full and hearty farmhouse breakfast – egg, bacon, home made bread, plenty of butter – the works! It was a rare farm who hadn't made provision for themselves and could produce all that was required to start a day off on the right foot.

On April 3rd 602 teamed up with 65 and 19 Squadrons as escort for a dozen Venturas which were bombing the docks at Brest. A trio of FW190s sniffed the air and tried long range shots at 65 but then disappeared. On the 4th John scrambled in EE721 but saw nothing. On the 5th 602 were top cover (with 65) to Venturas bombing Brest again. Once again FW190s appeared and 602's Flt Sgt Robinson had a go at two of them but made no claims to destruction or damage. On the 7th the Squadron conducted an uneventful sweep to Brest – other than the fact that John's erstwhile shooting partner, Jimmy Yates, failed to return. His disappearance was a mystery although Jimmy was another one like 74's Peter St John – he wouldn't keep up with the rest of the formation. The last patrol that John flew from Perranporth was on the 8th and once again it was an NTR sortie – nothing to report. A few days later 602's Sgt Eames suffered engine failure and ditched during a shipping recce. He would survive in his dinghy on nothing but the contents of his ration pack for two weeks before he was rescued!

– o O o –

Accommodation at Perranporth was in a comfortable hotel but a rude awakening was now in store. Orders came for the squadron to relocate to Lasham near Andover where it would become a component of the 2nd Tactical Air Force, working up in the ground attack role. John remembers the transit to Lasham over a bleak snow swept Dartmoor on April 14th and contemplating the severity of the conditions there, little expecting conditions at their new home to be comparable. It was after all April for goodness sake and it was a brand new station! Land had been requisitioned as recently as September 1941, the original intention being that it would be a satellite for the bomber OTU airfield then being built at nearby Aldermarston. McAlpines were the contractors and they made rapid progress (including the diversion of a main road) and within a year it was taken over by 38 Wing, Army Co-operation Command, the OTU plans having been cancelled. Lasham remained unused for six months: facilities remained largely unbuilt for six months too and still hadn't been completed in sufficient quantity to cater for 602 when they moved in. Accordingly a tent village was erected. Not only were there few facilities, there was little equipment of any sort either. Not expecting to ever need it John had sold his camp kit to 34 Squadron pilot Johnny Allan who, when with 54, had accompanied Al Deere as top cover on the Laurie White rescue mission at Dunkirk. Johnny had missionary connections and John's kit was probably in the depths of Africa at the very time he needed it in the depths of a late English winter. The cold was bitter and penetrating and all personnel resorted to sleeping fully dressed with beds piled high with any additional blankets that could be scrounged topped up with the odd greatcoat. When it rained tents began to leak, mainly because people touched the sides releasing a deluge of water onto the incumbents. It was a truly unhappy stay although the Squadron record shows an initial optimism about the whole situation.

At Lasham with 602 Sqn in the cold April of 1943. John wears his pyjamas over his uniform in an attempt to keep warm in the tented camp seen in the background. The mugs were for tea for John and CO Mike Beytagh. The pail was for water for washing in

Today we all moved into tents and we all agree that at the moment... it is a fine experience. We just expected huts – but dug ourselves in and took things easy.

Within a few days though it was only the perverse sense of humour that invariably surfaces at these times that kept everyone going. And innovation of course. Home made fires started to be seen, and even electricity was tapped from an obscure mains supply to provide light. It didn't take crews long to learn how to live off the land. The only transport available was an ancient motorbike and side-car: but this was put to good use by raiding parties into the surrounding countryside in search of game. One of the Squadron pilots was a Frenchman – known to all as Henri – who could turn his hand to cooking and pheasant, liberally smeared with butter liberated from the Mess, became an essential supplement to the poor tack sent across in 'honeyboxes' which were supposed to keep food warm but which never did. Commissioned and Non Commissioned Officers shared the same Mess and contributed the sum of 3/- a week to provide the 'extras' which they all considered very much worth the money.

602 Squadron's Doctor, Intelligence Officer and Adjutant at Lasham, the latter John recalling as being a power boat racer in peacetime

Conditions at Lasham notwithstanding training commenced for its new 2nd TAF role (although Lasham itself would not be transferred to the TAF until the end of August), but not before John was ordered back to Perranporth on the 17th for that most important of sorties – collecting the mail! On the 18th cross country flying was on the agenda. On the 19th they conducted a practice attack on an army convoy with tragic results. During the course of the 'attack' some army co-operation Mustangs got mixed up with 602's Spitfires. A collision occurred and the tail of a Spitfire was sheared off sending it spinning into the ground. The Mustang unsuccessfully attempted a controlled crash landing: its pilot didn't survive.

Mercifully 602 were not at Lasham for long – by the 29th April they were on the move again – for not only were conditions bad but relationships with the Station Commander were not happy either. He seemed impervious to 602's plight and was not committed to improving their lot. In return 602 became somewhat 'anti' themselves. The result – life for both sides became difficult. It was a relief to all concerned when the Squadron moved again, this time to Fairlop near Romford, one of a succession of eight fighter squadrons to use it during 1943. It was however a case of frying pans into fires, for Fairlop was not adequately provisioned either in terms of accommodation and crews found themselves under canvas once more.

602 Squadron at Lasham. John Topham is standing on the left with the Squadron MO next to him. John is fourth from the left with the Frenchman, Henri the pheasant chef, five from the right. The Squadron Adjutant is sitting just in front of John. As for the rest, time has obliterated memory of the names...

Originally developed as a satellite for Hornchurch, Fairlop had at one stage before the war been earmarked by the Corporation of London as the site for its airport, plans which were shelved thanks to gathering war clouds and its subsequent taking over by the Air Ministry. It was hardly reassuring that Fairlop was at the centre point for shrapnel falling from the London barrage, shrapnel which had to be cleared from the airfield every morning before flying could begin. Thus it was a case of taking to the shelters each night, air raids or no raids. Small comfort was to be had from the companionship of a navy wife whom John found, a relationship which ended when the husband turned up unexpectedly one night and very politely asked John to leave. A simple 'you are not welcome here' showed considerable restraint on the aggrieved husband's part although John was obviously always hopeful that nothing more physically damaging was suffered by the girl.

Missions of other kinds were quickly taken on although in John's case he was not in the air again until the 15th when he flew with 602 down to Hawkinge to refuel and then escort Bostons to Pol: on the 16th it was to Tangmere, refuel and escort Mitchells to Caen, both days uneventful in terms of enemy interference. But it is a sad fact that no contact with the enemy was necessarily needed to promote loss. Exercises with the army again on the 18th this time involved a pair of Spitfires intercepting and 'shooting down' a 90mph army co-operation Auster. In its strenuous efforts to shake off the attentions of the Spits the Auster manoeuvered too low and hit a tree. The aircraft burnt out and the occupants were killed. Bad weather put a halt to flying for the next seven days before escort work was undertaken again – on the 25th six Mitchells (two of which were lost) were taken to Abbeville. On the 29th 602 were back at Tangmere to join 121 Wing as close escort for Venturas to successfully pattern bomb the airfield at Caen. On the 31st a dozen Mitchells were escorted to the benzole works near Zeebrugge. Despite constant attention these works always seemed to survive the bombing inflicted on them for reasons John has never been able to fathom.

A spot of leave followed and whilst he was away a posting notice came through. His short association with 602 was about to come to an end for on June 17th 1943 John was posted to Spitfire Vb equipped 118 Squadron at Coltishall and his first command.

Chapter 11
118 Squadron – Coltishall

602 Squadron were certainly sorry to see John go. John didn't particularly want to go either as he liked the camaraderie of 602 immensely. But go he must!

He is well overdue for a squadron but we are sorry to lose one of our social stars. He is also sorry to find that 118 are equipped with Spitfire Vbs with long range tanks and bombs.

John was hoping for Spitfire IXs at least. Vs were OK but despite the clipped wing which many Vbs sported (endowing a very respectable roll rate) and a bigger engine, it turned out to be something of a clod of an aeroplane. It was underpowered for, quite simply, too much was hung on it. John had been spoiled by his beloved Mk II which handled better and went quicker than any other variant. The Spitfire V had first appeared in February 1941 and was to be built in different versions. The Mk Va, based on the Mk I but with a Merlin 45 engine producing 1,515hp at 11,000ft and armed with machine guns, was built in only modest numbers. The Vb was cannon (two 20mm) and machine gun (four .303) armed and, as with the Va, could carry a 35 gallon drop tank: it carried a bomb load (two 250lb bombs under the wings or a single 500 pounder under the fuselage) almost as heavy as the Blenheim could cope with. The Spitfire Vc was similarly armed bombwise but toted four cannon and a 90 gallon drop tank.

118 and its Vbs was particularly good at *Roadstead* strikes against enemy shipping. The Squadron, when it was made up of mostly of Dutch and Free French pilots, had gained a fine reputation for this kind of work whilst operating off the Cornish coast with Coastal Command. It was also doing a lot of bomber escort work when John arrived – American Eighth Air Force Marauders out and Fortresses back, the latter a sorry picture when the extent of the damage inflicted by the Luftwaffe on the B17s was seen. Such were the types of formation flown by the Americans that collisions occurred with some frequency as well, particularly when in cloud. Bombing accuracy was also suspect and the feeling was that the types of raid flown were generally not effective in relation to the damage they did to the enemy.

Ramrods – straightforward bomber missions designed to simply bomb the enemy rather than acting as decoys to get enemy fighters into the air – involved in the main aircraft of 12 Group as escorts. Rendezvous with Bostons or Mitchells would, for example, be over Beachy Head at 0900 – and invariably the bombers were there on the dot if they were 2 Group RAF. Transit to Beachy Head by 118 Squadron from Coltishall would be at *very* low level to avoid any chance of a build up of aircraft being picked up by the Germans – across Essex aerodromes almost between, rather than over, parked aircraft, under power lines and across Kentish fields where haymakers atop their haywains could almost be looked in the eye – all at speeds of up to five miles a minute. John relished this sort of flying! Transit across the Channel, with 118 in its customary close escort position on the left of the leading group, was at low level too: then, two thirds of the way across, the formation climbed through to 10,000 feet as it crossed over the enemy coast. The RAF's Bostons and Mitchells had a different bombing manner to the Americans: they would pass the target at 14,000 feet, turn, approach the target at descending altitude, bomb (usually very accurately) and then get out of the area as quickly as possible. The Spitfires carried 35 gallon drop tanks on these missions which, once the fuel was used, were dropped, often indiscriminately by those flying top cover so that dodging falling fuel tanks became an integral part of the mission! Once the Bostons were homeward bound the Spitfires would relax their close escort, although keeping the bombers in sight.

If it was the Americans and their massed ranks of Marauders who were to be escorted, RV procedures and the subsequent bombing effort were far more lax and unpredictable. (One statistic that John recalls is that just 3% of American bombs hit their intended targets on these raids). Simply throwing numbers into the fray was not the answer unless accompanied by some sound tactical thinking – and perhaps better training for the crews. It took the Americans a long time to formate and typically 118 would leave Coltishall bound for Tangmere at roughly the same time as Marauders were taking off from their various bases looking for their brightly coloured rendezvous ships, spend an hour on the ground at the Sussex airfield and then take off to join the Americans.

If the aircraft to be escorted were Venturas then they would invariably be of Australian manned squadrons

Bostons, Mitchells, Venturas and Marauders were all light/medium day bombers of American design and manufacture. The Boston came from the Douglas factory and first entered RAF service with 88 Squadron at Swanton Morley in 1941, replacing Blenheim IVs. They were used by 2 Group (and the 2nd Tactical Air Force) on antishipping strikes and for raids on Continental targets. Bostons were twin engined (Wright Double Cyclone radials) and had a top speed of just over 200mph at 13,000ft with a range of 1,000 miles and could carry a bomb load of 2,000lbs. The Mitchell (known as the B25 in USAAF service) was a twin-finned North American design of which 800 were delivered to the RAF. As with the Boston they were used by 2 Group and the 2nd TAF, with the latter making pre-invasion attacks on northern France. Performance was considerable better then the Boston – a top speed of 292 mph at 15,000ft: a range of 1,635 miles with 4,000lbs of bombs (or 950 miles with 6,000lbs.). The Lockheed Ventura first entered service with 21 Squadron in October 1942 but proved to be not particularly successful on daylight raids and by late 1943 had been withdrawn from this role to re-emerge as a Coastal Command reconnaissance aircraft. With a pair of Double Wasp engines it had a top speed of 300mph. The USAAF's Martin B26 Marauder first appeared in Britain with the Eighth Air Force in early 1943: its initial performance was disappointing and it quickly became apparent that the aircraft was vulnerable to ground fire after many losses were recorded – an entire flight of ten aircraft was wiped out during an attack on the Velsen generating station at Ijmuiden on May 17th for example. After this it was moved to medium and high level operations. At the end of 1943 the B26 was transferred to the 9th Air Force (eventually twenty eight squadrons of the type were formed) as a medium altitude strategic bomber against targets in preparation for D Day.

A lot of aircraft were involved in escort work and typically they were layered around and above the bombers' formations. 118 with its Spitfire Vs was literally 'close' escort and as such the last line of defence were enemy aircraft, invariably Focke Wolf 190s, to penetrate the rest of the defensive screen. Immediately above the bombers were Spitfire XIVs and above them Spitfire IXs, which could match the 190s performance, as top cover – usually 11 Group aircraft. These were the squadrons that always got to mix it with the Luftwaffe. Rarely did 118 have the opportunity, for the enemy would have already been picked off or driven off – which is one reason why John scored no further air to air victories after his time as a Tiger. Others got to them first!

– o O o –

118 Squadron – with a motto of *Occido Redeoque* – had a badge depicting a flaming galleon, thus illustrating the Squadron's shipping strike role, which had been authorised by the Chester Herald shortly before John's arrival. 118 had existed only briefly as a training squadron during the First World War before disbanding in November 1918, not to reappear again until February 1941 at Filton as a fighter squadron equipped with Spitfires and being engaged on convoy patrols, offensive patrols and as escort to coastal strike units. For the first half of 1942 118 was located at Predannack in the West Country, working with Coastal Command and flying convoy patrols again before moving to Tangmere as part of that Wing and being heavily engaged on *Ramrods*, *Rodeos* and *Rhubarbs*. Equipped by now with Spitfire Vbs it was soon found that they were at a disadvantage when they came up against FW190s so the Squadron was moved to Coltishall in January 1943 where in effect it became a 'spare' squadron which, whilst for the moment maintaining Coltishall as home base for shipping strikes, became something of a peripatetic outfit moving to where its escorting skills were required.

Sqn Ldr Bertie Wooton DFC, John's predecessor on 118, had left him with two rather hostile Flight Commanders. These John moved on as soon as he was able with Station Commander Vere Harvey's backing ('we'll get them a DFC and they'll go quietly!') and replaced them with Tony Drew and John Shepherd. Tony was a great rugby player (Northampton had been his team pre-war) who was to stay with 118 after John's departure as Commanding Officer. He came to the Squadron from Malta where he had been involved in the flying off of Spitfires from the *Ark Royal* to reinforce that island's defences. John needed the support and expertise of men such as these as he set to in knocking 118 into shape. It seemed to him to be in a pretty poor and undisciplined condition when he arrived. In John's eyes they were an unkempt outfit too so, having smartened them up pretty quickly dress wise – John's tidy man, tidy mind principle was at work here – he smartened them up on the parade ground as well. Then it was down to the real business and John was determined that there would be little sleep for anybody until everyone on the Squadron could prove to him they were able to do the job asked of them. They all knuckled down – even the Engineering Officer came to terms with the demands placed upon him for availability of aircraft. Harking back to his Tigers' days, formation take offs and landings became the norm: air to air and air to ground firing was always carried out with a camera gun: and every spare moment between flying actual missions was taken up with training of one sort or another. Whenever a Spitfire flew it had to attack something – for real or in training – and bring back the film to prove it! A sense of pride in a job well done was engendered.

As an aside, here we have one of the few instances in our tale where John's memory and official records cannot be reconciled. He recalls John Shepherd as leaving the squadron early in his time as CO with Mike Giddings coming in then rather than at the somewhat later stage that the 540s show. Record keeping was a matter of how committed those detailed to do it were. Some were very good – others recorded the barest information and then only sat down to do it days after the event. It was ultimately down to Commanding Officers to ensure that records were accurately and conscientiously kept – after all they had to countersign them at the end of each month – but the truth was COs themselves often had more pressing matters on their agendas and record keeping wasn't a top priority for them either! As far as our story is concerned we will keep an open mind and go with the record whilst acknowledging John's reservations about their accuracy sixty years after he signed them off!

It didn't take long – barely a month in fact – to achieve the proficiency that John demanded. The material with which he and his Flight Commanders – particularly the latter to whom the training task was fully delegated – had to work was essentially sound and this soon manifested itself in a squadron that began to be noticed. Able assistance and support in the task was given by the Squadron Intelligence

Officer Fl Off G A le Mesurier – fondly nicknamed 'Misery'. A tea planter from India (his time there left him with considerable stomach problems which required frequent hospitalisation) and a great fun merchant when off duty, le Mesurier also found time to write the slang entries for the Oxford Pocket Dictionary. Another stalwart at the time was Adjutant Henry Mallory, in civilian life a jeweller from Bath. Henry was a charming but fussy man who was always impeccably dressed and at the drop of a hat would don his best blue in case he met someone of importance!

There were lighter moments on the Squadron too of course. The story of the WAAF, for example, who doggedly clung to the tail of a Spitfire as it was being run up to full power to test its brakes and then refused to let go as the aircraft began to taxi – and then take off! The pilot got a bigger fright than she did when his awkwardly handling aircraft was found to have an unwanted passenger at the rear end! Flying a gentle extended circuit, an equally gentle descent to land was made and it was only when the Spitfire touched down and slowed that she fell off. There are few documented instances of WAAFs taking such unauthorised rides. It is known, however, that a Spitfire Mark V currently flying with the Battle of Britain Memorial Flight was involved in a similar incident. It is just possible that this was the aircraft that John recalls.

WAAF's at Coltishall were an enterprising bunch in many ways. John's personal driver was a brawny girl with an eye for a quick buck. Perceiving a definite need at the isolated place that was Coltishall with its almost total lack of facilities at this stage of the war, she set about recruiting some fellow WAAFs and set up a discrete, but increasingly well patronised, house of ill repute in Cromer on the North Norfolk coast within easy reach of camp and giving clients the excuse for an evening out a well! It was not long though before the whistle was blown, the brothel was raided, the girls were caught and sent off to the remote northern outpost of Skeabrae where, it was thought, they could come to no harm. But the powers that be had reckoned without the Pioneer Corps who hitherto had only had sheep for company. Soon business was booming and a few months later when 118 itself had moved north and were operating detachments from Skeabrae John came across his former driver again. Business, she declared, had never been better and she thanked the day that her Cromer operation had been raided and she had been given this new opportunity!

– o O o –

The following resume of ops in the main covers those in which John participated with 118 Squadron which, incidentally, was the only squadron based at Coltishall at the time. 402 and 416 were both Royal Canadian Air Force squadrons flying Spitfire Vbs from Digby in Lincolnshire (friendly outfits they were too) and 118 flew with them regularly. The Wing, of which the three squadrons were the components, was often led by John. On 21st June he flew his first operational sortie with 'his' Squadron (in AR447 which was to be his allocated Spitfire until it was lost at the end of July – on this occasion John wasn't at the controls – when it collided with EP191 in a formation break). This was part of a ten aircraft shipping strike but for John and Fl Off Dunning it was curtailed by engine problems and they were both forced to return as they were crossing the English coast. The other eight continued, looking for shipping reported to be off Den Helder. Nothing was seen there, but to compensate a convoy came into view near Texel. 118 attacked an escort vessel which responded with heavy flak which downed two Spitfires. Both pilots were killed – Fl Off Handley managed to bale out but there was insufficient height for his 'chute to open. Flt Sgt Caxton hit the sea still in his cockpit. Damage to the escort and a couple of minesweepers was scant compensation for this loss of life. The following day John and the Squadron were up again, this time to provide withdrawal support alongside 402 and 416 Squadrons for 100 B17s returning from a raid. No enemy aircraft were seen.

The men of 118 as John arrived on the Squadron in June 1943. Sitting atop the Spitfire is the popular Sinhalese, Fl Off Tallala. Back row from left to right– W/O Faulkner; three unidentified individuals: Ken Paal (RAAF): Flt Sgt Spencer: unidentified: Fl Off Burglass (killed in a collision with Flt Sgt Hollingsworth on 29th July). Front row from left to right – unidentified: Pl Off Roy Flight (shot down and captured on 15th September): the Norwegian, Lt Liby (who ditched on 15th August but successfully made it back to England): unidentified: Fl Off Murray (later killed in action): Flt Lt Dicky Newbury, OC A Flight (replaced by Tony Drew): Flt Lt John Shepherd, OC B Flight: unidentified: Flt Joe Hollingsworth (killed in the collision with Burglass): Flt Lt Doe (supernumerary): Engineering Officer Fl Off Spinney Merewood
[Photo: RAF Coltishall History Room]

A little later on the same day, the 22nd, 118 was escort to 16 Group Beaufighters attacking a convoy off the Hook of Holland. Once again the RAF lost two aircraft in exchange for an escort set on fire, two mine-sweepers damaged and four merchant vessels raked with cannon fire. Beaufighters were powerful aircraft with twin Bristol Hercules sleeve valve engines. Armament of four Hispano-Suiza 20mm cannon and six .303 machine guns represented formidable fire power in itself but with the additional capability of carrying eight rockets (which when fired were the equivalent to a broadside from an 6" cruiser) and a torpedo it became positively evil! The Beaufighter was based on the Beaufort. Service trials began in 1940 and despite some early problems (underpowered and a tendency to swing on take off as well as being longitudinally unstable at low speeds) Bristol worked hard on their rectification and aircraft started to enter squadron service from September of that year, the first of 5,500 eventually produced. Its biggest continuing weakness was an asymmetry problem that manifested itself when one engine was out.

Wing Commander Rabagliati led a formation consisting of aircraft from 118, 402 and 416 Squadrons as an escort to twelve Bostons bombing Albert as a diversion on an 11 Group *Ramrod* mission on the 23rd. On the return leg half a dozen FW190s made contact near Abbeville and they attacked the bombers but were driven off without loss to the RAF. One 190 which had been first intercepted by 402 and 416 as it tried to get amongst the Bostons was engaged by 118's 2nd Lt Liby.

Liby opened fire at 600 yards closing to 300: the German's mainplane was damaged – panels could be seen falling off – and then its dive angle increased to the vertical and it entered a series of uncontrolled spirals and hit the ground. Liby was a Norwegian who as with many of his countrymen didn't particularly like the British because of a perceived superiority complex on their part. Nevertheless he had come across after the German occupation of his country and was doing a good job. One thing that sometimes rankled with having foreign nationals serving in British squadrons was that they continued to be paid at the rates they would have received were they still flying with their own air force – which was invariably better than the RAF were! The Canadian situation was a particular case in point where, John recollects, Pilot Officers received the equivalent of an RAF Group Captain's pay! And there were considerable benefits for the Canadians in other areas too – welfare included.

On June 26th the Squadron was down at Hurn and took off in the early evening with the intention of providing withdrawal cover for B17s returning from bombing Le Mans but cover was not possible as the Americans were not seen! 118 returned to Coltishall ready for a 16 Group *Roadstead* the next day led by Rabagliati. Twenty one Beaufighters were involved this time and along with 402 and 416, 118 acted as rear cover. Three mine-sweepers were attacked and were left burning by the Beaus but they were in turn intercepted by 190s and 109s before being driven off with a 190 shot down. This helped counter the loss of a Beaufighter to heavy flak. On the 29th 118 flew down south again to join the Tangmere Wing in another withdrawal cover operation. Once again the B17s they were to escort did not materialise.

John's involvement in operations was curtailed at the beginning of July when he was admitted to Station Sick Quarters with a bad dose of 'flu (he always seemed to be catching it at Coltishall) where he languished for four days before being discharged and sent on three weeks leave. On his first day incommunicado (6th July) Wing Commander Rabagliati crashed into the sea sixty miles from home after trouble with his aircraft's Napier Sabre engine, whilst leading a seven aircraft shipping strike – Typhoons of 195 Squadron from Ludham. Other members of 195 saw a dinghy floating near the crash site and were hopeful the Wing Commander had managed to get out. A Walrus, escorted by six 118 Sqn Spitfires, set out from Coltishall on a rescue mission but by the time the search area was reached the weather was horrendous. With squally rain showers, thunderstorms and high seas, nothing was found of the Typhoon or its pilot. In all sixty aircraft were involved in the search. A further Walrus rescue mission was launched when another Typhoon was lost, this time to a FW190. Unfortunately 118 Squadron's Spitfire Vb EP124 itself crashed soon after take off.

It was not until 27th July that John was back in the air and this was as close escort to Mitchells bombing Schiphol in the Netherlands. Taking up position above and to starboard of the bombers 118 engaged attacking Messerschmitts and the Norwegian Liby came up trumps again, destroying one. 118's Sinhalese pilot Fl Off Talalla – 'a splendid fellow and a great character,' John recalls, 'black as the ace of spades, from a wealthy ruling class family in Ceylon which had modelled itself on the British Raj and with an accent as British as British could be' – shared another with Pl Off Flight. The 28th was a glorious day weatherwise, a day on which 118 and a formation of eighteen Marauders created a diversion which involved flying to a point ten miles off the Dutch coast, turning north for a while and then returning to base. If it was hoped to draw enemy fighters it didn't succeed as nothing was seen.

The 29th July was not only a day on which 118 lost two men and two aircraft in a tragic accident, it was also a busy one in terms of sortie generation. It had started from Matlaske in north Norfolk, one of Coltishall's satellite airfields, as part of an escorting force to Marauders attacking a target near Amsterdam. Things, as so often

124

seemed to be the case, didn't go quite according to plan and the bombers for some reason steered a very erratic course – 'behaving most extraordinarily' as the 540's state – before deciding to abort the mission. Bombs were dropped into the sea and whilst the top cover suddenly found themselves under attack, Marauders and close escort returned safely to their respective bases. In fact 118 landed at Matlaske again before returning to Coltishall after lunch. It was as they broke to land that Pl Off Burglass and Flt Sgt Hollingsworth collided, crashed and were killed. John, in formation with Hollingsworth and Burglass and leading the Squadron, had called 'break, echelon right', the intention being that the Squadron would land in threes. As he called he pulled the stick back to allow his No 3 move to the right of his No 2: unfortunately Hollingsworth flew into Burglass. It was not as if these two were inexperienced for they had been with the Squadron a long time and had flown many ops. Both left a family behind. Indeed, to compound the tragedy was the fact that their wives saw the whole thing from the ground – of all the pilots on 118 at Coltishall these ironically were the only two who had their wives with them. Station Commander Gp Capt Arthur Vere Harvey dealt with the distressing situation and in so doing demonstrated what a compassionate and kindly man he was. He was later to leave the RAF to become Secretary of State for Air.

As ever such events could not mean a cessation of the job in hand and in the early evening 118 were on the move again, this time to Bradwell Bay in Essex, escorting bombers attacking St Omer. Unbelievably a repeat of the morning's experience manifested itself with an erratically steered course by the bombers after an early arrival at the rendezvous point. On this occasion though the target was hit after avoiding heavy flak as landfall was made – but then as they came out of their bombing run the formation turned right instead of the planned left which caused considerable confusion to the escorting fighters! However, fortune smiled on them: no enemy aircraft were encountered and France was left behind with Cap Gris Nez sliding beneath them. All reached home safely.

– o O o –

August – and after the loss of AR 447 in the Coltishall collision, BM 628 became John's favoured aircraft and he set about having it personalised. Coded, as ever, 'C' all the pop rivetting was filled and made flush: the joints at the wing's leading edges were filled too: and it was polished – and polished again. Over 400 man hours were invested in the aircraft and there is little doubt that it must have looked beautiful – an aesthetic looking aircraft anyway, this extra attention would have made it something very special. Nobody was allowed to fly it other than John: a felt mat was laid on the wing so that the latter wasn't marked as John ingressed and egressed the cockpit and when ground crew needed access. And there was a significant benefit in speed too – an extra 25 mph thanks to the aerodynamics of a highly polished surface.

Fifty one Spitfires from four squadrons (118, 402, 416 and 611) acted as escort and top cover to thirty three Beaufighters on a *Roadstead* from North Coates, successfully attacking an eighteen ship convoy, steaming south at eight knots in three lines and flying balloons, off Den Helder on the 2nd August with several ships sunk or damaged and a Bf109 claimed as a probable by 118's John Shepherd. Three were destroyed by the other escorting squadrons. 611, incidentally, was the Auxiliary West Lancashire squadron which had recently moved into Matlaske with 609, both with Spitfire Vbs. Later the same day 118 were airborne again, this time in company with Typhoons of 195 and the Spitfires of 609 Squadron. Led by Wg Cdr 'Laddie' Lucas they were on a further shipping strike. Overflying the scene of the mornings' sortie they saw tangible evidence of its success with a balloon still flying from a sunken vessel and other ships lying in Den Helder roads. Incidentally John maintains to this day that Lucas got a DSO which had been promised to him by Vere Harvey! Unfortunately before this could be recommended 118 travelled south to Westhampnett and Merston leaving behind a Laddie who was pleased to be awarded it instead! The medal though was obviously a 'Coltishall' award rather than an individual one, as merited as it might have been by either Freeborn or Lucas!

Four days later 611 Squadron lost a man and a Spitfire V off the Dutch coast and 118 were very involved in the search for him. A second patrol spotted a red flare as light was fading at 2130 which was thought to be him but darkness fell and this precluded following it up. Next day the search proved to be abortive. On the 12th, 118 were flying with the Tangmere Wing, escorting Marauders on a raid on the aerodrome at Poix. On the 13th they were back at Coltishall escorting Beaufighters to attack four mine-sweepers reported by Mustangs to be operating off Ijmuiden. There were no mine-sweepers, only fishing boats.

– o O o –

This was the day that 118 learned that they were to be moved to Westhampnett just to the north of Chichester and become a component of the Tangmere Wing. This made sense and was something which had been argued for for some time. Most of 118's escort work originated off Beachy Head which necessitated flying down from Coltishall to land and refuel before getting on with the job in hand. At least now the Squadron would be on the doorstep.

Nowadays known as Goodwood, Westhampnett is, and always was, an attractively sited airfield which had been requisitioned in December 1938 from the Duke of Richmond's Goodwood Estate and opened as a Tangmere satellite in July 1940. Three years on and 118's Adjutant was furiously packing up at Coltishall and making out the requisite movement orders to Westhampnett. A basic problem, not uncommon, was the lack of packing cases and scrounging became the order of the day to stand any chance of securing the important stuff at least. But then there was no guarantee that what was scrounged would be adequate. The Intelligence Officer for example was provided with a rather flimsy three ply wooden case in which to cart important documents from one end of the country to the other. There were doubts as to its integrity and these were well founded for during the handling necessary to get it onto one of the railway waggons provided for the move it burst. 'Ah well,' sighed an exasperated diarist. '118 Squadron always somehow gets there in the end.'

Impending moves notwithstanding, ops continued unabated. On the 15th they were at Martlesham Heath and formed part of the close escort to Marauders attacking Woensdrecht. It was a shambles. The bombers were late at the RV point and the second box was trailing badly so the whole affair was called off. Which at least meant that on their return 118 could concentrate on getting down to Westhampnett which they did by air, airlift and rail. There was no chance to settle in though for scarcely had the aircraft touched down at their new home than they were airborne again, escorting a raid on Bernay airfield – a sortie on which their successful Norwegian Liby was lost after his engine failed and he was forced to ditch. The Squadron didn't hear of him again until they were languishing in the far north of Scotland three months later when they found out he was back in England and had had time to get married to boot!

Two days later there was a second attempt on Woensdrecht but whilst this time the attack was pressed home, cloud and rainstorms hindered the effort and the results were described on the return as 'indifferent'. Woensdrecht survived largely unscathed. A big show was mounted on the 22nd when in company with their Canadian friends from 402 and 416 once again 118 provided close escort to thirty six Marauders attacking Beaumont le Roget. This proved to be a tense mission with top cover engaging enemy aircraft as the bombing was underway. FW190s managed to break through and get into the Marauder stream with 118 battling furiously to protect their charges and the Marauders themselves putting up some concentrated defensive fire. Whilst their own tangling with the enemy proved to be inconclusive, the 190s eventually decided to call it a day and left the scene but not before a Marauder and 190 shot each other down. It was Marauders again the next day, the 23rd, with the Gossnet electrical plant the target but lousy weather over the French coast meant that the operation was called off.

This gave 118 an opportunity to react quickly to a totally unexpected order for them to move yet again. They had only been at Westhampnett for a week – long enough for them to decide they liked the place. But likes didn't come into it and Merston (only a few air miles away to the south of Chichester and another Tangmere satellite) became their new home. All that had so recently been unpacked was frenetically repacked and the goods and chattels of 118 Squadron were transferred! This move came a result of the rather obvious conclusion that it made sense to group the same mark of Spitfire together – thus 118's Vbs should link up with other Vbs at this Tangmere satellite and these just happened to be their old friends of 402 and 416 Squadrons from Digby. Actually 118 had got wind of the fact that they had been due to re-equip with the Spitfire IX but these were diverted to Polish squadrons. John was livid but despite vehement objections to losing the new Spitfires he was overruled and ops continued with the Vbs.

On the 26th, 118 flew to Exeter to act as rear cover to Bostons bombing (successfully) a power station at St Brier Dren. 118 didn't cross the coast on this one but circled off the Brier estuary until the bombers returned. But when Bernay was the objective again on the 27th poor weather intervened and the operation was scrubbed. Then Venturas bombed the forests to the north of St Omer where, it was believed, ammunition dumps were concealed. There were no gigantic explosions much to the disappointment of all those watching but fires were started and this had to suffice. As it was 118 were more concerned with avoiding the heavy flak which had accompanied them into the target area and certainly escorted them out again. There were no enemy aircraft to contend with though which was probably just as well. Then on the 31st they made contact with eighteen Mitchells at the pre-arranged co-ordinates to escort them to Manchy Breton airfield. 'It is believed the airfield bombed was too far to the north of Pol to be Manchy Breton,' the day's report comments. 'But wherever it was a neat stick fell across it!'

September 3rd 1943. 'An historic day – the anniversary of the outbreak of war and the day Italy was invaded.' 118's diary keeper recognised the significance of the date, something which was reinforced to all at Tangmere when Lord Trenchard visited after an early sortie had been flown escorting Marauders to Beaumont le Roget airfield. The 'Grand Old Man' (as many in Fighter Command referred to him) was up to his inspirational best as he insisted on being introduced to all pilots of the Wing and then went on to give the type of morale boosting address for which he was renowned. But nothing stops even for a Marshal of the Royal Air Force and he was cut short when the Wing was ordered to Coltishall at fifteen minutes notice for a shipping strike. As it happened they were recalled shortly after getting airborne and all aircraft returned to their respective airfields to spend the remainder of the day untroubled. There was some diversion though in the sight of large numbers of B17s flying over as they returned from a mission – enough, as far as the size of the formations were concerned, to quicken the interest of even the most blasé of observers.

On the 6th September John led the squadron on close escort work with Marauders which were attacking the marshalling yards at Rouen – and attacking it well as John saw sticks of bombs laid right across the target. Accurate flak from Dieppe meant that for a while it promised to be an interesting trip home. Later in the day the stakes were raised and a formation of seventy two Marauders formed to attack more marshalling yards, this time at Serqueux. Pol was visited the next day with the same number and type of aircraft to escort. The bombers on operations of this size were in four boxes with 118 on this particular occasion escorting the first box with a position on the port side of the formation. It was an 0800 hours start for the ten Spitfire squadrons employed from various Wings – all Spitfires of different marks, mainly Vbs, IXas and 'bs. Quite a formation and quite a sight! In position at its head, 118 was able to see the initial results of the lead bomb aimer's laying in of the target and on his command the complete formation let its bombs go. Unfortunately John saw nothing hit the yards but the surrounding areas were plastered. A solitary FW190 came up – a brave man – and had a go at the Marauders, disappearing into the midst of the formation box in the process. A claim of fifty enemy aircraft destroyed was subsequently submitted – one aircraft for each of fifty Marauders!

Numbers were reduced to more familiar levels on the 8th as eighteen Mitchells attacked Vitry en Artoise – accurately and, being the RAF says John, with the correct target selected this time. As the Mitchells pulled out half a dozen or so Bf109s were spotted. It was left to 402 and 416 (who were top cover for the formation) to engage the Messerschmitts. One was claimed as destroyed.

Next day there was an early start – everyone was called at 0330 and by 0415 had tucked into a good breakfast. 118's brief was to patrol a convoy of landing craft and escort vessels (corvettes) off Dungeness. Suddenly tension was raised. Could this be the beginnings of the long anticipated and talked about invasion of Europe? Considerable colour was lent to the idea when a high flying German – obviously reconnaissance – was shot down into the sea off the Isle of Wight by 124 Squadron. However that was to be the last German shot down by anyone that day and by the end of the second sortie pilots began to smell a rat and shortly thereafter it became apparent that this was not an invasion force, merely an exercise on the grand scale! Disappointment was rife! Abandoning the convoy for routine Boston escort duties (they were bombing Manchy Breton again) only confirmed this. On the way home a pair of 109s tried very hard to formate with the Spits but were promptly driven off by 416 Squadron.

Chapter 12
118 Squadron – North of the Border

A fundamental change in the establishment of the Squadron was now promulgated when the powers that be decided that in order to increase mobility it should only consist of pilots, the Intelligence Officer, Adjutant, MO, one sergeant fitter and one clerk. The Engineering Officer and ground crew would be posted out – to 3051 Servicing Echelon – and would no longer accompany 118 on its wanderings. The intended objective of the change – increased mobility – would certainly be realised for there would be less personnel to uproot, pack and transfer as the Squadron moved around but the down side was that many ground crew who had been with 118 since its reformation in 1941 would now be lost to them. Instead of their own groundcrew the Squadron would be serviced by a permanent establishment at each station they operated from. It was around this time that WAAFs started to arrive as groundcrew – flight mechanics, armourers and radio mechanics. At this stage of the war at least they were not Fitter 2s but they were certainly good at what they did and aircrew were more than happy to see the girls on the wing. There was little evidence of male chauvinism here.

There was a certain prescience to all this talk of manning changes for within twenty four hours of being informed of it they were told to be ready to move again – but with all groundcrew. Establishment changes could wait! This time it was to what for many equated to foreign parts – Peterhead. Were the natives friendly they wondered? And was the move possibly a reaction at senior level to John's vehement tirade at losing the Spitfire IXs to the Poles? Probably not. Its switch from escort work to what was fundamentally a training role was more likely a reflection of the fact that most of the pilots at this time were tour expired.

Before they could find out about hostile natives there were a few cases of the abandoning of aircraft – metaphorically in the case of two Americans that had been attached to 118 (Captain Weaver and First Lieutenant James) who were moved on, but literally in the case of Pl Off Flight who parachuted out when his aircraft's engine caught fire – not as the result of enemy gunnery but of a very fast dive when he was chasing an FW190 whilst on escort duty to Merville on the 15th. He came down behind enemy lines and it was later confirmed he had been taken prisoner. Weaver and James had been welcomed onto the Squadron with open arms for they each brought a jeep with them! They had arrived on 118 virtually out of the blue and were perhaps the start of an exchange programme which didn't get off the ground until peacetime and which flourishes to this day.

The move was due to take place on the 18th but it seems that things were to be made as awkward as possible when Group insisted that the Squadron be briefed for two missions and a recce. One of the former materialised in the morning of moving day – Marauders to Beauvais. The weather recce at lunchtime reported 10/10ths cloud but that didn't seem to matter to the planners who set up an attack on Beaumont le Roget with the Wing to escort. Inevitably given the results of the recce the whole thing was called off – but only after everyone, bombers included, got airborne! Now was their chance. Back on the ground everyone – but everyone – was enlisted to help with packing and in getting the accumulated crates to the local station for the jour-

131

ney by train northwards. Then, at last, it was time for pilots to climb into their cockpits for the transit to Scotland – or so they thought. New orders came through – fly to West Malling and exchange the Spitfire Vbs they had been flying with long range tanks for Spitfire Vbs without the tanks – except for one of the weather recce Spits that is that had crash landed on its return to Merston with undercarriage failure! This late change in plan led to a scramble back to the railway station, hoping that their crates had not yet been loaded, to delve into the depths of who knows which crate to find the aircraft's log books! Luckily memories were good and the crate was quickly identified. But time had run out – and daylight. It was not until the morning of the 19th that the Squadron took off for West Malling, effected the aircraft exchange, then flew on to a very unco-operative Church Fenton, who seemed to resent the presence of the Squadron, for an overnight stop. Ground crews were airlifted by a stately, fixed undercarriage and be-spatted Handley Page Harrow – or rather some of them were. There should have been two Harrows but, one becoming unserviceable, the remainder of the groundcrew entrained for what was to be a twenty five hour journey! Two pilots – he of the previous day's undercarriage collapse and another whose aircraft was undergoing maintenance – took the Squadron's hack, a Tiger Moth.

Routing up to Peterhead from Church Fenton via Turnhouse, the reality of Scotland's east coast was a harsh one. It might as well have been Siberia and John's immediate memories of the place are of a Canadian Station Commander who left as soon as they arrived, of John's taking that role on as well and indeed doing multifarious other things as directed. 'It was', John recalls, 'a wonder that they didn't give me broom to sweep the runways too!' One mission from Peterhead does stand out though. John was summoned to No 3 Group HQ at Inverness and informed that his Squadron was to act as escort to Mosquito nightfighters who were directed to intercept and force down a Ju88 which was purported to be carrying a German spy for parachuting into the UK. Just where did this information come from? No matter, the Junkers was intercepted, was brought down (it landed on a beach) and the crew and passenger detained.

But we jump forward. Within two days of their arrival eight aircraft were detached to Skeabrae and both here and at Peterhead itself any apprehensions about the Scots were quickly allayed when it was found that the natives were indeed friendly and very welcoming! Skeabrae was on the northern shore of Scapa Flow in the Orkneys just across the Pentland Firth, an airfield used by the Fleet Air Arm for training and whose runway was thus marked out in the form of a carrier's deck. There were one or two narrow squeaks for 118 whilst operating under the Navy's auspices from here. Whilst it was RAF practice to refuel an aircraft immediately it landed so that it would be ready for an emergency departure, for the Fleet Air Arm it was not. At sea where aircraft were taken below decks and consequently didn't want to be full of fuel where fire could be catastrophic, it was the practice to reful prior to a sortie taking off. This was the norm on shore bases too. The problem for the RAF was that now and again it was forgotten an aircraft hadn't been refuelled and on more that one occasion it was only by sheer good fortune that diversion airfields were near and handy and disaster was avoided.

On September 24th Sgt Pilot Graham was posted to 118 from 52 OTU. Graham was a West Indian and he added to the growing list of nationalities who had hitherto served on the Squadron – Canadian, New Zealander, Australian, Sinhalese, French, Dane, Dutch, Belgian, Norwegian and American. There had been and still were a lot of good men on 118. But there were also those who had been forced into the RAF and would never fit in – and not always for want of trying. This was an inevitable consequence of the wartime need to man the Services and usually the result as far as units were concerned was inconvenience rather than danger. As in the case of the batman who had been assigned to John by this time. He was an

Oxford don who was truly a fish out of water if ever there was one. The harder he tried the worse it was for him. Sent on leave on one occasion he got as far as Peterhead town itself and failed to salute an officer he passed at the station. The officer took umbrage and ordered John's batman back to camp. His story was that he had been too shy to salute! Determined to get him away John arranged to have him flown done to Oxford in the Proctor. What stories did he tell his university colleagues of his exploits in the RAF once he got there?

At the other end of the spectrum to John's batman was the Squadron Medical Officer, Sqn Ldr Pettigrew. Here was a man who had come to his profession late in life and who never tired of taking the opportunity of bettering himself. Starting his working life pre war down the pits he had soon had enough of that. Craving more excitement he joined the French Foreign Legion! But the reality of this was not the romantic notion he had imagined it to be and he contrived his escape and found his way back from north African deserts back to England where he became a lorry driver delivering dairy products before a sideways move took him into a factory as a manager. It was at this stage of his life that Pettigrew enroled at night school and qualified for university and went on to become a doctor. After wartime service he reached the top of his particular tree in the medical profession. Such are the characters that were found throughout all three Services – fascinating people who found themselves thrown into alien environments. Some coped – others didn't.

118 quickly settled into a routine at both Peterhead and Skeabrae of dawn and dusk patrols, navy and army co-operation and affiliation exercises, sector reconnaissance, weather reconnaissance, occasional escorts (although of personnel such as Sir Alan Brook in a Dominie to and from Sumburgh as opposed to bombers *en route* to France) and air to ground firing. There was sometimes night flying too and Air Sea Rescue exercises alongside Coastal Command Walrus's and Ansons.

There was occasional contact with the enemy – but usually at a distance. On a very grey 28th September, for instance, Sgts Capel and Miller were off Aberdeen at 400ft and just below cloud base when they spied a 'speck' about ten miles away to the east. They promptly gave chase, closing to within six miles at which distance the 'speck' became a twin engined aircraft whose shape and behaviour suggested a Ju88. At this juncture though the '88 spotted *them* and promptly climbed and hid in cloud. Such was the rarity of such sightings that the pair were congratulated by higher authority on seeing off an unwelcome intruder in trying weather conditions! There were scrambles fairly regularly to investigate radar plots which couldn't be identified – on the 7th October the sirens at Peterhead sounded and a section was put up to intercept a bogey coming in off the sea at 500ft. It was a Beaufighter.

Flt Sgt Anderson was awarded his first good conduct badge on the 9th – but why was it the Squadron's only such badge to date? The Squadron diarist was rather repentant about it – 'this is the first, we regret to say, which has been earned by our pilots' he notes, although there is no indication as to why this should be!' Then the matter of the Squadron establishment was raised again when the fitters and armourers were finally posted out of 118 to be attached to the station servicing echelon. But the arguments for and mainly against continued. Whilst there was a certain sense to having permanently based groundcrew rotating between squadrons as they came and went instead of the logistical effort required to move them as well, the general consensus was that a squadron with its own echelon would be a far better concern than a squadron with an echelon which didn't specifically belong to it, wasn't integrated with it and indeed could only belong body and soul with its previous master – in the early stages of any changeover at least.

– o O o –

Once again, talk of echelons prompted a move. 118 hadn't been long at Peterhead when instructions came to proceed to Castletown on the north coast, the Spitfires at Skeabrae flying across to join the main body of the Squadron. 504 Squadron were to take on 118's duties at the latter and Peterhead although 118 would continue to send aircraft to stand in for or supplement 504 on a regular basis.

We were made very welcome on our arrival and everything was done for our comfort. It is a pretty place with a Mess on the seashore, fishing on the doorstep and shooting around the corner. It is the ideal place to send a squadron for a rest.

This was Castletown which was under the command of a Wg Cdr Barrett who proved to an enlightened CO who always had the interests of everybody under his charge at heart. This interest was probably prompted by the fact that he had his wife and daughter with him and was quite content to make Castletown his own, perhaps for the duration. Personnel were billeted on the estate of Sir Archibald Sinclair, Secretary of State for Air, and they got to know the family very well, particularly Sir Archibald's sister Stroma who worked for the local coastguard and who had been awarded the OBE as a schoolgirl in World War One after she had spotted a German submarine offshore and had promptly reported it to the authorities who themselves acted with commendable speed and sank it. 118 undoubtedly had a very good time at Castletown and John together with his Flight Commanders and a young Pilot Officer, Paddy Harbison, who would later rise to considerable Air Force heights, regularly dined at the Big House in the company of this lovely family. Another guest at the Sinclair dinner table was a peg-legged Navy Staff Captain from Thurso who turned up late for dinner one night in a rather excited state having just played a significant communications role from his shore base in the sinking of the *Scharnhorst*.

118 were welcomed by the Sinclairs despite some escapades on the Estate which were akin to poaching – using a Tiger Moth! They had actually been given *carte-blanche* as far as shooting and fishing was concerned, the only proviso being that no rabbits should be touched as these were strictly for the crofters. But a Tiger Moth?! The technique was simple: string a net between the wings and undercarriage and as duck flew off the water of a local loch fly through them and bag 'em! How did they get the duck to fly off? By roaring down the loch at low level in a Spitfire one way, and fly the Tiger Moth up the loch the other way as the birds rose. Simple, but effective – and very damaging to the Tiger Moth whose prop and fabric were done no good at all. Further damage was avoided after the Tiger Moth's exploits became known and the practice was quickly banned by those who knew better! So 118 resorted to shooting duck in the conventional way – if creeping on all fours along the estate wall until coming to a raft of birds, standing and shooting as one – a veritable 12 bore broadside – can be counted as being conventional. Paddy Harbison proved his worth here too for once the duck were downed he would act as retriever, whatever the weather and however cold the water!

Paddy was quite adept at rescuing humans as well as wildfowl. 118 were able to use one of the Estate's boats for fishing – hardly surprisingly rarely in the conventional sense but by illegal use of hand grenades which were very effective at stunning the fish and ensuring a big catch everytime. Also hardly surprisingly these escapades could conclude with cries of 'man overboard' – John included – at which Paddy would leap in as if he was unable to restrain himself and effect a rescue. Paddy was unable to rescue the boat itself though on the night it was lost after an engine failure and was abandoned to the Pentland Firth. John's Navy friend came to the rescue on this occasion as far as finding a replacement was concerned, even going so far as to arranging having it towed in by mine-sweeper! Not that the swap was not noticed by the Estate – but the replacement was obviously an acceptable one and it continued to be used for fishing by 118.

The weather was one of the definite minuses at times at Castletown.

There is always a gale blowing in these parts which no doubt accounts for the ruddy complexion of the local inhabitants. Most of the men have blue noses and purple cheeks. The women can only be described as scarlet!

But one of the big plus points was the fact that there was no food rationing in force. This was largely a consequence of distribution and the fact that population was sparse and it was certainly more than self sufficient. Indeed there were considerable food surpluses. (An Air Commodore from Air Training Command was a regular visitor for a while, flying up in an Oxford and loading it up until the tyres were flat. It was never discovered exactly what his ruse was but whatever it may have been he was shopped at the other end and the visits, and probably his career, came to an abrupt stop.) The crofters around Castletown were lovely people who would always invite visitors in to share their table. Indeed there was little to choose between the hospitality at the Big House and the simple but warm welcome afforded by the crofters. Both were equally appealing to 118 – particularly because the Mess itself was, in the Squadron's early days at Castletown at least, in pretty poor shape. It may have been attractively sited but the standard of cooking and presentation, compared with what everyone became used to outside the camp, was abysmal. John's appointment to Mess Presidency meant that improvements were soon underway, most noticeably with the arrival of a steady trickle of WAAFs (some of them familiar faces from Coltishall days as has already been recounted) and evidence of the feminine touch quickly became apparent.

Rugby became a much played game whilst at Castletown. After lunch with Miss Catherine Sinclair at the beginning of November, John was expected to turn out for a practice match – but he had over-indulged and had to cry off! John had never been a sportsman but, as with his pilots, a player or not, you turned out if you possibly could! As he did with football. Le Mesurier was the referee for the regular encounters with a team from the based ASR squadron and he was a tough one. Counting over twenty players on the opposing side John demanded of his Intelligence Officer cum referee what sort of football match this was. 'Never you mind,' came the reply. 'I'm the ref and you'll do as you're told!' All symptomatic of the spirit of the Squadron under John's leadership.

The ASR unit in question was 282 Squadron flying the Supermarine Walrus – one of seven UK based ASR squadrons which did so – and the Avro Anson. The Squadron had formed at Castletown on January 1st 1943. John quickly got his feet under their particular table with invites to private dinners in the Officer's Mess! The wooden hulled mostly Saro built Walrus's which were affectionately known as Shagbats by their crews were available to 118 pilots for euphemistically termed familiarisation flights although for some reason lost in the memory John never did take up the offer – surprising given his predilection for flying anything he could get his hands on! That included of course the Squadron hacks – and here there were two, a Proctor and a de Havilland Dominie as well. This latter was not always the most reliable of aeroplanes as witnessed by an unfortunate erk who had cadged a lift from Skeabrae across the treacherous Pentland Firth to Castletown. An engine failed – but the Dominie was perfectly capable of flying on one. Unfortunately the second engine began to falter too and the order went out to throw out anything that could be moved in an effort to maintain height. The ground crewman became convinced that he was the next to go – but his bacon was saved by the fact that the Dominie was able to land in the grounds of the Castle of May. Water in the fuel was found to be the cause of the double failure.

It was in the Proctor though that John soon made the short flight across to Kirkwall to meet Sector boss Gp Capt Pearson-Rogers who in turn reciprocated by visiting Castletown and the Station HQ, showing particular interest in 118's unofficial squadron diary. This had been kept since the reformation of the Squadron at Filton by le Mesurier. It was a very full record, both official and private, that covered operational, social and personal matters and there were high hopes, such was its quality, that it could be published after the war. Sadly during the Squadron's subsequent moves it seems to have been lost.

– o O o –

With the wide open uninhabited spaces at Castletown, the Squadron revelled in the opportunity for uninterrupted *low* flying training. Their tasking at Castletown though was for *high* level interception of recce Ju88s (rarely seen) or the shepherding of American B17s and B24s en route to East Anglian bases from the States which had drifted somewhat off course – a not uncommon occurrence. Apart from their Spitfire Vbs, they had managed to temporarily get their hands on a few pressurised VIs at Peterhead (which soon had to be given up) and unpressurised VIIIs, optimised for high altitude operations – both types being fitted, as they were, with extended wingtips. These aircraft could be landed at 45mph – they simply floated down to earth! But there were some troubles with them. A Sgt Pilot returned from one sortie and reported an awful juddering as he was coming down from height in a gliding turn. He was convinced the wings were about to detach themselves. However he landed safely and there being nothing obviously amiss externally John took it up for a test flight himself and experienced the same problem – so he returned and immediately put a grounding order on all the VIIIs he had. The main spars were examined and it was found that instead of using high tensile steel bolts, mild steel had been used – which were nowhere strong enough. 'Which really goes to prove,' says John, 'that Singer should really have stuck to making sewing machines and not built aeroplanes.'

Here again we have an instance of conflict of memory. Records show that 118 operated Vbs throughout their time north of the border but John's recollections of these new marks are so vivid that they cannot easily be discounted. He is hardly likely to forget the sight of tethered, picketed, prop-secured Spitfire VIIIs at Castletown in a howling gale, with the wind getting under their long wings and lifting them off the ground against the secure but stretching rope that held them down!

On October 20th popular B Flight Commander John Shepherd DFC was posted out to HQ Fighter Command. Whilst with 118 he had destroyed four aircraft with another probable, had damaged three, had made five attacks on shipping and undertaken seven *Rhubarbs*. His place was taken by Flt Lt Mike Giddings, like Tony Drew ex Malta. Mike proved to be a very competent person who would work out solutions to problems in sometimes unorthodox ways. He was always willing to innovate too – sometimes in unexpected areas outside his direct remit. He spent time with Bofors gunners who had been emplaced around airfields in the defensive role teaching them to deflection shoot. He also taught himself to play the piano by analysing the finger numbering system with which sheet music is marked.

It wasn't very long before another fundamental change was made – the Squadron Adjutant (Henry Mallory) was posted to RAF Castletown itself where he would act as Adjutant to the station overall rather than 118 specifically. As with the changes with ground crew, the loss of an Adjutant was keenly regretted.

In most squadrons the post of Adjutant has been filled by well-to-do businessmen of breeding, tact and experience of life whose work on squadrons has been invaluable although unappreciated. Their absence from squadron life will be felt in many ways, particularly by the pilots whose interests they have so unselfishly served.

Such statements today smack of a wicked snobbery which also serves to make it easier to understand why there would always have been an unbridgeable gap between air and ground crew – their breeding would not have been up to scratch no doubt! – but it also demonstrates the way in which the Air Force worked in the 1940s, for these were the mores and attitudes of the age. However it reads today, there is little doubt that 118 missed Mallory and his expertise in keeping the Squadron together (John could vouch for the importance of that from his time in a similar role with 74): there is little doubt either that Mallory missed 118 as well.

One story about Henry, a highly intelligent man, is worth the telling and centres on co-operation with Coastal Command Sunderlands. Walking to the Mess with John one day one of these Shorts behemoths of a flying boat was circling Castletown. 'What's he doing?' asks Henry. 'Well, he's waiting for Spitfires to go up and play with him!' 'But everyone's at lunch.' 'I know. We'll send a signal for him to land and wait instead of flying in circles.' 'But the sea's a long way away and we shan't see it!' 'No, not the sea Henry. Why do you think this aerodrome is saucer shaped? They flood it!' 'Oh! I never realised...'

The gullibility of intelligence!

– o O o –

Routine at Castletown was very much as it had been at Peterhead with rather more cine gun practice on the agenda. A convoy patrol was undertaken on the 27th and those who flew it were intrigued to see that it included a huge three funnelled vessel, probably one of the Empress class ships. Convoys were a regular feature around the north of Scotland and were often major assemblies of shipping numbering thirty five vessels plus. At the beginning of November much to John's fury the Squadron managed to put up a tremendous black. Three Spitfires took off to rendezvous with AOC 3 Group who was coming to inspect Castletown and stay for lunch. The three Spits sighted a Dominie, closed in and escorted it onto the airfield. There was more than a little embarrassment when the welcoming detail discovered that there was no Air Vice Marshal on board – but rather the mail! AVM Henderson arrived shortly afterwards, completely unheralded, in an Oxford.

On the 7th John took the Squadron up three times on formation work, during the course of one of which they were instructed to investigate a plot of three aircraft which they chased to a point eighty miles to the east of Duncansby Head before they disappeared without being seen other than on the controller's tube. More enemy raids appeared to be forming in the same location a week later but once again no contact was made. On the 8th Sgt Piper was scrambled with high hopes again of finding a swastika marked aircraft – it had been so long since a German interception – only to find a Mosquito with its port engine stopped. Piper trailed the Mossie to Wick but was unable to catch it – which really didn't say too much for the Spitfire! There was another scramble on the 17th – Grant and Freeman this time – to intercept an alleged enemy aircraft approaching to within twenty miles of Kirkwall at 30,000ft. It wasn't seen.

Caricature of John scowling at WAAF officers in the Mess at Castletown as it appeared on the reverse of the 1943 Christmas Dinner Menu as drawn by le Mesurier

John himself was away from base later in the month, leaving the Squadron in the hands of Tony Drew, to attend an Army Co-operation course at Old Sarum. He never quite worked out why he was picked to do this other than as a break in routine, entertainment and for the experience. It certainly had no bearing on his next posting but proved to be highly interesting. Amongst the things he was involved with were the testing of a new GPO system whereby mail was packed into rubberised containers and snatched off the ground by a Dakota, flown to its destination and dropped out of the aircraft. Being protected by the rubber, the mail came to no harm. The GPO objected to it, declaring it to be not safe – whereupon a volunteer rigged himself up to be successfully snatched in a similar way. The GPO still objected. Also tested while John was there were self propelled British 25 pound and American 90mm guns on the Salisbury Plain ranges, the latter mounted on a Sherman chassis. With three charges the former could throw a shell for fifteen miles: with a single charge you could actually see the shell leave the muzzle of the latter. Strange the detail that memory recalls sometimes! The third experience of Old Sarum involved early Martin Baker ejection seats: John volunteered to be fired up a test ramp – but only the once!

There wasn't much activity on the northern Scottish coast whilst the Boss was away, for the weather deteriorated alarmingly to a succession of howling gales and days of incessant rain. 118's popular Sinhalese Talalla was no doubt pleased to escape what was for him particularly abhorrent weather (although he was not necessarily pleased to escape his colleagues) when he was posted to 9 Group. With 118 he had destroyed one enemy aircraft and shared another, had taken part in almost 100 sweeps, 27 recces, five *Rodeos* and three *Rhubarbs*. His career had seen him rise from the rank of Sergeant to that of Flying Officer and the award of the DFC (on the day John took command of the Squadron). For a long time he was the only Sinhalese in the Royal Air Force – until the day his brother, affectionately known as Jimmy, joined.

Perverse as these latitudes could be weather wise, gales gave way to sharp frosts and beautiful starlit nights as December progressed. This was excellent flying weather and over the course of a week over a hundred hours night practice was clocked up at Castletown by the remaining Flight, the other having been sent to Peterhead to supplement 504 Squadron. This was a period of good serviceability and no accidents which met with the obvious approval of Gp Capt Pearson-Rogers who sent his congratulations. This was coincident with the fact that 118 did more camera gun and cine filming during the month than all the other squadrons in the Group put together. More congratulations! A little praise from such quarters from time to time went a long way in 118's eyes!

Christmas 1943. Traditions were closely followed at Castletown with a church service conducted by the Station padre and a dull sermon by the local Scottish pastor! Officers descended on the Sergeants/Airmen's Mess where they served lunch and where appreciation was shown by the licking clean of all plates! The Officers enjoyed their own Christmas dinner in the evening followed by fun and games until the small hours. Boxing Day weather was bad – as bad as the Squadron's collective hangovers – including even those who were selected to fly a dawn patrol! But this was soon done and much looked forward to then was the arrival of Sir Archibald Sinclair and the whole family for tea in the afternoon. The New Year was celebrated with gusto as well with a Fancy Dress Ball (thank goodness for the WAAFs to partner!) and much admiration of the ingenuity of costumes made from scrap material.

Thus ends 1943 in a spirit of gaiety and rejoicing with every hope that the war will be over within the coming year with Germany at any rate blasted off the face of the map…

– o O o –

A couple of aircraft were scrambled on New Year's Day 1944 but, as usual, their intercept turned out to be friendly. Which was as well. Once again there were more than a few sore heads after the festivities of the night before! These effects were soon dissipated as gales roared in and rain lashed down for a couple of days before better weather allowed resumption of dawn and dusk patrols and a series of low cross country training flights. John very often led these himself. He was a fine low flier – one of the best in fact – and was keen, and able, to pass on a great deal about hedge hopping to his younger Squadron charges. The feeling was that many of these youngsters, acknowledging the first class start to squadron life they had been given by 118 after their posting in from OTUs, were subsequently wasted for very often they would then be posted on to Flying Instructor Schools. Two cases in point were Dunning and Jones. Fl Off Willison was another. All were fine pilots but, excellent training notwithstanding, they had not had the opportunity of real operations. It seemed odd that youngsters who were wanting to get to the front line and utilise their new found skills for real should be posted to a job far better suited to pilots who had already done their stuff and were ready for a well earned rest.

Willison was a bit of a character. He was of rather diminutive size and during the first week he was with 118 he caused some consternation when he was barely visible in the cockpit to those watching as he came in to land – to the extent that everybody was initially convinced that a Spitfire had landed without a pilot!

> *One day a pilot lands*
> *A Spit which looks quite silly*
> *In horror we throw up our hands*
> *Then out hops Little Willy!*

Thus was Fl Off Willison immortalised!

John's days as CO of 118 Squadron now swiftly came to an end. On January 12th he was ordered to the Air Ministry on special duties and Sqn Ldr P W E Heppell DFC was appointed in his place. Within a week the Squadron was ordered south to Detling – and new Spitfire IXs! John had missed the opportunity again to fly this superior mark of the type! He meanwhile had made his own reputation with the men under his command and they regretted his leaving. The Squadron Intelligence Officer and diary keeper, le Mesurier, summed up everyone's feelings:

A man of strong personality he has wrought many changes during the period he has been our CO. It was unfortunate that during the major portion of the time he commanded the Squadron it should have been resting at Castletown. Under him though we have broken all local records for cine gun practice and night flying and have kept up a high standard of efficiency despite the appalling ravages of a posting mania....which makes it difficult for any commander to hold his Squadron together as a unit. Despite all difficulties...he has succeeded by sheer determination in keeping up a maximum effort. A fine flier and a good friend, he is a man who has the outlook expected of a regular officer. Amongst us he leaves many good friends who will watch his future career with the keenest interest. There was a cheery farewell party at the Mess which should have left him in no doubt as to the affection in which he is held...

John could expect no such affection at his next posting.

Chapter 13
Italian Wing

January to June 1944. Grottaglie

When John's tenure as CO of 118 Squadron came to an end his posting, when it came through, sent him to the Middle East. Travelling down to London and thence to St Mawgan, a civilian operated cold, noisy and uncomfortable DC3 took him to Gibraltar and thence to Algiers. Here he and his kit were unceremoniously dumped. The base at Maison Blanche where he found himself was fifteen miles outside of the city and there was no apparent way of getting there. Joining forces with some others who didn't know where they were going either they hitched a lift and once in Algiers sought out the office which would arrange their onward transportation. This they finally did and John was amazed to find that they knew all about him and furthermore that he was not bound for the Middle East but for Italy. Not that it moved him on any quicker. Kicking his heels for a few days he was eventually taken back out to Maison Blanche where he caught an American transport which flew the Casablanca – Algiers – Tripoli route. It diverted to the former airship station at Grottaglie near Brindisi via Tunis where it landed on a road outside the city. Flying low over the desert John saw dozens of Spitfires and Hurricanes, the former of many different marks, with nobody to ferry them! And in prospect for John in Italy were Spitfire Vs again, this time the version optimised for desert operations with a bulky air filter beneath.

Grottaglie was now home to 286 Wing. After reporting to 242 Group HQ at Taranto on 30th January 1944 (the Group had moved to the Italian seaport from North Africa in September 1943) John was told by his new AOC that he was to be Wing Commander Flying of 286 Wing – so 'get back to Grottaglie and get on with it!' In fact he was to remain merely 'attached' to the Wing until May 2nd, a permanent posting only coming through at that stage. Once done, John stayed on for barely a further month before engineering his return to the UK. Another interesting factor is that the Wing records consistently refer to John as acting Flight Lieutenant before his promotion to Wing Commander was confirmed at the same time as his confirmed posting! His Squadron Leader rank does not occur at all! Administration obviously hadn't caught up with him.

242 Group had two Wings under its control, 323 Wing with 73 Squadron Spitfires at Foggia and 286, the latter one of the largest in the RAF. 286 Wing's constituent squadrons were initially Spitfire equipped 126 and 249 at Grottaglie with 1435 at Brindisi. As at December 1943 it also controlled a detachment of 608 Squadron Hudsons at Montecorvino, the Spitfire Vcs of 253 Squadron at Naples (Capodichino), Warwicks of 284 Squadron at Brindisi, a detachment of 14 Squadron Marauders at Grottaglie (specially adapted to high speed, low level, anti U Boat ops) together with 255 Squadron Beaufighters also operating from Grottaglie. As part of the Group's port and shipping defence briefing, a host of barrage balloon squadrons were deployed around Naples, Taranto, Brindisi, Bari, Barletta and Manfredonia. On top of that were Italian Cant 2506/S seaplanes at Taranto. Looking forward six months to the time of John's departure, the complement had changed a little. 126 Squadron was by then back in the UK but 249

Squadron was still there as were 1435, the 14 Squadron detachment and 255 Squadron Beaus. Hurricane IV equipped 6 Squadron had arrived, a detachment of 39 Squadron had replaced 416, and 221 Sqn Wellingtons had made their presence at Grottaglie very much felt.

– o O o –

This is not the place to undertake an evaluation of the complicated Balkans situation at the time of John's arrival – for it was with the war in the Balkans that 286 Wing was increasingly concerned as opposed to the northwards advance up Italy – but a few lines do help to put into context the war theatre in which they found themselves operating. In Yugoslavia, under the leadership of Draza Mihailovic the Chetniks had from the beginning initiated a campaign of harassment of the occupying German lines of communication. At the same time a communist backed group, the Partisans, under the leadership of Josep Broz, known otherwise as Tito, began operations: sadly the conflicting ideology of the two groups led to their embarking on a campaign, one against the other. The Chetniks politically found themselves to be more in line with Hitler's brand of national socialism than Tito's communism and this in the end led them, after an initially secret accommodation with the Germans, into open collaboration with the Axis, their guns and equipment supplied by them. The Allies in general and Britain in particular were not initially aware of Mihailovic's shifting allegiances and for a while the distinctly bizarre situation existed whereby British aid and British liaison officers were being received by both Chetnik and Partisan.

Over the winter of 1941-1942 Tito's forces were almost annihilated. Hounded by German, Italian and Croation troops as well as the Chetniks he managed nevertheless to break out and form a provisional federal Yugoslav government which guaranteed the rights of the minority groups and which thereby held great appeal for a great many people. However the German *Operation White* which aimed to secure the Balkans in anticipation of an Allied invasion forced Tito into Montenegro where he was completely surrounded but from where he nonetheless contrived to escape and headed north once again – he was proving to be a clever tactician and something of an escape artist! In 1943 Churchill finally opted to back Tito – they were 'killing more Huns' than Mihailovich's Chetnik 12,000 strong army which was in any event beginning to disintegrate. Mihaolovic could not control his officers: there was widespread desertion from the ranks, men who were in the main country people who were not interested in political manoeuverings and who viewed the Partisans as brothers fighting the German invaders as they should be doing. The Partisans were indeed a tough breed who fought a dirty war, who would leave their wounded to die, who would certainly take no prisoners, who would pick the battlegrounds and fight largely on their own terms and of whom the German soldiers unfortunate enough to be pitted against them were terrified. There were large numbers of exhausted, war weary Jaeger Division soldiers from Bavaria on the ground and they must have longed to be fighting a conventional war again, not this incessant game of hide and seek in the mountains.

When the Italians dropped out of the war Tito managed to disarm their forces in Yugoslavia before the Germans could do so. He ultimately established a new HQ under British protection on the island of Vis. By this time his army numbered close on 300,000. From bases across southern Italy the Balkan Air Force dropped supplies, evacuated the wounded, provided air transport and cover and initiated constant strikes at targets of opportunity, on Germans and the remaining Chetnik forces alike. The British navy and army (which provided a commando force for the defence of Vis) also had units actively co-operating with the Partisans. Tens of thousands of wounded and civilians were evacuated by the British: over 10,000 tons of supplies were dropped to the Partisans and although this was never as much as they would have liked it did undoubtedly play a role of some significance in the later stages of the war in Yugoslavia. One of the Navy intelligence people with whom John worked ran high speed launches from Brindisi to Albania, taking and bringing back partisans, POWs and shot down aircrew.

Meanwhile the Royal Yugoslav government in exile in London was persuaded by Churchill to recognise Tito's Partisans as the official Yugoslav army and by the end of 1944 a communist dominated coalition government was empowered. As the Russian's entered Yugoslavia on October 11th 1944 Tito entered into negotiations with Stalin and the Reds aided the Partisans in the final victory drive to Belgrade.

Albania largely followed the Yugoslav pattern and Enver Hoxha established a provisional government along similar lines to Tito's, a government which was soon to be superseded by a ruthless dictatorship. Further south, Greece posed a particular problem. Long before the defeat of the Germans in the Balkans it was clear that Greece would be plunged into a bloody civil war, as with Yugoslavia, between communists and conservatives. Here Churchill was determined to prevent a communist takeover and thus he sanctioned *Operation Manna*, the direct involvement of British troops which did nothing to appease the protagonists.

– o O o –

Such was the background to 286 Wing's effort in the Balkans. Its (and indeed 242 Group's) main tasking was initially one of the defence of ports, convoys and airfields on the Italian peninsular and reconnaissance and offensive operations in Yugoslavia, Albania and Corfu with the emphasis shifting further to the latter as the weeks passed by. The Wing's constituent squadrons did some training with the American B24s when they first arrived as they worked up to attacking the Ploesti oil fields (they never escorted them for real on these missions) – but a look through the record books show that by March 1944 286 was dedicated almost wholly to operations over the Balkans with the bombing and strafing of enemy transport and radio installations in Albania and Yugoslavia: and that in April 249 Squadron was wholly engaged in attacks on transport, barracks and shipping in the Adriatic with 6 Squadron similarly employed. Royal Navy Intelligence ultimately oversaw operations and all orders came from them or at least had to be directed through them. The Partisans had arms caches throughout the mountains and through the Navy the Wing were told where the next engagements were likely to be and very often were able to have its squadrons in position in the aftermath ready to pick off the remnants. One of the Partisans favourite ploys was to catch a German patrol on a road, blow up sections before and after them, thereby blocking their advance or retreat, and then set to with weapons or simply by setting off boulder avalanches. 286's squadrons would then be called in to strafe. Targets became as increasingly diverse as HQ buildings, radar sites and shipping and as 1944 progressed detachments from the squadrons at Grotagglie were sent to islands off the Yugoslav coast. These rarely had natural sources of water and so the Wing was always on the look out for caiques and schooners that might be supplying them. Working with his staff from a school in the nearby village, John and his colleagues co-ordinated all this: but at other times theirs was a free ranging brief in terms of the targets they hit. The only proviso was that Navy liaison people were kept in the picture.

John found that as Wing Commander Flying the squadrons were somewhat reserved when it came to his relationship with them – they were not hostile and indeed were welcoming to a degree but nevertheless made it plain that they would prefer not to see too much of him socially. It certainly wasn't the same relationship as between a Squadron CO and his crews. They were probably a little wary of John's reputation as a disciplinarian and perhaps there was a certain feistiness about him which didn't always endear him to those responsible to him! But he did fly with them – and frequently in weather that was gin clear (until Vesuvius blew in which case the fall-out caused some problems) with Greece itself often visible as the climb out from Grotagglie was initiated. They tended to be long, uncomfortable sorties of up to three hours duration sitting on a parachute and dinghy pack and which could reach as far as the Bulgarian border in search of targets. Sometimes they would be airborne as a squadron, sometimes in smaller numbers. There were occasionally prearranged sorties – the Partisans captured the airport at Tirana for example to enable DC3s to fly in with arms which were quickly offloaded after which both aircraft and Partisans melted away and the Germans returned – then 286 Wing were involved in continuing strikes which knocked hell out of them. As far as damage assessment was concerned, the Partisans themselves played a part in this by reporting back to Navy Intelligence with results of attacks.

On the longer sorties wooden 90 gallon drop tanks were carried but these were not to be jettisoned as they were in short supply. The smaller aluminium 35 gallon tanks were by comparison expendable. There was a lot of over water flying involved and with engines that were serviced in Egypt and which were prone to surging when back in theatre it was not a comfortable feeling. But it was exciting, adrenalin surging stuff – low level, fast, in company with up to a squadron's complement of aircraft, crossing the blue Adriatic at 1,000ft, pulling up as the Albanian or Yugoslavian mountains grew large in the 'screen, shaving the slopes and skimming the tops or tracing the course of rivers through the foothills, mountain sides closing in as valleys were traversed, racing in to a target if predetermined or constantly looking for tell tale signs of German movement on the roads if not (staff cars were always a good target for they invariably meant persons of some importance), your mind focused on what lay directly ahead but well aware of the position of your colleagues around you, releasing your bombs or letting fly with cannon, armour piercing high explosive or incendiary ammunition creating havoc, death and destruction in the course of a frenetic few minutes – then pulling up, round and away. There were never any collisions – and to those on the receiving end it was just a melee of noise and a blur of speed as the Spitfires screamed overhead.

Anything that moved on the ground was considered legitimate game and was shot at. And there were many targets of opportunity. On one occasion John and his Flight caught a roadside conference underway at Ioannina on the Greek/Albanian border, a gathering dominated by grey Wehrmacht uniforms. With tables out, maps on tables and surrounded by cars and armoured vehicles and an ambulance, as soon as John's Spitfires put in an appearance the latter sped off at considerable speed – but not fast enough to escape. Knowing that ambulances were used to carry arms and ammunition to units in the hills, this one proved to be no exception and it blew up spectacularly. The following day the Wing was amazed to hear the raid and its result described on the BBC's World Service. It must be remembered that the first months of 1944 saw something of a lull across Europe and it was in the Balkans and Italy that most activity was for the moment concentrated. Thus the interest in this what to John and his Wing was a routine sortie. A slow news day brought some fame to Grottaglie! It was in the aftermath of this attack that John saw a large number of German armoured vehicles concealed in a wood and being worthy of further attention he made careful note of its position. A further strike was set up the following day but the armoured vehicles had disappeared, the Germans no doubt realising they had been seen. Dispersal must have taken place overnight – but it was surprising no word of this had been sent back to Grottaglie by the Partisans who normally monitored such movements very carefully to the British and Americans. The Germans were certainly very good at camouflage in the mountainous terrain. On more than one occasion tent laagers were spotted but having pulled round to attack they couldn't be found again.

On another early sortie four trucks were caught on the edge of a plateau with men around them seemingly enjoying their breakfasts. John was leading a Flight of three on a reconnasissance on this occasion, looking for a reported camp in a wood and was checking to see whether it was still occupied and whether it would be worth setting up an attack. When the Germans saw the Spitfires racing towards them they dived beneath the trucks for cover. But there was no escaping the strafing attack which followed. The Spits peeled off into the adjacent valley, identified the hill atop which the Germans sat, and raced *uphill* towards them, opening fire and killing those under the trucks outright. High Explosive Armour Piercing cannon shells put paid to the trucks. There was no sentiment about such sudden and destructive attacks. As John recalls:

The Germans were real bastards to the poor peasants in the hills. It was always very satisfactory seeing them get their dues.

It was a demoralising time for the Axis forces all round because there was little or no air cover and attacking aircraft roamed almost at will although there were a few places that they did avoid – the larger towns and cities such as Dubrovnik were well defended with 88mm guns for example. German aircraft were not regularly seen – indeed there was no air opposition because Allied air superiority was total. One of the few occasions on which John saw the Luftwaffe was on returning from a strafing run in Yugoslavia during which all ammunition had been expended and they came across a formation of glider towing Ju52s. Without the means to shoot them down the only alternative can best be described as aggressive posturing which the Germans took very seriously and abandoned their gliders and the troops they carried. Subsequent intelligence suggested that they were part of an attempt to capture Tito. On another occasion John's Flight stumbled across a solitary Ju88 at 2,000ft. The plucky German flew straight at the formation of Spitfires and took one out before he himself was shot down.

– o O o –

Grotagglie, set in the flat southern Italian countryside characterised by olive trees and scrub, was in the early months of the year a cold, wet place and operations from the grass airfield were frequently disrupted by flooding. Indeed it was a salutary experience to find that the Italians had neglected to make provision for the winter rains and had merely accepted that if it got too wet flying would be abandoned. For 286 Wing the same principle frustratingly applied initially and there were weeks when very little if any flying could safely take place. Thus from an early stage there was considerable discussion at 242 Group level as to what the constituent squadrons and aircraft types at Grottaglie should be. Particular concern had been voiced at the beginning of 1944 that the impending arrival of American B24 Liberators would cause problems – the cutting up of the landing area by these heavy aircraft would make it impossible to operate Spitfires, the main issue being mud thrown into radiators causing overheating. At the same time plans were set in motion to improve facilities although this did not really get underway until April when the eventual appearance of the 449th Bomb Group prompted the calling in of the 809th Aviation Engineer Battalion of the United States Army to construct a 6,000 by 200 foot fighter runway to the west of the main runway which itself was improved. Suddenly Grottaglie possessed the nearest approximation to an all weather surface that it had ever had! After the landing areas, perimeter tracks and dispersals were created, levelled and graded. This latter task fell to the 1898th

Engineering Battalion of the US Army – the first negro ranked, white officered battalion to operate in Italy. These negroes found an old German bomb dump whilst engaged in this work. They found no bombs but did find a large number of the attachments which the Germans clipped to bomb's fins that gave the awful shrieking effect that frightened the living daylights out of those targeted. The negroes were determined to give the Germans some of their own medicine and fixed the shriekers to Allied bombs destined for them. Not a big thing in itself but a morale booster at the time.

It was uncanny that soon after the cessation of the rains Grottaglie became a dusty devil of a place and special oil spraying machines had to be used on the runway which were quite effective in dampening down the dust. A similar treatment applied to the peri track did not fare so well – the constant flow of vehicles as well as aircraft along it soon began to raise clouds of dust again and it was not long before the windward side of the airfield was covered in a white film. Aircraft suffered as much as everything else for there were no hangars in which to house them. All aircraft at Grottaglie were out in the open.

Buildings around the airfield and in the adjacent village were put to immediate use. The local School of Ceramic Art housed Ops and was John's base for the duration of his stay. Admin was in a building nearby. A small former olive factory provided space for MT. Requisitioned Rosario's Farm buildings accommodated 126 Squadron and provided their HQ and the Officer's Mess. Ex Italian Air Force huts accommodated the 14 Squadron detachment. Additional building work was set in place – cook-houses for example to feed the expanding population of Grottaglie, but with Italian workmen on the job progress was painfully slow! And the workmen's children became a nuisance as did those youngsters who were with the women who came to collect the camp's laundry. They seemed oblivious to moving transport and taxying aircraft and it was more by luck than anything else that there wasn't a serious accident.

When 1435 and 249 Squadrons initially arrived from Malta they had to go under canvas having begged, borrowed and perhaps stolen what they could. John's uncomfortable Lasham experiences were repeated for these two units when it did rain and they were literally washed out! 249 and 1435 soon moved to Brindisi where there was more room for them although 249 returned a little later when 126 flew back to the UK and they were able to take over the farm accommodation. Lingering Italian Air Force units were then withdrawn as well to make the maximum amount of accommodation available for 286 Wing. 6 Squadron arrived in late March. They too went under canvas adjacent to their allotted dispersal. 221 Squadron and their Wellingtons arrived at around the same time and they immediately became the largest unit of all. It was tents for them too!

Thus, to recap, 286 Wing's component squadrons changed somewhat during the six months John was with it but essentially it was made up of 126 and 249 Squadrons with cannon armed and bomb carrying Spitfire Vcs and 1435 Squadron with Spitfire IXs. 126 had been in the Mediterranean theatre since June 1941 when it had reformed on Malta. It moved into southern Italy behind the advancing ground forces but by April 1944 had been earmarked to return to the UK and participate in the build up for D Day. 249 too had been in the Mediterranean theatre since mid 1941, moving into Grottaglie from Malta in October 1943. 6 Squadron arrived with its rocket firing Hurricane Mk IVs from North Africa where its success in tank busting has since been commemorated in its famous flying can opener badge. 1435 Squadron is interesting because of the out of sequence number plate it carried which came about after it took on the designation from a disbanded night fighter Flight at Luqa – but with its complement of Spitfires being of squadron strength 1435 Flight became 1435 Squadron. From October 1943 to April

1945 it spent its time moving between Grottaglie and Brindisi with the bulk of its sorties flown from the latter during John's time which accounts for the fact he never flew with them. As a Spitfire IX squadron they were more on air defence and protection of harbours duties. John divided his time between Grottaglie and Brindisi but with the bulk of his assets at the former that is invariably where he spent most of his operational days. He was of course sorely tempted by the prospect of flying a Spitfire IX – he had been trying to get his hands on one for a long time! – but when it came to it he would be depriving somebody else if he brought one back to Grottaglie. What did turn up at Grottaglie though was a Spitfire V with a cropped supercharger – the blades had been cut down – and this produced 24lbs of boost to 12,000ft which endowed fantastic low level performance compared with the unmodified V. Produced to combat the FW190 it certainly gave the pilot quite a kick on take off then exhibited an impressive 7,000 feet per minute climb rate as opposed to the normal 1,500 feet. But that was essentially that. 12,000 feet was to all intents and purposes the limit for this aircraft – it would climb another 2,000 feet or so but only slowly. John flew this modified Spitfire whenever it was available, and if John was flying it was usually available!

There were units other than those that were Spitfire or Hurricane equipped at Grottaglie too. These included detachments of 14 Squadron Marauders used for non offensive reconnaissance, aircraft which patrolled the Adriatic looking for submarines, and sometimes 608 (North Riding) Squadron Hudsons. These were based on Sicily and were tasked with convoy patrol work. By far the largest RAF user of the airfield both in terms of establishment and in the size of aircraft they flew was the Wellington equipped 221 Squadron on anti-submarine work. Aircraft frequently visited from other Wings too to participate in specific operations – Beaufighters of 255 Squadron for example or Spitfires of 87 and 185 Squadrons. Cover was sometimes flown by the Grottaglie based Spitfire squadrons for Air Sea Rescue Cant Z506s crewed by Italians. And then there were the Americans – the four constituent squadrons of the 449th Bomb Group with their B24 Liberators – but these had their own agenda and whilst John enjoyed a very good relationship with them, spending many a pleasant evening in their company and enjoying their food, they operated independently of the Wing.

Discomforts and inconveniences aside, there were some facilities for off duty moments. There was a NAAFI – but for the most part it was a NAAFI without beer and indeed at times soft drinks as well so local brews were discovered and sampled, sometimes with unfortunate consequences! Italian wines could be potent – the locals always drank it with a carafe of water to dilute it – but this was something to which the Brits did not always subscribe! Oddly there were good supplies of spirits of which the Americans didn't appear to have much so a good trade was initiated whereby bottles of whisky and gin were exchanged for crates of fruit juices. Much of the recreation was of the men's own making but some was also provided by the authorities. The civilian population played their part for in the village, just 300 yards from Station HQ, there was a 800 seater cinema albeit with only one projector which meant frequent disruptions to the film being watched as the reel was changed! In time US Special Services built a small cinema on the aerodrome itself. The village cinema also had a stage and dressing rooms and these were put to good use, particular by the entertainers amongst the men and by the occasional visiting concert party.

John doesn't admit to sharing in, or taking advantage of, the illegal trafficking of the rogue Irishman he encountered at Crotone as will be recounted in the next chapter, but certainly at Grottaglie he had his own quasi-mafia operation, albeit in the relatively innocuous field of catering. The food on camp was abysmal – essentially corned beef for every meal in every conceivable shape and form. His first move was to find a friendly local butcher who wouldn't be averse to slaughtering the odd sheep or lamb if it was found from amongst local flocks – in fact a herd was targeted and, being honourable mafia, the shepherd was paid off! There is little doubt that menus improved after that. There were, however, things other than sheep in which members of the Station establishment dabbled. Crews from RAF transport aircraft flying in from Africa always looked for Grotagglie's accountant. These men were lira rich having accumulated great quantities of the currency in Africa – you didn't have to flog many gallons of petrol at 10,000 lira a gallon to find your fortune running into millions! What the crews wanted was to convert their lira into a more stable currency – sterling for example! – and this is where the accountant came in. Lira would be exchanged for BMA (British Medical Assurance) certificates which would subsequently be cashed back in the UK. The accountant would in turn cash in the lira at the local bank.

There was a roaring black market trade at Grotagglie. 40 gallon drums would be filled with water except for a couple of gallons of octane which would be floated on top and sold to the Italians as drums of fuel. The test was to dip paper into the drum, making sure that it was immersed in the fuel floating on top, and set fire to it. The Italians were convinced, the RAF boys were richer! There was a good trade in hydraulic fluid too – the locals seemed to want gallons of this for whatever reason.

Italians working on camp were quite intimidated by the British and Americans – hardly surprising given their recent reversal in the fortunes of war. And sometimes a perverse pleasure was taken in baiting the locals. Such as the day one was seen crossing the aerodrome carrying a huge basket of eggs. Challenged as to where he was going by a gaggle of Brits, and getting the response 'to the Americans', he was accused of not telling the truth and indeed of being a spy! He stepped back – apprehension etched onto his face. 'No! No! Not a spy. Eggs are for Americans. Not a spy!' 'You know damned well you are a spy. You'll be punished.' Apprehension turned to concern as the group bore down on him. 'Not a spy! Eggs are for Americans. I do not spy.' The wicked baiting continued and indeed took a step further when he was made to dig a trench. 'Your grave Giuseppe. You will dig your grave.' 'No! No!' By now he was losing control of his senses and probably his bodily functions. A Sten gun was produced. 'Dig!' So Giuseppe began the back breaking work from which he was granted no respite. Every so often, to spur him on, a shot was fired into the air. Crying with fright the 'grave' gradually, but only gradually, took shape. The Italian was tiring. But finish it he must. More shots were fired which seemed to galvanise him into renewed frenetic digging for a while until his muscles tired again. Finally, the trench was finished and the Italian was backed up to its edge. 'Now Giuseppe. You are a spy. This is your grave.' And they pushed him in, burst into laughter and left the luckless Italian to crawl out, now crying with relief but hating every last Briton on the camp – and in the world. 'Wicked bastards,' chuckled John as he recounted the story.

John managed to acquire his own hack at Grottaglie – a Fiat CR42 Falco which had been abandoned by the Italians. The engine had expired but a few slabs of chocolate acquired a new one in the same way that a few packets of cigarettes were exchanged for a replacement propeller. Having got the little biplane back into the air again John found it a delight to fly. Almost 1,800 had been built by Fiat, including 150 for night ground attack duties with the Luftwaffe, and with the Italian Air Force they served in Europe (a few even operating from Belgium alongside the Germans in the Battle of Britain), in the Greek campaign, over the Adriatic, in Libya and East Africa as well as on the Italian mainland. By the time John arrived their numbers were few: at the time of the September 1943 armistice only 60 or so remained serviceable so John's refurbished example was a relatively rare bird! Men from the American B24 Liberator unit saw this Falco buzzing around the airfield and curiosity compelled them to go across to the British flight line to see what it was. Having seen it they wanted to fly it – but John very understandably resisted. He got on very well with Americans – indeed it got to the stage that he was a welcome guest in their Mess which he tended to patronise in preference to his own – but he had spent too much time and effort in getting the Fiat airworthy again to let a bunch of maverick Yanks get their hands on it! The Americans pulled in the big guns and their Brigadier joined the queue. He wanted a go! Still John resisted and could only be persuaded to change his mind when a Liberator was placed at his disposal for use whenever he wished. This however was a short lived enterprise – an enterprise which included using the aircraft to fly men of his Wing back to the UK for leave – when the AOC at Taranto commandeered the aircraft for his own and his Command's use!

– o O o –

John's first Station Commander at Grotagglie was Cranwell graduate Gp Capt J R Rhys-Jones, an efficient and amiable individual – a gentleman of the old school – who ran his camp with a very firm hand and who went on to become AOC Malta. Rhys-Jones had flown into Grottaglie from TAF HQ in Sicily on September 13th 1943 in a Hurricane and became the first British pilot to land there with the Germans, at that stage, rapidly evacuating south east Italy and being pushed north by the Airborne Division that had been landed from naval vessels at Taranto.

Having enjoyed a first class relationship with Rhys-Jones, the Americans found they had as much trouble with his successor, Gp Capt P Prosser Hanks – he arrived from Malta on February 17th – as John did and John found that along with Sqn Ldr Plunkett, the Admin Officer, he spent an increasing amount of time trying to keep the peace between them. The new Group Captain was an unknown to the men already at Grottaglie, including Rhys-Jones, and so nobody knew what to expect. John had had some hope that he might have been put up for Rhys-Jones' job: as it was, when Prosser Hanks arrived he seemed to resent the Freeborn/Rhys-Jones friendship.

The quickly growing friction with the Americans was not a happy state of affairs given the latter's propensity for co-operation and assistance and, incidentally, given that Grottaglie was an American base and the RAF were there as the lodger unit! To give an example, Halifaxes would come into Grottaglie for refuelling having been on supply dropping sorties to the Partisans. A Halifax would take 4,000 gallons and the Americans had the pumps to facilitate its transfer. After the falling out they were far less inclined to help – in short, they often wouldn't – and 4,000 gallons per aircraft had to be delivered by hand pumps. The problem from Prosser Hanks' point of view was that the American Liberators were damaging the graded earth runway, rutting it badly, particularly after rain, which he perceived as being a threat to the ability of the RAF to operate. This in truth was not a problem for the Spitfires and Hurricanes were able to use the secondary strip on the huge airfield – and regularly did – as has already been explained.

Gp Capt Prosser Hanks and John never did see eye to eye and this led to a very uneasy relationship. John got on with his job as Wing Commander Flying as best he could and indeed oversaw an increasingly busy and varied programme with little time for relaxation as the Spitfire and Hurricane squadrons under his control clocked up an impressive sortie rate as the Italian Winter gave way to Spring.

Chapter 14
Italian Wing Operations

January to June 1944

286 was a busy Wing. Unless weather was particularly bad the strike squadrons were constantly patrolling and looking for targets. Squadrons flew many sorties each day, not all at squadron strength but often in components of four or six and often in concert with similar numbers from sister squadrons. Other Grottaglie based squadrons and detachments of Marauders, Beaufighters and Wellingtons had their own agendas of reconnaissance, anti shipping strike, U Boat patrol and so forth and they often operated in conditions in which the single seaters could not. The picture overall is of a constantly active airfield with not many quiet moments, a diversity of aircraft types and all the necessary support that that entailed, the American Bomb Group with its very different agenda and own command structure and Italian personnel still somewhat bemused, albeit relieved, by their change in role and allegiance.

Scrutiny of the Wing records confirms this and contributes to a fascinating picture of the war in the Adriatic in the first half of 1944. Taking operations month by month during John's tenure of the Wing Commander Flying post, we see that John flew from time to time with both 126 and 249 Squadrons. He did however allow a few days after his arrival before he climbed into the cockpit of a Spitfire again and left it to four of the type from 126 Sqn and six from 249, each carrying a pair of 250lb bombs, with top cover by 185 Squadron which had flown in from Malta, to conduct an offensive sweep over roads in Albania on the 1st February. This part of the sortie met with little success with just a pair of trucks seen. An attack on Berat airfield fared no better. There were no parked enemy aircraft to be seen and the flak was so intense that violent evasive action had to be taken which precluded any bomb dropping. This was finally done at an RDF Freya site at Fier instead where intensive fires were started which immediately gave off great outpourings of smoke. This was accomplished with a great deal of AA fire once more, from the target area itself as well as from the surrounding hills. The following day a convoy escort in the Gulf of Taranto was flown by aircraft of the two squadrons – convoys were identified by alphabetically listed codewords: this one was *Register* – and then in the afternoon 249 was tasked with escorting B24s from Gioia del Colle on a raid on an RDF site near Durazzo. No enemy aircraft were seen and the target was hit. Back at Grottaglie a 221 Squadron Wellington, operating on detachment before their permanent move in, crashed on take off and burst into flames, killing four of the crew in the process. Such events were saddening but not uncommon.

On the 4th John finally got into the air himself by leading four 126 Squadron Spitfires, with the Squadron CO Sqn Ldr Swinden alongside, on a low level recce to Valoria and on to Corfu. Despite not seeing anything it did give him the chance to orientate himself and to look at the area. Small arms fire from the Corfu harbour area was ineffective against the low flying Spits. On the 8th after a few days grounding because of the weather, John flew his first mission with 249 Squadron, 126 flying top cover. With 249's CO, Sqn Ldr Colvin, leading and John as his number two they crossed the Albanian coast at 10,000ft north west of Fier where the RDF site was again the target. Approaching from the north, Colvin and John half

151

rolled and dived but did not bomb as they found the radar site to be obscured. The other four in the formation did, releasing their 250 pounders as they passed through 5,000ft. John and his leader meanwhile reversed course and came in from south to north, bombing at 4,000ft. They saw bursts in the target area and on the hillside just beyond but the pilots were unable to see the results as the flak was as effective as previously and forced a speedy exit. One of the Spits crash landed on return to Grottaglie but the pilot, Flt Sgt Fox, walked away unscathed. The aircraft was returned to service within forty eight hours.

The 10th was a very busy day amongst busy days. Four aircraft from 249 conducted an offensive sweep in the Durazzo – Bari area, bombing and strafing four flak barges in the process, recording 'near misses with bombs and cannon strikes.' Four 229 Squadron aircraft, detached from Malta, hit lorries laden with wood near Durazzo and destroyed one and set two alight. Both the Wing's Commander, Rhys Jones, and Wing Commander Flying, John, flew with 126 on a two hour coastline sweep from Port Palermo to Corfu, noting a Swedish relief ship in harbour there – a ship which became a familiar feature over the ensuing weeks. More immediately a Ju88 was intercepted and one of the Squadron was detailed to move in from a head on position, ineffectually as it happened with the '88 turning east away from the line of fire. A second Spitfire, flown by Pl Off Greenwood, then attacked from astern but was promptly shot down into the harbour by the German's rearward firing MG131. A pair of Spitfires next closed in from beam astern and dead astern – this time silencing the rear gunner and setting the port engine on fire until finally the whole aircraft burst into flames, turned over and itself crashed into the sea north east of Korakiana. W.O. Saphir and Fl Sgt Rae had delivered the coup de grace. The German had fought hard – but lost.

And so the pattern was set – convoy patrols, weather recces, standing patrols, occasional offensive sweeps, sometimes with nothing seen. On the 15th John led fifteen aircraft from 126 and 249 with a quartet of 185 Squadron Spits as top cover when they attacked a radar site on the Bari headland. They approached the coast and turned southwards to bomb from 5,000ft down to 2,000ft with spectacular results as 50% of the bombs dropped fell in the target area and sheets of flame and thick black smoke erupted skywards from wrecked buildings and the Giant Wurzburg and Freya equipment. Following the bombing they strafed the site, silencing sporadic light flak in the process. As they exited the area one pilot saw twenty or thirty armoured vehicles parked in a field off the main road which he made one pass at with cannon blazing.

On the following day 249 were over Igoumenitsa on Corfu, bombing buildings and strafing a tug and a pair of schooners in the bay. They were back the next day for more of the same and then 126 joined in the assault with direct hits on what Intelligence had discerned were barracks. Any building seen with enemy M/T parked in the vicinity were adjudged to be legitimate targets for following sorties, some of which were specially mounted very quickly to strike at them. On the 21st John flew with 126 again. The formation flew south of the Fanos Islands then hugged the west coast of Corfu at sea level to within ten miles of Paxos where they climbed rapidly to cloud base at 2,500ft. Targeting Paxos harbour they dive bombed flying from the south west to north east down to 1,000ft. Four bombs burst harmlessly in the water, two landed on a small island just to the east of the harbour and two fell very close to a schooner and damaged it. A white building behind the barracks was hit and blown up, leaving the area swathed in brown smoke. The barracks themselves were severely damaged and were left blazing fiercely. On the 22nd convoy *Vellum* was escorted into Brindisi. Consisting of just two destroyers, they had been patrolling off the Yugoslav coast but had been attacked from low level by a pair of Bf109s, fortunately without a great deal of damage being inflicted. 126 were back attacking Corfu harbour on the 23rd, the day that a 14 Squadron Marauder on air test crashed at Grottaglie killing the crew. On the 25th a pair of 126 Squadron Spitfires with a pair from 185 from Malta streaked across the Adriatic to Albania for a strike on a camp at Varrazen which they dive bombed from 6,500 to 3,000 feet and were rewarded with a great orange flash, a huge explosion and billowing white smoke. With no AA fire, they turned for a low level strafing run which precipitated a further explosion of such ferocity that it violently rocked the attacking aircraft. Now was the time to withdraw!

Of 286 Wing's Spitfire squadrons, as we have seen 1435 alone flew the Spitfire IX, operating in the main from Brindisi. On the 28th they conducted a sweep to Dubrovnik where they found a pair of sixty foot motor barges at the harbour's entrance, barges with guns in the bows which put up a spirited defence but paid for with the gunners' lives and wrecked barges. A 5,000 ton motor vessel, which also replied with tracer fire, was also silenced and damaged. 1435's cannon fire picked out jagged patterns down the vessel's starboard side. With Grottaglie again made unserviceable by heavy rain 1435 were busy once more the following day from Brindisi when they attacked an E Boat close by Corfu harbour to such determined effect that the crew abandoned ship. They carried on to Kotor seaplane base where the control tower became the focus of their attention, the bridge of a two masted schooner was destroyed and the radar station at Ostri point was strafed. A tug and its coal laden barge was hit in Tivat Bay and two fifteen hundredweight trucks and a fuel dump were left smoking to the south of the bay. This was in no uncertain terms a particularly successful strike and one can only imagine the feelings of the Germans on the ground when they heard the powerful roar of approaching Merlins at low level day after day. This was unusual tasking for 1435 Squadron – in the main they operated at higher levels but the weather at Grottaglie which had precluded any operations over these few days meant a temporary change of emphasis for the Spitfire IXs.

– o O o –

E Boats were on the agenda again at the beginning of March with another success at Tivat – the vessel was attacked from astern and the beam, its Oerlikon was silenced and it was left smoking and moving slowly in a circle. The attack was accompanied by intense flak from all around the bay but 1435 escaped damage. 126 Squadron returned later the same day, the 2nd, but found no more E Boats. Instead they attacked the dockyard area and recorded four near misses on the mole, two bomb bursts amongst the lighters inside the mole and four bursts amongst the wharf's sheds. John was aloft with 249 on a two hour sortie on the 3rd to attack a two masted schooner creeping into Corfu harbour, catching it near the boom. Return Bofors fire was pretty accurate here so the formation moved on to Sarande to attack six vehicles on the road leaving one on fire, another smoking badly and three damaged.

On the 3rd March Grottaglie saw the landing of 6 Squadron with its Hurribombers: the initial echelons of the groundcrew had been steadily arriving since February 24th. Coming from Egypt (Fayid) this was the first time that 6 Squadron were to operate from European soil since 1919! Wing Commander A E Morrison Bell was CO. With the lack of anything other than tented accommodation to look forward to the Squadron set to making themselves as comfortable as possible. The almost immediate onslaught of another bout of heavy rain couldn't have been farther from conditions they had become used to in the Egyptian desert. And to accommodate a different set of operating criteria Ops and the Squadron hierarchy had soon got their heads together and had decided that the Hurricane

IVs should carry a long range tank in place of one set of rockets in a bid to increase endurance. Once this had been established 6 Squadron could be given the roving commission of its new sister squadrons with the opportunity to range the length of the Albanian coast in search of trade. Their numbers were to be reduced however with one Flight being detached almost immediately to Corsica for anti shipping strikes. Or that was the plan. It was to be May before the move materialised although this was to a degree recognition that the Squadron was at a low ebb and exhausted after its time in the desert and needed to recuperate and acclimatise to very different operating conditions. As for John and the Hurricane – no go! He was not enticed by the appearance of this new type at Grottaglie and didn't avail himself of the opportunity of sharing a sortie with them remembering no doubt his earlier thoughts on the aircraft – and this despite the prospect of letting loose a salvo of rockets which equated to a cruiser's broadside.

But continuing bad weather immediately precluded any flying anyway. 1435 Squadron, still operating out of Brindisi had a good day on the 6th – crossing the coast north of Ragusa they attacked a motor vessel at Kotor before finding troop carrying trucks on the coast road which they set on fire. A W/T station near Dubrovnik was damaged and a goods train just leaving the station there was also damaged, its locomotive left smoking for reasons other than getting up a head of steam! In Port Cruz a two masted schooner was set on fire.

Given the number of sorties being flown and the amount of AA fire and other flak encountered, casualties inflicted on the attacking aircraft were in the main light. There were exceptions of course, days on which luck deserted the British. On the 8th three 1435 Squadron machines attacked Cattaro seaplane base. Two were hit. Fl Off Chandler baled out having pulled up to 1,000ft to do so. 1435's Boss, Sqn Ldr Clements, was also hit. He too managed to find some altitude but at that juncture, off Ostri Point, his aircraft stalled and crashed into the sea. He managed to pull the hood back and get out – but only just prior to impact and as he left his stricken Spitfire he hit the sea, having had no chance to deploy his parachute. A sad day for the Wing – during a lengthy period when the state of Grottaglie put it out of bounds to anything except the heavies. One such was a Polish crewed Halifax from 334 Wing with undercarriage problems which was diverted in from Brindisi to Grottaglie so as not to block the former's still serviceable runway. The Halifax made a text book belly landing on Grottaglie's soft earth…

It was from Brindisi that 1435 got airborne once more on the 17th with four aircraft to find a considerable amount of road transport near Scutari. The results were emphatic – six trucks left on fire or damaged, a troop carrier damaged and casualties inflicted, two staff cars strafed and one set on fire, the other forced off the road with its occupants hit. Later in the day 1435 were sent off on a Air Sea Rescue mission, looking for two dinghies reported twenty five miles north east of Brindisi. They found two with seven men aboard and called up a High Speed Launch, circling overhead to wait until it arrived. Close by the dinghies was a partially submerged B24 Liberator which was refusing to go down.

On the 19th ten 249 Squadron Spitfires flew from Grottaglie, finally serviceable again, in support of a commando raid on the island of Solta. They flew continuous air cover, refuelling near Termoli so as to be able to maintain the necessary cover before 1435 arrived sporting 90 gallon tanks to take over. The raid was a success with eighty prisoners taken. Neither 249 or 1435 encountered any problems from enemy aircraft. The following day John led 126 on a road reconnaissance between Fier and Valona, four aircraft at 3,000 feet acting as cover to three on the deck. A staff car was found, strafed and its five occupants killed between Fier and Mifol: a stationary engine and two waggons on the railway west of Selenica were strafed and a steam roller similarly treated at a road junction west of Valona, the driver jumping for his life. Here the formation encountered AA fire and what appeared to be rockets so they withdrew and carried on to Corfu to look for a newly reported RDF station on the west coast but without success. It was down to 249 Squadron to find it the next day – but 126 drew some consolation from the fact that it was not at the reported co-ordinates!

After more bad weather inactivity 126 had a busy 27th March. They put up four aircraft at first light for a road recce and a warehouse attack near the jetty at Budra. A three ship completed a further road recce later in the morning leaving a lorry in flames between Drin and Durazzo, bombing a bridge at Alessio (but missing!), strafing a lorry nearby and killing its occupants, flaming a six ton lorry, disabling an armoured car and hitting a staff car. Four more Spitfires took to the air late afternoon and destroyed a convoy of lorries near Alessio. Quite a day – but certainly not atypical.

– o O o –

249 were not inactive either on the 27th. They were in the air searching the area south of Crotone for their Wing Commander Flying who had been reported as being in difficulties. They didn't find him – but there was a happy ending. The story went as follows: John's relationship with Group Captain Rhys-Jones, formed in the short space of time before the latter was posted out, was such that during a period of leave he flew over to Malta to spend some time with him. On his return flight, and having landed at Catania in Sicily to refuel, the weather began to close in. Electing to carry on John was soon to rue his decision as snowstorms set in and he was forced to seek refuge. But this was inhospitable territory – there were far too many mountains for comfort. He looked for Crotone but without success and so put his Spitfire down in a field – within thirty two paces! There would be no way, however, that John would be able to fly it out. What to do? His immediate concern was to make contact with friendly forces. A railway line ran adjacent to the field which he followed until he came to a signal box and made contact with an Allied Military Government officer who had John collected and put up for the night before arranging his onward journey to Crotone. This proved to be one of the most frightening in his life with the Mercedes truck he shared with five others bouncing wildly across mountain roads and around hairpin bends on the approach to each of which John found that he was crossing himself! At Crotone he linked up with a disgraced Irish Flying Officer who with twenty or so other RAF rogues formed a refuelling and rearming Flight but also ran a very successful contraband racket. Taking a working party back to John's stranded Spitfire they dismantled it and low loaded it back to Grottaglie – a process which took a considerable time given the conditions – and the roads!

Whilst this was going on ops, of course, continued. On the 28th 249 strafed a hutted camp and two trucks near Kotor and a 150 ton auxiliary barge, heavily laden and flying the Albanian flag, which they found three miles off the mouth of the River Drin. A second sortie damaged two trucks on an offensive sortie to Corfu. In company with six Spits from 126 carrying fragmentation bombs they attacked Berat airfield but found the target obscured by cloud. Teaming up with 229 (in from Malta) their next briefing took them to Durazzo where they contrived near misses on a white house to the south of the town identified as an enemy HQ of sorts by the transport parked outside. At the same time 1435 Squadron were scrambling to intercept two hostiles but the plot faded and nothing was seen. The by now steadily increasing tempo was maintained the following day when 126 bombed the seaplane hangars at Cattaro recording six direct hits. A further four from the same squadron bombed Shijah airfield before damaging trucks and cars

155

on the Durazzo to Valora road. A quartet from 249 bombed a two span bridge just south of Valora and completely wrecked one of the spans. The day progressed with 126 returning to Shijah, this time hitting parked aircraft on the dispersal area. 6 Squadron with their rocket armed Hurricanes, each aircraft carrying four 60lb projectiles, hit the white house building at Durazzo that both 126 and 229 Squadrons had previously had had a go at. 6 Squadron succeeded where the others had failed – but at a price. One of the Hurricanes was hit by AA fire and crashed in flames, blowing up as it hit the ground.

On the 30th, 126 and 249 Squadrons carrying fragmentation bombs and 250 pounders flew into the heart of Albania to attack Tirana, diving from 8,000 to 4,000 feet to release their weapons in the teeth of intense flak which was bursting all around them all the way down. Mercifully they escaped unscathed. The airfield was not so lucky: one of the 250 pounders went clean through the roof of a hangar and exploded with devastating effect inside. The fragmentation bombs exploded amongst the airfield buildings and around the perimeter. As they left Tirana the two squadrons split to egress with 126 recrossing the coast south of Durazzo. 249 lingered to strafe a hutted camp and a truck full of soldiers it had found. This proved to be unfortunate for Lt McCardle, a South African flying with 249 at the time. He was hit by returning fire in the long range tank which burst into flames. Climbing to 1,200ft he baled out and came down in the sea. 87 Squadron were around at the time and one of their aircraft was called in to drop a dinghy to McCardle. He was seen to swim towards it – but not to reach it. Further Spitfires were called in to search as was the Italian Cant rescue aircraft, but they saw no sign of the South African. The conclusion was he had been hit by fire from the coast nearby – indeed several of the searching aircraft had been hit too, one of 249's pilots paying the ultimate price when he crashed into a wooded hillside by the seashore. The Americans lost men that day too and 126 were involved in searching for downed Liberators reported in the sea after a 700 aircraft raid on the Bulgarian capital Sofia, flying from bases in southern Italy.

This was 126 Squadron's Italian and Balkan swansong for on April 1st they were ordered to pack up and return to the UK in preparation for D Day.

– o O o –

April 1944. The tempo was maintained as a variety of targets were attacked including shipping in the harbour area of Corfu, hutted camps, bridges, RDF stations, gun posts, store houses and MT. Wing totals for the month would include five enemy aircraft destroyed together with 281 vehicles – 103 of which were damaged or destroyed on one day alone. Better Spring weather meant that Grottaglie was serviceable throughout although this was due to a considerable degree to good airfield management which worked on the premise that all except essential flying was curtailed whenever the surface became at all soft. Another quite different corollary to the advent of better and warmer weather was the beginning of a camp wide anti malarial campaign.

Meanwhile Greek sourced intelligence to 242 Group suggested that the Germans were preparing to evacuate Corfu. Accordingly on the 2nd April six 249 Squadron Spitfires and four 6 Squadron Hurricanes were sent to investigate and found up to twenty caiques in the harbour which suggested that something might be afoot, particularly as they appeared to be unladen and thus possibly ready to accept troops. This led to a series of attacks over the ensuing days. On the 3rd 249 returned three times, John leading on the last occasion. Twenty four aircraft sorties during the course of the day led to damage to both the shipping and the wharf, with a major oil fire darkening the skies. On the final sortie the number of vessels in the harbour appeared to have reduced which was confirmed the next morning when John and 249 returned to attack once more. More devastation was wreaked amongst the wharfside buildings and whilst the caiques were damaged again it didn't appear to be terminal damage. Great waterspouts erupting in the air as bombs exploded beneath the water obscured vision for following pilots and made damage assessment difficult.

Breaking off from Corfu for a couple of days 249 turned their attention instead to truck strafing near Durazzo and identifying what appeared to be a detention camp of sorts nearby, surrounded as it was by barbed wire and equipped with sentry boxes and machine gun posts. When they went back to Corfu on the 7th there were still a dozen caiques in port but they had been joined by two large barges. John's formation of four aircraft (he was in the modified ES720 which remained his personal aircraft on the remaining occasions he flew with 249) didn't have much luck – two bombs missing completely and ending up in the sea outside the harbour, two hanging up and four landing on the already very damaged jetty. Not to worry. Other sorties by the Squadron enjoyed better luck and what had been achieved over the previous week had been completely demoralising for those on the receiving end as a ground observer reported:

From 31st March to the 7th April Allied aircraft have bombed enemy positions every day with excellent results especially at Paleokastritsi and Krinyi where they killed 16 soldiers and 3 officers. On the 7th they bombed stores of petrol inside the town with great success and sank a ship used for mine sweeping killing all the crew and eleven soldiers. The same day they bombed a motor repair shop which was burnt out and killed eight soldiers and an officer.

However, by now the intelligence was becoming suspect and it seemed there was no evacuation imminent. That didn't stop further attacks the next day when the harbour took another pounding from 249. John was with them again as six aircraft took off at 0635 in company with a quartet of Hurricanes. Meeting little resistance in the form of flak they scored at least four direct hits on wharfside buildings and some near misses on shipping in the harbour. 1435 Squadron meanwhile, tails up from intercepting and destroying a Bf109 that had been found circling the airfield at Berat, were slated for a very different mission escorting fifteen Wellingtons from the Foggia area which were bombing (successfully) a strategic road junction near Niksia. 1435 themselves were sent to Corfu harbour the following day to assess the results of the previous week's bombing and found many of the vessels to be unsurprisingly waterlogged and lying very low in the water. A ferry was included in this assessment. The wharfside itself had been blackened by fire for two hundred yards along the water's edge with the skeletal remains of buildings and equipment much in evidence. The ground observer's report had certainly been accurate.

On the 12th John led another bombing sweep against Igoumenitsa barracks but finding the target obscured by cloud turned to the harbour and its shipping once more. In the afternoon 249 returned to have another go at the barracks but this time John was thwarted by a pneumatic system failure and was forced to turn back. The following morning they inflicted a further pounding on an RDF station on the island, the full results of which were not properly seen through the dense clouds of smoke from the target area. Returning from this sortie 6 Squadron unusually found themselves on a U Boat hunt, nineteen of its aircraft committed to this, each taking off singly at thirty minute intervals and flying once around a course covering a prescribed area. The pattern was repeated the following day with twenty aircraft committed and the day after that with twenty one alongside 14 Squadron and Cants of the Italian Wing. A U Boat had been seen in the area by a 14 Squadron Marauder a few days previously but despite this very persistent search it was not sighted again.

John and twelve aircraft from 249 returned to Igoumenitsa on the 15th where they bombed a camp of an assessed thirty to forty huts just outside the town scoring direct hits, setting the area ablaze and leaving it smothered in smoke and dust. A large truck parked within the compound exploded spectacularly. AA fire forced 249's withdrawal but as a parting shot they found another RDF station which they strafed. Later in the day they strafed again, this time roads leading to Durazzo and Scutari, before following the railway line inland from Dubrovnik and attacking a train of fifteen waggons outside Trubjela. In concert with 1435 it was another day of road strafing on the 16th leading to wooden huts at Jergusat in which a number of troops taking refuge were killed. Motor transport in some profusion was discovered by John and 249 on the 17th – forty vehicles parked at twenty yard intervals at Ymerfindiu which after bombing they raked until all their ammunition was exhausted on two passing runs. The column was left wrecked and smoking. They had not been unopposed for there were AA batteries nearby which put up a screen of intensive fire – but such was the speed and indeed the surprise of 249's low level incursion that they all escaped unscathed. Keeping at very low level the squadron were quick, and indeed sharp eyed, to see more motor transport parked, this time amongst olive trees north of the town six of which they left in flames and ten damaged.

1435 Squadron flew along the course of the River Drin on the 18th to the east side of Lake Scutari where they strafed and destroyed a staff car before coming to Podgorica aerodrome where they destroyed a Bf109 and damaged a Ju88 on the ground. A further Bf109 was destroyed at Scutari itself. 6 Squadron were back in action on the 19th when four of their number set off to attack coastal guns at Cape Kiephati: sadly these guns were not to be found but they did destroy a coastguard hut as consolation. Judging by the severity of the resultant explosion it seems to have been a munitions store as well. John was in action again on the 19th when he led eight 249 Squadron and four 87 Squadron Spitfires on a road strafing mission in the south and east of Albania. They caught cars and lorries at several locations and created havoc with a flamer and two destroyed near Gramash and five in flames out of nine at Barmash. The remaining four were damaged, two of which soon fell apart. The same pairing of squadrons (but without John who was leading practice formation flying over Grottaglie as a sop to ops!) repeated the same exercise later in the day with similar success. He was however with them again on the 21st when, with a pair of 87 Squadron aircraft as top cover, half a dozen Spitfires from 249 attacked a three span road bridge over the river east of Bicak. They succeeded with two or three direct hits but failed to demolish a span – it was a tough bridge and the crossing remained intact. Frustration was vented on trucks and a couple of hutted camps south east of Pajengo. Fires were started and casualties inflicted. Inexorably pressing on they then destroyed a car at Pegin and left a large lorry blazing west of Elbason. Several hutted camps were found as they transitted and here fires were started and more transport disabled.

– o O o –

And that, flying wise, was metaphorically that for John. On May 2nd he was officially posted to the Wing rather than being merely attached to it – a little late in the day as within a month he would be posted back to the UK. But after April 21st he flew no more operational sorties in the few weeks he had remaining in Italy although as Wing Commander Flying he orchestrated some more pretty active sorties for his squadrons. South west Albania and north west Greece were visited on the 22nd with successful strafing attacks. On the 24th 1435 went chasing the Luftwaffe when they were scrambled for two aircraft reported near Bari. They found a pair of Bf109s at sea level at full throttle and heading eastwards towards safety. The Spitfires gave chase and managed to close to 1,000 yards. As they reached the

Albanian coast they were showing an ASI of 320mph. But the 109s were destined to escape. Approaching Saseno island they fired a double green flare which was the signal for an intensive barrage of AA fire to be thrown up. 1435 withdrew.

In a month in which convoys of motor transport had been frequently sighted and attacked either on the road or hidden and camouflaged, it came as almost no surprise to 249 Squadron that they should find 150 trucks and cars in and around Elbason. They had a field day, streaking in at their customary low level, canons blazing, repeatedly running the length of the convoy, until all ammunition was expended and forty one of their targets were either in flames or destroyed and damaged. Sitting targets indeed – and no resistance on this occasion. On the 27th they were looking for an oil dump south of Scutari but failed to find it. They did find and shoot down a Fiesler Storch though, flying sedately at 3,000 feet to the south of the River Drin. For a small aircraft it blew up pretty spectacularly as it hit the ground.

The Wing tally for May reads enemy aircraft destroyed – nine plus one damaged: motor transport destroyed – forty plus ninety nine damaged: ships destroyed – twenty one plus thirty two damaged: and locomotives – two damaged. On the 1st a quartet of 249 Squadron aircraft swept Yanina, Valona and Tepelene without finding any targets, a pair located a chromium mine near Elbason which would be worthy of future attention, a trio carried out a patrol of Brindisi harbour and six, together with six from 1435 Squadron, set off to rendezvous with Italian Savoia-Marchetti SM82 Canguru bombers but as the Italians were late in taking off the Spitfires landed again to wait for them. Confusion then set in for when they took off again they met the Italians returning from the RV! Everyone thus returned to their respective bases and then tried again the next day. This time contact was made and the SM82s were escorted thirty five miles inland from Dubrovnik where the Italians separated into pairs or went in singly to supposedly drop their bombs on their target – a target the identity of which was not privy to the RAF. The Italians were in the end left to it for the Spitfires were running low on fuel (they were not kitted up with tanks). Apparently a signal to bomb was due to be transmitted from the ground and the Italians were waiting for this – hence the delays. It later transpired the signal was never received and the Italians themselves turned for home without bombing. The SM82 was an interesting aircraft which didn't really look the part as a bomber which is hardly surprising as its primary role was as a troop carrier and only a few were reconfigured for the bombing role.

Meanwhile 6 Squadron Hurricanes attacked shipping at Ploca and returned the next day as part of a far larger force (eight Hurricanes with a pair each of 73 Squadron Spitfire Vs and 32 Squadron Spitfire VIIIs) and severely damaged a schooner as well as attacking a train and a house on the jetty. One of 6 Squadron's Hurricanes was hit by AA fire and the pilot was forced to bale out into the Neretljanski Channel. Sadly, despite intensive ASR efforts, he was not recovered. Meanwhile 249 were concentrating on a stores dump near Elbason, sending in eleven Spitfires in two waves to attack it. Direct hits on buildings and materials left clouds of orange smoke over the target.

The opening of an airfield on the Adriatic island of Vis on May 5th meant that the length of the Adriatic coastline could now be covered by using the island as a refuelling and rearming point with aircraft flying to Vis for operations in the morning and returning to Grottaglie in the late afternoon having undertaken one or two strikes in the meantime. 249 strafed a hutted camp near Mize, starting fires in the process, and then on to Scutari where motor transport was strafed, trucks were set on fire and troops killed. A pair of 70 foot schooners on the River Drin and a hutted camp near Kavaje were also at the receiving end of 249's guns on what was a busy day for them. They returned later to the same river accompanied by 6

Squadron where they destroyed one of the schooners they had previously damaged and also barges and a motor boat at Ulcinj. It was a different mission the next day when the squadron was committed to searching, alongside Warwicks of 293 Squadron, for Wellington and Liberator crews reported to have ditched seventy miles north east of Bari. Five of the Wellington's crew were located and picked up by High Speed Launch. On the 7th six Spitfires set off for a bridge near Palermo and scored hits on the approaches to it. Four aircraft were committed to a continuing search for the B24 without success but instead sighted two dinghies as they flew back towards Bari with eleven men aboard, the crew of a B17. Here again a High Speed Launch was despatched to pick them up.

There was no let up in the pace of, or variety of, operations that 249 Squadron were tasked with. On the 8th they strafed motor transport at Lushanje Progradec. On the 9th they were escorting Italian bombers. On the 11th with a pair of 185 Squadron aircraft they bombed a bridge at Babie and cut its centre span as well as inflicting considerable damage on trucks nearby. Contact with the enemy continued to be made. Four Bf109s were found by 1435 Squadron 60 miles north of Brindisi, one of which was shot down. Two more were then intercepted north of Bari and both of those were despatched in short order. Another bridge, this time at Bicak, was destroyed on the 12th thus hindering the movement of enemy vehicles still further. They were back at a stores dump at Kavaje on the 13th. On the same day 6 Squadron were back in action, a radar station on Corfu the target. They wrecked the aerial but also destroyed a nearby house when a salvo of rockets overshot their intended target. On the 15th 249 killed at least fifty Germans when they hit a camp at Velican. Trucks and a pair of steam rollers were destroyed as well. On the way back to Grottaglie they strafed the radar station at Cape Gacil. On the 16th 6 Squadron went after a schooner at Ploca and another at Mjlet Island.

From the 19th 249 were tasked with searching for E Boats in an area from the Gulf of Kotor to Valona. None were seen during the course of the fifteen sorties flown although five barges were strafed as a consolation prize. Three dark grey vessels were spotted under camouflage netting in Durazzo harbour during the course of these sorties and later in the day six of the Squadron's Spitfires returned to attack them with some success. A further E Boat search the following day found one which was attacked but which returned very accurate fire bringing down one of the attacking aircraft. The pilot baled out and was later picked up by Catalina. 6 Squadron Hurricanes found another later and left it sinking. 249 bombed a motor transport yard and workshops just outside Tirana and on the 22nd Hurricanes a 1,500 ton coaster at Bajkastaro. They scored nine direct hits, one salvo hitting the waterline, and returned to strafe it. By the time they left it the vessel was listing and burning fiercely.

– o O o –

The intensity of operations in February, March, April and May had taken their toll on John. Not that he flew particularly frequently over those four months but the pace of life as Wing Commander Flying was showing. He hadn't had a break from operations, first with 602, then 118 and now 286 Wing, for eighteen months. Furthermore, when he did fly much of the time was spent over the sea and this factor, which had always made John uneasy, increasingly became an issue for him. The thought of coming down in the water was a terrifying one. He always felt a little better knowing that he had a trusty Merlin in front of him, albeit one probably overhauled by Egyptians, but experience had shown that they were more reliable than he might have expected. All of this, allied with his difficult working relationship with Gp Capt Prosser Hanks, finally prompted a request to the Station MO and the Admin Officer after barely five months in Italy to engineer a return to the UK. On June 1st he was posted to No 3 APCD 'for disposal as tour expired' as the Wing's records so elegantly put it – a posting which made John a very happy man. He was not concerned as to where he went as long as he went somewhere other than operational flying. On June 6th John's position as Wing Commander Flying was taken by a Wing Commander Hopkins.

Return was scheduled to be by ship and embarkation was at Naples. Billeted in a transit camp overlooking the harbour and waiting for his transport to arrive, John awoke one morning to find the glorious sight of a vast armada of shipping inclusive of the Cunarders *Queen Elizabeth* and *Queen Mary* together with cruisers, destroyers, aircraft carriers and battleships – all there to embark a large part of the 8th Army for return to the UK. It was whilst at Naples that John met up with some American aircrew in a local bar. Rather than wait for sea transport to be arranged, which could have taken weeks as there was no place for him on any of the fleet of ships he could see from his rather luxurious flat window, he obtained a movement order from the local Transit Office. They were quite relieved to give him one as he had been plaguing the life out of them during the weeks he had been in Naples. Thus was organised the first leg of his return by air – by USAAF C47 on a cold and uncomfortable flight to Casablanca, minus his kit which he had left with clear instructions that it was to be sent home on the next available flight that had luggage space. He never saw it again!

From Casablanca John hitched a ride in a Liberator – but not before having to spend some days in the North African city (whilst an engine was changed) in the hotel in which Churchill stayed after his meeting with Roosevelt and Stalin. This was fine and in complete contrast to Casablanca city itself which John did his very best to stay out of – a rough and ready place in which no-one could be trusted and in which the locals were involved in every sort of skulduggery imaginable. But having seen how they lived – poor, destitute and lacking most things – he quickly understood why they resorted to thievery. If you have nothing you seek every way of getting something.

After a couple of abortive attempts – faulty magnetos the main culprits – John's VIP configured B24 (rather more comfortable than the C47) finally flew him into St Mawgan from where a Hudson took him on to Northolt. Sharing the B24 with him was a Flight Lieutenant who had been given the rank despite a criminal past (he had been languishing in a gaol in Glasgow) in deference to the role he now played – that of parachuting into enemy territory, allowing himself to be captured and once ensconced in a POW camp sharing his forgery skills – and those of lock picking and key making too – with his fellow prisoners. Having done this his brief was to escape (hopefully his teaching would have facilitated the escape of others also) and repeat the process elsewhere. He successfully did this five times.

A very different side to war that John had thus far experienced. But then, his war would take on a very different aspect from now on too beginning with a peripatetic period of a few months where he was not allowed to settle to anything for more than a week or two…

Chapter 15
The Final Years

For the next six months John seemed to be forever on the move. Once back on British soil and having reported to the Air Ministry, after leave John found himself in the world of Spitfire OTUs again – as Chief Flying Instructor at Tern Hill first (where the Station Commander, Gp Capt Finlay, was an Olympic medallist and the students were mainly Poles), then CFS at Acklington and finally to Hawarden once more where as a supernumerary he was available for any job necessary – anything other than flying in fact and in reality simply a dogsbody! By this stage of the war John was quite happy to play out the remainder of hostilities on the ground (although he did take advantage of any non combat flying he could using aircraft of the various Station Flights of the establishments he was assigned to). To this end he was next posted to Morpeth for an administration course (this was a happy stay!) before returning briefly to Hawarden as Station Administration Officer and then his final posting in the RAF, to Netheravon, in the same role on 8th December.

Netheravon was one of the largest stations in the Royal Air Force and it had an interesting history. In 1912 a few sheds for aircraft were built near the village of Netheravon, the rides of an unused Cavalry School being deemed to be suitable for the landing of aeroplanes. No 3 Squadron RFC moved in in June 1913 followed by 4 Squadron. When these two squadrons departed for France, 1 Squadron arrived in November 1914 and acted as a training unit until March 1915 – and this was the role that Netheravon would largely henceforth adopt, for the truth became apparent that its large undulating fields would certainly be of no use for aircraft on operational duties. When John arrived Netheravon was, although of very large complement, still essentially a First World War station with a single line of hangars from that era.

Starting with No 1, Netheravon continued to concentrate on the build up of new squadrons and as such became a major facility which by 1918 was flying types as diverse as the Avro 504K and Handley Page 0/400. Between wars 1 FTS was formed here and by the outbreak of the Second World War was operating with the Harvard and a motley collection of Hawker biplanes, largely training pilots for the Fleet Air Arm. Associations with the units which were present when John arrived began in 1941 when 296 (Glider) Squadron with Hectors and Harts towing Hotspur training gliders and 297 (Parachute) Squadron with Whitley Vs from which ten parachutists could be dropped, moved in as part of 38 Wing. By now the Fleet Air Arm had moved the largest part of its training effort to the States. 296 and 297 Squadrons moved out to be replaced by 295 whose brief was the training of ex bomber crews to tow Horsas. The Glider Pilot Exercise Unit formed in August 1942 but moved in and out of Netheravon a few times before finally disappearing by the end of 1943 at which time 38 Wing had become 38 Group and resident units were the Operational Refresher Training Unit, 1 Heavy Glider Maintenance Unit, 235 MU and the RAF Regiment. The Air Transport Tactical Development Unit (ATTDU) arrived in early 1944 followed by 1677 (TT) Flight which used Martinets to train air gunners on the new breed of glider towing aircraft. In preparation for D Day Horsa and Hamilcar gliders were made ready: post D Day glider parts were brought back from France for refurbishing plus thirty nine complete gliders which had been snatched from their Normandy landing sites. 38 Group HQ moved to East Anglia in October 1944 and activity at Netheravon continued with the ATTDU trialling glider snatching and pannier drops with Dakotas and Halifaxes. Two unusual aircraft they had on strength were Buckinghams undergoing tests as high speed couriers and which were capable of flying to Cairo and back in a day.

– o O o –

Tenants on Netheravon's wide-open Salisbury Plain spaces when John arrived included the ATTDU (later renamed the Transport Command Development Unit), No 1 Heavy Glider Servicing Unit, 46 Group School of Air Transport and 38 Group Parachute Maintenance and Servicing Unit. Mobile Parachute Servicing Units were deployed to surrounding airfields used for para dropping. The WAAF tailoresses of these parachute units were an iniquitous bunch and their 'factory' – one of the original World War One hangars – operated on a twenty four hour a day three shift basis. It was nothing short of a den of vice with the girls showing off their bodies at the windows during the night shifts to brazenly attract the soldiers of the Small Arms Unit into their lair – and they needed little attraction! To try and put an end to the practice one of the station fire engines would be regularly positioned nearby to hose down the soldiers as they approached – but this was no lasting deterrent! The parachutes the girls produced were not only for dropping soldiers but for dropping equipment too – from small arms canisters to Bren gun carriers. And John's windows. His flat sported some very flamboyant green silk curtains!

There was nothing of the supposed glamour of a front line station at Netheravon (or its satellites at Thruxton and Shrewton) – rather the hard graft of a second line support organisation. Netheravon had been built with accommodation for 500. From 1939 this steadily rose to 5,000 men and women, military and civilian – 1,000 of whom would regularly present themselves for Wednesday parade – at its peak. These population levels (there were 1,765 military personnel when John arrived) threw up all sorts of logistical problems which it was John's job to sort out. To help him he had a staff of men and women from all the professions – barristers, accountants, solicitors – as well as less vocational walks of life.

Catering for example. The canteen could cater for 500: the camp held thousands! Given a free hand to make the best possible provision, John started a farm! On it he grew produce and raised beef cattle, sheep and pigs: under the auspices of the NAAFI, all that the farm produced was sold to the RAF with John retaining 10% of the profits for re-investment in livestock and equipment. In the canteens he increased staff numbers – and quality! He organised visits of the catering section to outside institutions such as bakeries in a bid to improve the fare offered. There are always stories which centre around Service food of course and what went on behind the scenes was perhaps suspected but not, probably thankfully, common knowledge. The time, for example, one of the cooks cut her finger, bandaged it and lost the bandage only to find it in her own helping of plum duff, the odds of which happening must have been considerably greater than coming up with the football pools. It was just reward for her insensitivity and carelessness of course! And John took great pains to ensure she was disciplined for it.

It wasn't only camp personnel that John fed however: local residents also benefited and this extra income helped swell the coffers of the Service Institute (which was growing to a value of thousands of pounds). However his efforts were not, it seems, always appreciated. A local bobby, who regularly received a portion of John's bounty, had no compunction in stopping John for failing to display a rear light on his cycle. The case went to the local magistrates and John was fined 5/-. Not always one to let bygones be bygones – and in this case he felt particularly aggrieved – the bobby was summoned to the camp and his NAAFI ration book taken from him. No more would he metaphorically sit at John's table. He had lost the right to rations far in excess those of the normal allocation.

Station and Service Institute funds were not the only ones that accrued thanks to the efforts of John and his staff (distribution of the money the latter held was agreed by a Committee which was made up of men and women from all sections and ranks on the station). Individual savings were greatly encouraged amongst service personnel and records show some months when as much as £767 was placed in RAF schemes and as little as £155 during others – the declining amounts reflecting the end of the war and reduction in numbers. The exodus started almost immediately after VE Day having reached a peak of 2,329 in March, bolstered by troops returning from the Continent. Forty Dakotas had arrived during late February, for example, bringing in 800 and had flown straight out again to collect more. Another 3,000 passed through in May, all courtesy of Transport Command.

Entertainment was crucial for a large work force that was active round the clock. A cinema was a necessity and when John arrived the existing facility was totally inadequate and could not meet the demand. He bought new projection equipment from his funds – the latest state of the art kit – and new seating. Films were shown twenty four hours a day. He also organised concerts and dancing at station level (these were apart from those organised by individual units) – and once again to accommodate the never sleeping work force these could take place anytime within the twenty four hour clock. ENSA paid regular visits. And concerts were held – everything from military bands to the local choral society.

The money was well spent in other areas too: in education, £60 a week was allocated to the purchase of books and other necessary material and equipment. Indeed education figured large in the station's planning and increasingly so as the war came to an end and service personnel had to anticipate a swift return to civvy street. Resettlement courses began and EVT (Educational and Vocational Training) took on a new urgency. Tutorial courses in Higher Education were organised. Outside of these a plethora of opportunities became available for those of a more practical disposition and for those who merely fancied trying their hand at something completely different purely out of interest's sake or indeed to indulge a particular interest. Thus there was general handicrafts, leathercraft, carpentry, household repairs, joinery, cabinet making, embroidery and domestic science. There was a discussion group, a debating society, a drama group, a new class in matriculation geometry, music circles (for 'heavy' and 'light' classical), a swing club (to strike a balance with those of a classical bent) and a lecture theatre.

Sport, as ever, played a major part in station life. For Netheravon's football, rugby and cricket teams, strip and equipment was all paid for – and Freddie Mills the boxer who was at Netheravon at the time could be relied upon to always spend more than he was allocated! Freddie was a tough little NCO who would regularly box with the Canadian Gp Capt George, a devout Catholic who became the new Station Commander four days before John's arrival. The Group Captain could never get the better of him! Freddie was simply too quick! Many other sports were catered for as well – swimming, hockey, badminton, squash, netball for the WAAFs and physical training in the gym. There were inter-squadron matches, inter-station matches and inter-service matches as well as the opportunity for playing your chosen sport just for the hell of it – and it was all encouraged.

But despite all this there was too much in the steadily accruing fund which John had inherited (there were, for example, £12,000 worth of war bonds from the first conflict). Sometimes too it seemed as if John couldn't help himself from thinking up ingenious new ways of making money. He had traps fitted to all the camp's drains which collected the fat from the soap and other waste which he collected into 45 gallon drums and sold to ammunition manufacturers who came and collected it on a weekly cycle! But Gp Capt George was horrified. How the hell were they to reduce the amount of money they had and not let it fall into the hands of the service auditors who, if they became aware of the riches at Netheravon, would confiscate it? New schemes were dreamed up – hiring trains to get people to London and buses to get people to the trains. Not that this was free – they were prepared to pay well for the service but perversely this didn't help Institute Fund levels of course. Money would be put into the Station Commanders' Fund for expectant WAAFs and the truth was, with so many at Netheravon, pregnant WAAFs were the norm! Each new mum was given a pram and £30 when their time came. But this again didn't significantly reduce the Fund. In fact during John's tenure of it he never could get it down below £30,000 – and wonders to this day whether the auditors ever got their hands on it or whether his successors managed to successfully hide it from inquisitive minds…

– o O o –

What of the day to day operations at Netheravon? Because of the size and diversity of the units that were tenants at the station, it was indeed a hive of activity – particularly the glider units. King George VI and Queen Elizabeth visited to see them at work – he in full military dress including highly polished riding boots which a stray piece of barbed wire, John recalls for some obscure reason, scratched terribly. It was decided that a demonstration of how a Horsa glider broke in two upon landing the easier to disgorge its cargo should be laid on. Aware that sometimes the mechanism that enabled this to be done did not always work successfully, a glider was specially rigged. Consternation all round when a canny King George walked into the hangar and insisted that the demonstration be carried out with a glider other than the one to which his hosts were trying to direct him Experience no doubt told him that plenty of fail safes had been engineered and he wanted to see a truly representative machine used. Consternation transmuted itself to relief when the King's chosen glider performed exactly as designed

In fact Netheravon was no stranger to demonstrations and exercises. In May 1944 during *Exercise Exeter* the King and Queen had been shown the aircraft and equipment soon to be used in the invasion of Europe. All the operational units of 38 Group and some of 46 were involved: 300 Canadian troops were dropped from Dakotas and Halifaxes towed in tank carrying Hamilcars and troop carrying Horsas. A tactical landing was made on the airfield. The royal couple had also previously been at Netheravon in May 1942 to see demonstrations by detachments of the Parachute Regiment and in April 1943 to inspect units of 38 Wing. Netheravon was increasingly being used as a large scale exercise and training area particularly with the forthcoming invasion of Europe in mind. Tactical landings by large numbers of gliders during exercises became a regular feature of life there which continued after D Day.

Netheravon was a remarkably accident free place flying wise – certainly during the time of John's tenure, although the flying, of course, was very much incidental to his new role. Inevitably though he could never resist the chance to watch and observe. In the first month of his stay he would have seen that flying was restricted on a number of days when the grass airfield became thoroughly waterlogged thanks to thawing snow (shades of Grottaglie in winter here!). February 1945 was similarly affected. In March Wg Cdr J W White took temporary command of Netheravon when Gp Capt George was posted out. 38 Group's School of Weapons Training was added to the Station complement of lodger units. 150 gliders were ferried out of Netheravon to various 38 Group Stations and a dozen United States Troop Carrier Command C47As arrived for a week for para dropping duties, each aircraft making at least one sortie each day carrying twenty troops – which meant that 8,000 were disgorged over the Divisional Dropping Zone during their stay. John recalls one famous incident which occurred during this exercise when the rigging lines of Lance Corporal Phillips, 6th Airborne Division, caught on the tail-wheel of a C47 and he was left spinning helplessly in the buffeting slip-stream. While the pilot flew as slowly as he dared, the jump instructor, a Sgt Beamish, hitched together several nylon strops and tied a kit-bag to the end. This lifeline was paid out to the parachutist. Somehow he managed to cling to it while the remaining men in the stick hauled him back to the door against the slip-stream. This was the first recorded incident of anybody surviving such as ordeal. Such incidents were mercifully the exception rather than the rule.

Gp Capt H A Purvis DFC became John's new CO in April. He oversaw the returfing of part of the airfield to help repair the ravages of hard use and a hard winter. *Exercise Knockaround* involved the towing in from Tarrant Rushton of three Horsas and taking them out again the next day. Snatch pick up trials continued with 1 HGSU, not always successfully and with the gliders often coming off the worse for wear. The TCDU moved out to RAF Harwell and better facilities. The war may have come to an end in Europe but training exercises continued, perhaps with an eye on the need to get involved in the Far East. A mass landing of sixty four Horsas at Thruxton, code named *Exercise Reconnaissance*, was followed by *Exercise Residue* and ninety two Horsa landings at the same satellite.

On 15th September the first of the country's long ongoing series of Battle of Britain At Home Days began and Netheravon was amongst the stations to open its doors to the public for the afternoon of that day. Displays were modest compared with later standards. There were a few aircraft on the ground, representative of the types that operated, or had operated from the airfield, and most of the technical and domestic sections of the camp were opened up for viewing. There was a display of equipment and aircraft used on D Day operations in one of the hangars. A display by a helicopter from RAF Andover and a Dakota towing a Horsa constituted the only flying activity. 859 civilians attended: 150 from the army were also there and £11.5.0 was collected for the Royal Air Force Benevolent Fund.

During October the 38 Group Junior Leaders School moved in. Maintenance work on the airfield involved the marking of its boundaries so that they were visible from the air and this was done by cutting sections of turf and replacing it with chalk. At the same time the control tower was repainted. Administratively the WAAFs were moved out of married quarters into airmen's barrack blocks in anticipation of the arrival of married service families. The WAAFs on any RAF Station had their own senior officers of course and the relationship between them and the Station Admin team could be fractious at times although at the end of the day some harmony was maintained! A pair of Wellingtons arrived in November to act as glider tugs – a new type in this role for Netheravon – together with the necessary support and servicing equipment. And it was found that the explosives and small arms store was 80% overstocked by peacetime standards and so the surplus had to be moved to 202 MU for storage. Over Christmas and the New Year period staff were given a four day leave pass where possible – those that didn't take Christmas got the New Year instead. Netheravon's kids were well catered for at a party where a mass of toys made on the station were handed out…

– o O o –

… And so Netheravon settled into a peacetime routine with there suddenly seeming little point to it all any more and little attraction for the future. Wing Commander John Freeborn DFC and Bar elected to come out of the RAF in 1946 –

a service which in his opinion 'was at that stage run by nincompoops'.

He remembers: *One station commander had stones lining the roads on camp whitewashed, took great delight in turning out the fire engines just to see how fast they would go but thereby killing a young fireman who fell off such an engine and cracked his head on a whitewashed stone: and who stood up, put his cap on and saluted whenever his AOC came on the line to him*

The Crown Prince of Sweden visits Netheravon in 1945. He faces Group Captain Harman with John to his left. Behind them are members of the RAF Regiment

So he resigned, the story having perhaps come full circle because the reader will recall that one of John's characteristics from the very beginning was not to suffer fools gladly.

Were there any regrets that this decision had been forced on him? Perhaps – but having had a busy and often stressful war John felt it was the right time to get out anyway. There was no telling what would happen with the RAF – peace had broken out and a reduction in personnel and equipment on a drastic scale was sure to follow. It was not that he hadn't had the chance to get back to operational flying – not only was he actually on an early warning for India, possibly to command a station, but the previous year he had been offered a position (via the Commander of a small signals detachment at Netheravon) with the Fleet Air Arm as Wing Commander Flying Far East for the build up to the conclusion of the Japanese war – but had turned it down for various reasons. He was relatively happy at that stage at Netheravon. He was getting on with the job and finding it curiously satisfying. And he didn't trust the Navy any more than he had come not to always trust the RAF! There was every likelihood that he could have ended up in the jungle somewhere and that certainly didn't appeal

Netheravon had been a challenge. He had arrived to find the camp run down and lax in discipline, systems and procedures which was a tragedy, for so important an establishment relied heavily upon by the army for its glider, paradropping and transport requirements. But John had made it work and was proud of it. He had inaugurated a twenty four hour, three shift system The secret, if it was a secret, to

168

his success was finding the right people to do the jobs he needed them t included professionals such as accountants and solicitors. John built up good rapport with Army liaison officers – after all a large part of Netheravon *son d'etre* was support of the Army. He controlled the postings in and out of t camp. And he also sat in on briefings for exercises and other operational matters. In fact John continued to fly, albeit only on training sorties. The lure of the air was too great to stay away from flying for long. It was the Dakota which John mainly got behind the controls of.

This was one of the nicest twin engined aircraft I've ever had the fortune to fly. It was pretty docile. In rough weather the wing tips would flex through a nine foot arc! And in turbulence dropping the undercarriage was a very good trick to know to stabilise the aircraft!

The Dakota – the military development of the DC3 of course – was the mainstay of RAF Transport Command during the war and it served in every theatre. 1,900 of various marks were supplied under lend-lease to equip twenty five squadrons. Apart from glider tug and paratrooping the Dakota was also used as a personnel carrier, freighter and air ambulance. It served with the RAF until 1970 when the last one was eventually retired and an example still flies as a component of the Battle of Britain Memorial Flight. At Netheravon it was thanks to 'Chalky' White, boss of the HGSU, that John was able to fly the Dakota as much as he did. And Charlie Crawley who was in the glider repair shops and was, in off duty moments, John's fishing partner. Apart from the Dakota a silver Spitfire arrived one day – John is not sure from whence it came or what mark it was – and he was pleased to get back into the cockpit for a few local flights, but was forced to stop due to the lack of servicing records. The aircraft subsequently disappeared as quickly as it had arrived.

Before he left John attempted to give Gp Capt Harman, his last CO who had arrived in August 1945, refresher flying lessons in one of Netheravon's Magisters. He lost patience when the Group Captain insisted on repeatedly applying the handbrake instead of selecting 'flaps down' when coming in to land! That was the straw that broke the proverbial camel's back and he ordered the Group Captain out of the aircraft despite protests that he couldn't treat the Station Commander like that! As captain of the aircraft John of course was perfectly entitled to do what he did.

Actually John didn't get away from the RAF completely. He went into the Reserve of Air Force Officers again (the reader will recall this is where it all started for John) until 1954, participating in Annual Camps (usually at Doncaster) and flying Tiger Moths to keep his hand in. This brings us back full circle in another sense for such flying enabled John to indulge his railway interests as he took great pleasure in chasing the Flying Scotsman up the east coast line at full tilt, the train usually travelling faster than the Tiger Moth! This was better than administering grossly over inflated Service Institute Funds any day!

Suddenly he was enjoying himself in the air again… but even this was not to last for the day came in '54 when a medical revealed a hearing deficiency that was to preclude him from carrying on flying. So that, militarily, was that. John did continue to fly as a civilian though. When he later moved to Spain he joined a Flying Club there (where such Clubs were heavily subsidised by the government and where in times of emergency the military might find a ready trained source of pilots) and thoroughly enjoyed taking aloft the Rallye. This was a fascinating aeroplane for it had an extensively slatted wing which meant it could fly very slowly and land on the proverbial sixpence. In the UK John also joined a Liverpool flying club where he teamed up with Jim Hacking of Sun Valley Nuts fame to fly the latter's Beech Bonanza, an introduction which came about as a direct result of John's post RAF career…

Retrospective

We started this account with John's early family life and upbringing and it is fitting that we should conclude in similar vein. Having left the RAF John spent two years as a freelance vehicle inspector working for insurance companies that required his services. From there he took the necessary examinations and joined the Ministry of Transport as a vehicle and driving examiner. He had however meanwhile been pressured by the Managing Director of Tetley Walker, the brewers, into joining them and eventually, finding that the Ministry of Transport was not entirely to his liking, he did so as Regional Manager for their Minster soft drinks division (which is when he became friendly with Beech Bonanza owner Jim Hacking). Sadly though, after twelve years his career was brought to a premature conclusion by the increasing ill health and instability of Rita. John took early retirement to look after her and his daughter Julia. Rita died on 18th January 1980.

John had also become friendly with Jimmy Clinton. Jimmy was quite a character who had told his family that his war had been spent overseas on special assignments. It transpired that overseas was actually Holyhead! After Rita's death he and John decided on a visit to the Confederate Air Force at Brownsville in Texas which is the point at which once again fate stepped in. Booking tickets for this holiday they literally bumped into another old acquaintance, Mike Metcalfe, who in his day had been the youngest Chief Engineer in the Merchant Navy. The outcome was an abandonment of any plans to visit the States but rather a trip to Spain and the eventual purchase of an apartment at Mojcar near Almeria in the south west of that country.

It was in Spain that John met Peta. It was love at first sight for both of them. There is little doubt that John has always had an eye for a pretty girl as has perhaps become evident as these pages have been read, but in Peta he finally found what he had always sought – security, companionship and somebody with whom he wanted to fully share his life. They soon married and there began an exquisitely happy seventeen years, dur-

Peta and John at their wedding in 1983

ing fourteen of which they took great delight in discovering together the beauty of inland Spain, particularly in almond blossom time which they both loved. The lure of Andalucian villages was irresistible.

Peta had herself lived an interesting life. A talented painter, an early career with Mailings Pottery had to be cut short as she was allergic to the chemicals used. Plates that bear her artist's mark survive. She was also a talented dancer but chose not to pursue it as a career. Instead in early 1940 she married Donald who was a senior official at the Bank of England's Newcastle agency. Donald was also in the RNVR and he fought his war in the Atlantic and the Aegean – and a fascinating irony is that John is sure he knew him as part of the Royal Navy's intelligence team when he was at Grottaglie! After the war Peta and Donald moved from Newcastle to London and then, when Donald's health started to fail, to the warm climate of Spain.

Donald died in 1970 and Peta was left alone for the first time in her life. Her daughter Susan takes up the story:

After Daddy's death, Peta bravely spread her wings and with some good friends took off to see the world. In fact in Malaysia she spread her wings rather literally for paragliding was the latest thing and she just had to do it! Back in Spain she bought a house in the stunningly beautiful but rather remote valley of Cortico Grande. It was here that she met and fell for the man who would be at her side for the rest of her life... Peta was swept off her feet by John's adventurous spirit and they enjoyed the pleasures of Spanish life for almost fourteen years but a desire to be nearer their families prompted thoughts of a move back to their homeland. In 1996 they moved to a seaside home in North Wales. In 1997 Peta became ill and had to undergo

Margaret Ena Freeborn - John's beloved Peta

Peta, so named by her first husband Donald because he didn't like Margaret or Ena, seen here at their wedding in 1940

major surgery, always devotedly looked after by John who regularly drove the fifty mile journey to and from her hospital bed. She seemed to make a good recovery and even coped with the stress of another move, this time to Dorset. But then her condition worsened again and on Boxing Day 2000 she collapsed. Three weeks later she died.

The date was 18th January, exactly the same date that Rita had died. Peta was 83. John misses her terribly. It was Peta who in many ways prompted this account of John's life. Previously he had had little interest in telling his story but Peta persuaded him it was worth doing. It is as a memorial to her that this book has been written and published.

– o O o –

Many years ago, at the very beginning of his RAF career, John was waiting at Leeds Central Station to catch the train that would take him to Sywell and 8 FTS when he was set upon by a gathering of older boys who, as boys do, spotted John was by himself and started to take the mickey out this young Yorkshireman. They chose the wrong person – John got stuck in, they fled and honour was maintained. This was one of a number of practical lessons of life that John was learning. He was now making his own way in the world and part of that involved learning to look after himself.

Later, at Uxbridge en route to Montrose he watched a parade of Group 5 trades marching. They were in the hands of Warrant Officers. 'Look at this lot! We've given them one uniform: by the time we've done with them they'll have two when we fill them out a bit!' They too were embarking on a new career in a strange world. They too would soon learn that it was relatively easy to survive in new worlds but that you had to adapt and be prepared to accept new regimes, procedures and disciplines.

Behind it all for John were the words of his father, words he always remembered. *There's no one as good as you but you're no better than anyone else.*

Belief in yourself is important: but learn from others too. John practised this precept daily.

Discipline has been at the cornerstone of the principles by which John has lived. We have seen the effects of authority improperly used on John as a young boy and at times during his career. But discipline teaches everybody the rights and wrongs of this world. It teaches you that you must never be afraid to stand up for your rights. You must never let the standards that are established slip – something which John feels passionately about in relation to attitudes of professional activity today which he cannot equate with that of his youth. A metaphorical or literal clip round the ear never did anyone any harm – whoever you may be.

So, at Montrose, when John was given fourteen days confined to camp for dumb insolence, he outwardly accepted that punishment as the norm for the times even though he may not have fully understood of what insolence he had been guilty! It had been his Flight Commander, Fleming, who had spied spots of metal polish on John's belt whilst on parade. John looked down to see what was being talked about – but shouldn't have. Dumb insolence. A Flight Lieutenant – let alone anyone of higher rank! – represented legitimate Royal Air Force authority and His was the Word. But John's memories of Montrose are not clouded by incidents such as these: they are of a happy time, if a tough one. All his colleagues were of a like mind – determined to succeed in their chosen career. Discipline was part of that determination. In the years ahead John would apply the same principles to those under his command – being firm but fair didn't preclude anybody from being happy with what they were doing or indeed from having a good time. Everyone knew where they stood with John. He spoke his mind: he was respected for it: but everyone could let their hair down with him as well.

His early days with 74 Squadron were particularly impressionable ones and perhaps because of this his time with the Tigers is viewed as the best of his career despite the ensuing experience of the States, the camaraderie of 602 and the challenge of 118. Sammy Sampson in particular he adored – seeing him as his father but without the big stick. Life's obverse side soon became apparent with the likes of Paddy Treacy as his Flight Commander although John could always recognise the qualities even in men like these – in Treacy's case qualities as a pilot and officer. And Malan of course. A deep friendship undermined by Malan's intransigence after Barking Creek.

Looking back now to such a crucial character forming period of his life John knows that it was a time he would not in the main have changed. It was a memorable time, a life filled with individuals whom he recalls with fondness, characters who were totally trustworthy and honourable and loyal – as well as those few whom he recalls with considerable distaste. At higher levels, the one big mistake as far as he was concerned was the influence of the civilian, political heads on the way the Air Force developed. They certainly could not compare with the fighting and flying heads – the Dowding's, Harris's and Bennett's of the Service.

The Royal Air Force was a great character builder. In the main it was served by good commanders. It was, though, packed full of snobbery. When he first arrived at Hornchurch on that Sunday evening John was wondering how ever he would get on in this strange new world – a very young man surrounded by so many older and wiser men...but not that much older in the main of course. Little did he realise that within months he would be flying Spitfires, the amazing new aeroplane of the time, and that within a few more months war would take a terrible toll on his new friends and colleagues. He was thrust into positions of unthinkable responsibility and found himself in situations that he couldn't have imagined. It focused his life: he lost his youthfulness very quickly. Outside he still looked inordinately young, round faced, freshly complexioned and cheerful with his cap set at an increasingly jaunty angle! Inside very quickly a man had replaced the boy. War does that to everyone. It also created the impetus that enabled him to rise in rank and prestige. For that he is eternally grateful.

The Royal Air Force served me well:
I hope I served the Royal Air Force as well.

Index of Aircraft Types

Airspeed Horsa   163, 166, 167
Airspeed Oxford   135, 137
Armstrong Whitworth Siskin   3, 92
Armstrong Whitworth Whitley   4, 163
Avro 504K   163
Avro Anson   133, 135
Avro Lancaster   4, 110
Avro Manchester   4
Beech Bonanza   169, 171
Blackburn Roc   92
Blackburn Skua   92
Boeing B17 Flying Fortress   96, 98, 100, 119, 122, 124, 127, 136, 160
Boulton Paul Defiant   93
Bristol Beaufighter   48, 93, 123, 124, 125, 126, 133, 147, 151
Bristol Beaufort   123
Bristol Blenheim   4, 27, 28, 29, 32, 78, 80, 119, 120
Bristol Bombay   40
Bristol Buckingham   164
Cant Z506/S   141, 147
Consolidated B24 Liberator   96, 136, 143, 145, 147, 149, 151, 154, 156, 160, 161
Consolidated Catalina   160
de Havilland Comet Racer   80
de Havilland DH9A   109
de Havilland Dominie   133, 135, 137
de Havilland Mosquito   100, 104, 132, 137
de Havilland Puss Moth   83
de Havilland Tiger Moth   4, 5, 132, 134, 169
Dornier Do17   9, 40, 41, 51, 52, 54, 59, 65, 68, 78
Dornier Do215   39, 40, 46, 54, 59, 65, 78
Douglas Boston/A20 Havoc   100, 115, 119, 120, 123, 127, 128
Douglas C47/DC3 Dakota   138, 141, 144, 161, 164, 165, 166, 167, 169
Fairey Fawn   109
Fairey Swordfish   5
Fiat CR42 Falco   148, 149
Fiesler Storch   159
Focke-Wulf Condor   60
Focke-Wulf Fw190   46, 112, 120, 121, 123, 124, 127, 128, 131, 147
General Aircraft Hamilcar   163, 166
General Aircraft Hotspur   163
Gloster Gamecock   3
Gloster Gauntlet   2, 8, 9, 13, 14, 17, 20, 109
Gloster Gladiator   14, 17
Handley Page 0/400   163
Handley Page Halifax   4, 110, 149, 154, 164, 166
Handley Page Hampden   4
Handley Page Harrow   132
Handley Page Heyford   3, 60
Hawker Audax   5
Hawker Demon   7, 8, 9, 13
Hawker Fury   5, 9
Hawker Hart   5, 109, 163
Hawker Hector   109, 163
Hawker Hind   4, 109
Hawker Hurricane   3, 4, 9, 14, 21, 27, 31, 35, 39, 45, 48, 54, 77, 91, 92, 141, 142, 147, 149, 153, 154, 156, 157, 159, 160
Hawker Sea Hurricane   60
Hawker Tempest   3
Hawker Typhoon   3, 106, 124, 125
Hawker Woodcock   3
Heinkel He111   9, 32, 37, 40, 41, 42, 65, 67, 80, 84, 90, 92, 109
Henschel 126   32, 37, 40
Junkers Ju52   145
Junkers Ju87   59, 74
Junkers Ju88   37, 40, 48, 65, 78, 132, 133, 136, 145, 152, 158
Lockheed Hudson   4, 141, 147, 161
Lockheed P38 Lightning   100
Lockheed Ventura   110, 112, 116, 120, 127
Martin B26 Marauder   119, 120, 124, 125, 126, 127, 128, 131, 141, 147, 151, 153, 157
Messerschmitt Bf109   24, 33, 40, 41, 42, 50, 52, 54, 55, 58, 59, 62, 65, 73, 74, 75, 76, 78, 79, 80, 92, 124, 125, 128, 152, 157, 158, 159, 160
Messerschmitt Bf110   51, 52, 58, 65, 68, 78, 92
Miles Magister   20, 89, 90, 91, 93, 169
Miles Martinet   163
Miles Master   33, 64, 89, 91, 92, 95
North American B25 Mitchell   100, 110, 111, 115, 116, 119, 120, 124, 127, 128
North American Harvard   90, 96, 100, 163
North American P51 Mustang   99, 100, 114, 126
Percival Mew Gull   80
Percival Proctor   133, 135
Rallye   169
Republic P47 Thunderbolt   98, 99, 100
Savoia-Marchetti SM82 Canguru   159
SE5A   7
Seversky P35   99
Short Stirling   4
Short Sunderland   136
Supermarine Spitfire   3, 4, 9, 12, 13 17, 18, 19, 20, 21, 22, 23, 24, 35, 36, 37, 38, 39, 40, 45, 46, 48, 54, 58, 59, 62, 72, 75, 76, 77, 80 82, 84, 89, 90, 91, 95, 99, 109, 110, 111, 114, 115, 116, 119, 120, 121, 122, 124, 125, 126, 127, 128, 131, 132, 134, 136, 137, 139, 141, 144, 145, 146, 147, 149, 151, 152, 153, 154, 155, 156, 158, 159, 160, 163, 169, 174
Supermarine Walrus   124, 133, 135
Taylorcraft Auster   115
Vickers Vildebeest   3
Vickers Warwick   141
Vickers Wellesley   96
Vickers Wellington   4, 79, 89, 90, 92, 105, 142, 146, 147, 151, 157, 160, 167
Westland Wapiti   3, 109
Westland Whirlwind   110

Index of Personnel

Adams, Ronnie   58
Allan, Johnny   33, 113
Anderson, Flt Sgt   133
Armstrong, Bill   75
Aubert, Bertie   36, 37, 40, 41
Ayres, David   68
Bader, Douglas   38, 65
Baker, `Butch`   49, 62
Barrett, Wg Cdr   134
Bartley, Tony   78
Beamish, Sgt   167
Beamont, Roly   93
Beisiegal, Wg Cdr   65
Bennett, Air Cdre D C T   174
Bennett, Cpl   18
Beytagh, Mike   110, 111, 113
Black, Stanley   62
Bouchier, `Daddy`   33
Boulding, Roger   20, 47, 49, 60, 80, 81, 82, 84
Brittain, Susan   172
Brook, Sir Alan   133
Brookes, D S `Brookie`   8, 17
Brooks, Robin   71, 74
Brzezina, Flt Lt S   59

Buckland, Frank 59
Burglass, Fl Off 123, 125
Bushell, Roger 28
Byrne, Vincent `Paddy` 11, 17, 18, 23, 27, 30, 77, 41
Caldwell, Keith 7
Camm, Sydney 5
Capel, Sgt 133
Caslaw, Jack 5
Caxton, Flt Sgt 122
Chamberlain, Neville 9
Chandler, Fl Off 154
Chesters, Peter 12, 49, 67, 74, 75, 78, 79, 112
Churches, Wally 62, 72, 74, 78, 79
Churchill, Winston 35, 38, 58, 142, 143, 161
Clements, Sqn Ldr 154
Clinton, Jimmy 171
Cobden, Don 19, 36, 37, 40, 49, 50, 54, 58, 62, 79
Colvin, Sqn Ldr 151
Cooke, Sqn Ldr 13
Courtenay, Ron 5, 79
Crawley, Charlie 169
Crowe, `Jim` 7
Crown Prince of Sweden 168
Cunningham, John 93
Currant, `Bunny` 29
Cushion, Plt Off 90
Dales, Sgt 78
Darnley, Lord 80
de Havilland, Geoffrey 93
Deere, Al 33, 46, 113
Denley, Flt Sgt 18
Dennis, Capt. 103
Dodds, Hector 97
Doe, Flt Lt 123
Donaldson, Gp Capt 38
Douglas, AVM Sholto 76, 77
Dowding, ACM Sir Hugh 31, 35, 37, 38, 41, 76, 174
Dowding, Derek 19, 36, 37, 38, 40, 42, 52
Draper, Ben 19, 37, 41, 42, 49, 52, 55, 73, 74, 76, 86
Drew, Tony 121, 123, 136, 138
Dunning, Fl Off 122, 139
Eames, Sgt 113
Eisenhower, Lt Col 96
Elcock, `Chiefy` 18
Eley, `Tiger Tim` 54
Etheridge, Flt Sgt 18
Farmer, Flt Sgt 18
Faulkner, W0 123
Finlay, Gp Capt 163
Fisher, James 74
Fleming, Flt Lt 173
Flight, Roy 123, 124, 131
Flinders, `Polly` 14, 27, 28
Fonda, Henry 97
Fox, Flt Sgt 152
Franklin, Walter 49, 55, 74
Freeborn, Harold 1, 2
Freeborn, Jean 1, 64, 67
Freeborn, Julia 104, 171
Freeborn, Peta 104, 171, 172, 173
Freeborn, Rita 95, 104, 171, 173
Freeman 137
Freese, Lawrence 75, 78
George, Gp Capt 165, 166
Giddings, Mike 121, 136
Glendinning, John 74, 76, 78
Goering, Hermann 59
Grable. Betty 98, 103
Graham, Sgt Pilot 132
Grant 137
Greenwood, Plt Off 152
Grice, Gp Capt 72
Gunn, Harold 54, 55

Hacking, Jim 169, 171
Hales, Colin 13
Handley, Fl Off 122
Harbison, Paddy 134
Harman, Gp Capt 168, 169
Harris, Sir Arthur 174
Harrup 27
Hastings, Douglas 50, 54, 59
Hastings, Sir Patrick 28
Hawkins, Sgt 14, 27, 28, 30
Heinemann, Ed 100
Henderson, AVM 137
Henri the Frenchman 114, 115
Henshaw, Alex 80
Heppell, Sqn Ldr P W E 139
Heywood, Gordon 14, 18
Hilken, Clive 49, 73, 86
Hitler, Adolf 4, 7, 40, 59, 68, 142
Hoare, Sammy 10, 17, 18, 28, 36, 41
Hodges, Bob 76
Hogan, Gp Capt 96, 97, 102
Hollingsworth, Joe 123, 125
Hopkins, Wg Cdr 161
Howard, John 80
Hoxha, Enver 143
James, First Lt 131
Jones, Fl Off 139
Jones, Ira `Taffy` 7, 8
Kartveli, Alex 98
Kelly, Piers 50, 59
Kerr, Deborah 78
King George VI 49, 50, 58, 73
Lacey, James `Ginger` 92
Le Mesurier, G A 122, 135, 136, 137, 139
Leader, Sgt 18
Leathart, Flt Lt 33
Leigh Mallory, AVM T 38, 65, 77, 111
Liby, Lt. 123, 124, 126
Lillywhite, George 91
Lipman, Sqn Ldr 91
Llewellyn, Flt Sgt 12, 18, 19, 36, 81
Loud, Bill 10
Lucas, `Laddie` 125, 126
Lucking, Gp Capt 29
Mainwaring, Fl Off 14, 18, 23
Malan, A G `Sailor` 11, 12, 17, 18, 20, 21, 27, 28,
   29, 30, 32, 36, 37, 39, 40, 41, 42, 49, 50, 52, 53,
   54, 55, 56, 63, 64, 65, 74, 76, 77, 78, 80, 174
Mallory, Henry 122, 135, 136, 137, 139
Mannock, Mick 7, 58
Mayne, Ernie 11, 12, 18, 19, 30, 36, 40, 50, 58, 92
McCardle, Lt 156
McLane, Barbara 97
McTaggart, Flt Lt 101
Meares, Charlie 11, 18
Measures, `Tinky` 18, 19, 20, 32, 36, 37, 40, 42, 51
Metcalfe, Mike 171
Mihailovic, Draza 142
Miller, Sgt 133
Mills, Freddie 165
Mitchell, Philip 92
Morris, Derek 12
Morrison Bell, Wg Cdr 153
Morrison, Neil 76, 78
Mould, Tony 12, 19, 20, 36, 37, 42, 52, 54, 62, 81, 104
Mungo Park, John 19, 30, 36, 37, 39, 49, 50, 51, 52,
   53, 54, 55, 58, 61, 73, 74, 75, 76, 77, 78, 81, 83
Murray, Fl Off 123
Mussolini, Benito 3, 7
Neagle, Anna 102, 103, 104
Nelson, Willie 50, 58, 73, 74, 86
Newbury, Dicky 123
Northrop, Jack 100

Orde, Cuhbert   71
Paal, Ken   123
Park, AVM Keith   8, 29, 35, 38
Payne, Alec   78
Pearson-Rogers, Gp Capt   135, 138
Pettigrew, Sqn Ldr   60, 133
Phillips, Lance Cpl   167
Piper, Sgt   137
Playfair, AVM   23
Plunkett, Sqn ldr   149
Pooler, Norman   13, 17, 18
Pooley, Flt Lt   105
Poulton, Bob   62, 78, 81, 84, 85
Power, Tyrone   97
Prien, Lt   95
Prosser Hanks, Gp Capt   149, 160
Purvis, Gp Capt H A   167
Queen Elizabeth   166
Rabagliati, Wg Cdr   123, 124
Rae, Flt Sgt   152
Rhys-Jones, Gp Capt J R   149, 152, 155
Ricalton, Alan   53, 73, 81
Rice, Raymond   99
Richardson, Pl Off   49
Richmond, Duke of   126
Robinson, Flt Sgt   112
Rogowski, Jan   78
Roosevelt, President   161
Rose, Tommy   27, 28
Rothwell, Geoff   96, 97, 102, 103
Rowland, Tom   18
Sampson, `Sammy`   8, 10, 11, 13, 17, 18, 21, 22, 23, 27, 32, 38, 174
Saphir, Warrant Officer   152
Schmued, Ed   99
Shepherd, John   121, 123, 125, 136
Sinclair, Catherine   135
Sinclair, Sir Archibald   134, 138
Sinclair, Stroma   134
Skinner, Bill   37, 40, 42, 49, 50, 53, 58, 75, 76
Smith, Arthur   86
Smith, Dennis   50, 58
Smithers, Warren   72
Spencer, Flt Sgt   123

Spinney Merewood, Fl Off 123
Spurdle, Bob   62, 63, 67, 68, 74, 78
St John, Peter   40, 49, 51, 55, 73, 74, 78, 79, 112
Stalin, Joseph   161
Stephen, H M   19, 37, 39, 40, 42, 51, 58, 60, 64, 68, 73, 74, 75, 76, 77
Sterling, Judge Advocate 28
Stevenson, Air Cdre   58
Stevenson, Peter   19, 40, 42, 50, 52, 54, 58, 68, 79, 81
Strudwick, Plt Off   111
Summers, Mutt   92, 93
Surtees, `Butch`   5
Swinden, Sqn Ldr   151
Szczesny, Henryk   49, 59, 60, 61, 62, 76
Tallala, `Jimmy`   138
Tallala, Fl Off   123, 124, 138
Temple-Harris, Plt Off   18, 20, 30
Thoam, Don   62
Tito (Broz, Josep)   142, 143, 145
Topham, John   109, 112, 115
Treacy, `Paddy`   11, 12, 17, 18, 20, 21, 27, 32, 35, 36, 37, 40, 41, 174
Trenchard, Lord   76, 90, 127
Tuck, Bob   9, 20
Turpin, Richard   105
Vere Harvey, Arthur   121, 125, 126
Walkingon, Gp Capt   9, 15
Waller, Bill   98, 99
Watkins, `Dirty`   92, 93, 111
Weaver, Capt   131
Webster, Eden   17, 21
West, Mae   98
Whitaker, Sgt   18
White, `Chalky`   169
White, Laurie   19, 30, 32, 33, 37, 113
White, Wg Cdr JW   166
Wilcox, Herbert   102, 103
Willison, Fl Off   139
Wilson, Sgt   80
Wisdom, Tommy   104, 105
Wood, Sqn Ldr   47, 62, 78, 81, 82, 83
Wooton, Bertie   121
Yates, Jimmy   111, 112
Young, James   54

General Index

1 Flying Training School   163
1 Heavy Glider Maintenance Unit   163, 164
1 Heavy Glider Servicing Unit   167, 169
1 Squadron RFC   163
2 Group RAF   119, 120
2nd Tactical Air Force RAF   113, 114, 120
3 APCD   161
3 Ferry Pilots` Pool   92
3 Group RAF   132, 137
3 Squadron RFC   163
4 Squadron RFC   163
6 Squadron RAF   142, 143, 146, 153, 154, 156, 157, 158, 159, 160
7 Operational Training Unit RAF   90
8 Flying Training School   5, 173
9 Group RAF   138
11 Group RAF   8, 28, 31, 35, 58, 71, 73, 76, 77, 109, 120, 123
12 Group RAF   31, 38, 65, 119
13 Group RAF   31
14 Squadron RAF   141, 146, 147, 153, 157
16 Group RAF   123, 124
19 Squadron RAF   9, 17, 65, 112
21 Squadron RAF   120
32 Squadron RAF   159
34 Squadron RAF   113
38 Group RAF   163, 164, 166, 167

38 Wing RAF   113, 163, 166
39 Squadron RAF   142
41 Operational Training Unit   93
46 Group RAF   164, 166
52 Operational Training Unit   132
54 Squadron RAF   8, 14, 17, 33, 59, 113
56 Squadron RAF   27, 28, 29
56th Fighter Group USAAC   99
57 Operational Training Unit   82, Chapter 8
59 Operational Training Unit   77
65 Squadron RAF   8, 9, 13, 17, 112
66 Squadron RAF   73, 74
73 Squadron RAF   141, 159
74 (F) Tiger Squadron RAF   6, Chapter 2, Chapter 3, Chapter 4, Chapter 5, Chapter 6, Chapter 7, 137, 174
85 Squadron RAF   7
87 Squadron RAF   147, 156, 158
88 Squadron RAF   120
92 Squadron RAF   71, 74, 75, 76
96 Squadron RAF   93
101 Squadron RAF   78, 79
111 Squadron RAF   8, 79
118 Squadron RAF   60, 65, 99, 116, Chapter 11, Chapter 12, 141, 160, 174
121 Wing RAF   115
124 Squadron RAF   128

126 Squadron RAF   141, 146, 151, 152, 153, 154, 155, 156
145 Squadron   95
185 Squadron RAF   147, 151, 152, 153, 160
195 Squadron RAF   124, 125
202 Maintenance Unit RAF   167
221 Squadron RAF   142, 146, 147, 151
229 Squadron RAF   152, 155
235 Maintenance Unit RAF   163
242 Group RAF   141, 143, 145, 156
242 Squadron RAF   35, 38, 65
249 Squadron RAF   141, 143, 146, 151, 152, 153, 154, 155, 156, 157, 158, 159, 160
253 Squadron RAF   141
255 Squadron RAF   141, 147
257 Squadron RAF   106
282 Squadron RAF   135
284 Squadron RAF   141
286 Wing RAF   Chapter 13, Chapter 14
293 Squadron RAF   163
296 (Glider) Squadron RAF   163
297 (Parachute) Squadron RAF   163
323 Wing RAF   141
334 Wing RAF   154
402 Squadron RAF   122, 123, 124, 125, 126, 127, 128
416 Squadron RAF   122, 123, 124, 125, 126, 127, 128
449th Bomb Group USAAF   145, 147, 151
501 Squadron RAF   92
504 Squaron RAF   134, 138
600 Squadron RAF   28
602 (City of Glasgow) Sqn RAF   10, 17, 106, Chapter 10, 119, 160, 174
603 (City of Edinburgh) Sqn RAF   109
608 (North Riding) Squadron RAF   141, 147
609 Squadron RAF   125
611 Squadron RAF   65, 125, 126
693 Squadron RAF   17
809th Av Eng Battalion (US Army)145
1435 Squadron RAF   141, 146, 153, 154, 155, 157, 158, 159, 160
1578 ATC Squadron   90
1677 (Target Towing) Flight RAF   163
1898th Eng Battalion (US Army)   145
3051 Servicing Echelon RAF   131

* * * * *

Adastral House   41
Adler Tag   59
Air Firing School   5
Air Force Cross   11
Air Training Command   135
Air Transport Auxiliary   30
Air Tpt Tactical Dev`ment Unit   163, 164
Allied Military Government   155
Allison V-1710-39   99
Army Co-operation Command   113
Bank of England   172
Bastille Day   21, 22, 23, 32
Battle of Britain   7, 8, 22, 38, 41, 42, Chapter 6, Chapter 7, 92, 148
Battle of Britain Memorial Flt   169
Battle of France   35, 45
BBC World Service   144
Bevin Boys   3
Big Wing   38, 39, 65
Bishop of Truro   110
Black Varieties   62
Bomber Command   77, 96
Bristol Hercules   123
Bristol Mercury   14, 91
Bristol Napier Sabre   124
British Expeditionary Force   31, 35, 36, 40
British Medical Association   148

British Purchasing Commission   99
Brooklands Aviation   5, 81
Castle of May   135
Central Flying School   91
Channel Stop   78
Chester Herald   8, 121
Chetniks   142
Circuses   77, 110
Coastal Command   4, 31, 119, 120, 121, 136
Confederate Air Force   171
Convoy Register   151
Convoy Vellum   152
Crown, Knockholt   72
de Havilland Gypsy Major   90
Demon Flights   7
Diamond Horseshoe   102
Distinguished Flying Cross   29, 30, 41, 55, 56, 63, 64, 65, 66, 67, 68, 74, 77, 121, 138, 139, 167
Distinguished Flying Medal   76, 92
Distinguished Service Order   30, 33, 35, 76, 126
Ed. and Voc. Training (EVT)   165
Eighth Air Force USAAF   119, 120
Elementary Flying Training Sch   4, 5
ENSA   165
Exercise Exeter   166
Exercise Knockaround   167
Exercise Reconnaissance   167
Exercise Residue   167
Fighter Command   8, 9, 11, 27, 29, 31, 35, 36, 38, 41, 45, 71, 76, 77, 78, 80, 111, 127, 136
Fleet Air Arm   39, 60, 92, 132, 163, 168
Flying Scotsman   169
Ford   8
Foreign Legion   133
General Post Office   138
German RDF/Radar Sites (Balkans)151, 152, 153, 155, 156, 157, 158, 160
Glider Pilot Exercise Unit   163
H M Customs   23, 104
Hispano-Suiza   20, 123
HMS Ark Royal   121
HMS Hood   11
HMS Royal Oak   95
HMT Neuralia   7
IFF   28, 47
Irish Republican Army   17
Jaeger Division   142
Junior Leader`s School   167
Leeds Grammar School   1, 2
Link Trainer   92, 97
London Palladium   62
Louis Pasteur   95
Lufthansa   23
Mailings Pottery   172
Martin Baker   138
McAlpine   93 113
Mercedes   155
Ministry of Transport   171
Minster Soft Drinks   171
Minstry of Supply   104
Mobile Parachute Servicing Units164
Morris Motors   104, 105
MV Cavina   102, 103, 104
Ninth Air Force USAAF   120
North American Aviation   99
Officer Training Corps   3
Opel   64
Operation Dynamo   36, 40
Operation Manna   143
Operation Sealion   59, 68
Operation White   142
Op. Refresher Training Unit   163
Order of the British Empire   134
P& W Twin Wasp Junior   91

P&W Double Wasp   99, 120
P`chute Maint.& Servicing Unit   164
Parachute Regiment   166
Partisans   142, 143, 144, 149
Phoney War   31, 35
Pioneer Corps   122
RAF Benevolent Fund   80, 167
RAF Expansion Schemes   4, 8, 9, 31
RAF Regiment   163, 168
Ramrods   119, 121, 123
RDF Stations (British)   28, 31
Reserve Flying Training School   5
Reserve of Air Force Officers   3, 169
Rhubarbs   77, 210, 121, 136, 138
Riley Imp   37
RNVR   172
Roadsteads   119, 124, 125
Rodeos   121, 138
Rolls Royce   21
Rolls Royce Kestrel   91
Rolls Royce Merlin   17, 21, 30, 46, 48, 100, 119, 153, 160
RAF Volunteer Reserve   4
Royal Observer Corps   28, 29
Sassoon Trophy   14, 15, 18
Scharnhorst   134
School of Air Transport   164
School of Weapons Training   166

Service Institute Fund   164, 165, 166, 169
Seversky Aircraft   98
Singer Sewing Machine Co   136
Small Arms Unit   164
South Eastern Air Force Command   96
Southend Palace   80
SS Maihar   7
SS Queen Elizabeth   102, 161
SS Queen Mary   161
SS Rangitaka   95
SS Rangitiki   95, 96
Station Commander`s Fund   166
Sun Valley Nuts   169
Sunbeam Talbot   1, 73
Tetley Walker   171
TR9 Radio   14, 36
Transport Command   37, 165, 169
Tpt Command Development Unit   167
Treaty of Versailles   4
Twentieth Century Fox   97
United States Special Sevices   147
US Troop Carrier Command   166
Wright Double Cyclone   120
Wright R-2800   98
Yorkshire Evening News   78
Yorkshire Penny Bank   1
Yorkshire Post   56, 64, 95

Index of Place Names

Abbeville   77, 115, 123
Abbotsinch   109
Aberdeen   133
Acklington   163
Albert   123
Aldermarston   113
Aldwych   3, 104
Alessio   155
Algiers   141
Almeria   124
Andalucia   172
Andover   113, 167
Antwerp   68
Ashford   46, 48
Avonmouth   104
Ayr   7
Babie   160
Bajkastaro   160
Bari   141, 152, 158, 160
Barking Creek   Chapter 4, 56, 174
Barletta   141
Barmash   158
Bath   122
Beachy Head   119, 126
Beaconsfield   64
Beaumont le Roget   127, 131
Beauvais   131
Belfast   31, 104
Belgrade   143
Bentley Priory   28, 45, 77
Berat   151, 155, 157
Bernay   126, 127
Bethune   42
Bicak   158, 160
Biggin Hill   28, 39, 68, 71, 72, 73, 74, 75, 76, 77, 80
Bolt Head   105, 106
Boston (USA)   102
Boulogne   76
Bradwell Bay   48, 125
Brest   110, 112
Bridlington   1, 2
Brighton   54, 75
Brindisi   141, 143, 146, 147, 152, 153, 154, 159, 160

Brooklands   104, 105
Brownsville   171
Buckingham Palace   63, 65, 66
Budra   155
Caen   115, 116
Cairo   164
Calais   30, 32, 35, 40, 77
Canewdon   28
Cap Gris Nez   125
Cape Gacil   160
Cape Kiephati   158
Casablanca   141, 161
Castletown   134, 135, 136, 137, 138, 139
Catania   155
Catfoss   5
Cattaro   154, 155
Catterick   95
Chester   89, 91, 93
Chicago   100
Chichester   126, 127
Church Fenton   132
Cobham Hall   80
Coltishall   38, 39, 59, 63, 65, 68, 93, 99, 119, 120, 121, 122, 123, 124, 125, 126, 127, 135
Conyer Creek   75
Corfu Harbour   151, 153, 156, 157
Cortico Grande   172
Cowley   104, 105
Cranwell   32, 37, 78
Crewe   3
Cromer   122
Crotone   147, 155
Dagenham   8
Dartmoor   113
Den Helder   122, 125, 126
Detling   78, 139
Dieppe   111, 128
Digby   122, 127
Doncaster   169
Dover   30, 54, 58, 74, 76, 78
Dublin   11, 35
Dubrovnik   145, 153, 154, 158, 159
Duncansby Head   65, 76, 128

Dunkirk 17, 20, 21, Chapter 5, 61, 63, 92, 101, 113
Durazzo 151, 152, 155, 156, 157, 158, 160
Duxford 39, 65, 98
Eastleigh 17, 21
Eglin Field 97, 98, 100
Elbason 158, 159
Eltham 42
Exeter 105, 106, 127
Faeroe Isles 59
Fairlop 114, 115
Fanos Islands 152
Farmingdale 99
Farnborough 80, 82
Fayid 153
Fier 151, 154
Filton 121, 136
Foggia 141, 157
Folkestone 54, 55, 76
Gibraltar 35, 141
Gioia del Colle 151
Glasgow 05, 161
Goodwood 126
Gossnet 127
Gourock 95
Gramash 158
Grangemouth 109
Grantham 64
Gravesend 73, 80, 81, 82, 83, 84, 85, 91
Grottaglie Chapter 13, Chapter 14, 166, 172
Halifax, Nova Scotia 95, 96, 102, 104
Harwell 167
Harwich 58
Hawarden 82, 89, 90, 91, 92, 93, 95, 163
Hawkinge 59, 115
Headingley 1, 56, 78, 95
Hollywood 104
Hook of Holland 123
Hornchurch 6, 8, 9, 14, 15, 17, 18, 20, 23, 24, 27, 32, 33, 38, 40, 41, 47, 48, 56, 58, 59, 80, 91, 115. 174
Hurn 124
Iceland 59, 95
Igoumenitsa 152, 157
Ijmuiden 120, 126
Inverness 132
Ioannina 144
Isle of Sheppey 74
Isle of Wight 128
Ivychurch 78
Jergusat 158
Kavaje 159, 160
Kenley 109
Kiel Canal 24
Kirkwall 135, 137
Kirton in Lindsay 63, 64
Knockholt 72, 79
Korakiana 152
Kotor 153, 154, 155, 160
Krinyi 157
Lasham 113, 114, 146
Le Bourget 23
Le Mans 124
Leconfield 40, 41, 61
Leeds 1, 14, 56, 75, 95, 173
Lille 42, 47
Littlehampton 75
Liverpool 90, 104, 169
London 2, 3 47, 63, 64, 65, 68, 104, 105, 115, 141, 143, 166, 172
London Colney 7
Los Angeles 97
Lowestoft 67
Ludham 124
Lumbres 35

Luqa 146
Lushanje Progradec 160
Madrid 97
Maidstone 73, 75, 76
Maison Blanche 141
Malta 7, 8, 9, 31, 121, 136, 146, 149, 151, 152, 153, 155
Manchester 89, 95
Manchy Breton 127, 128
Manfredonia 141
Manston 12, 24, 32, 38, 47, 48, 49, 50, 52, 53, 54, 55, 56, 59, 78, 79
Margate 59
Marseilles 35
Martlesham Heath 126
Matlaske 124, 125
Merston 126, 127, 132
Merville 131
Middleton 1
Mifol 154
Milwaukee 100
Mize 159
Mjlet 160
Mojcar 171
Mold 90
Montrose 5, 14, 173
Montecorvino 141
Montgomery 96, 102
Morpeth 163
Mount Vesuvius 144
Munich 8, 9
Naples 141, 161
Neretljanski Channel 159
Netheravon Chapter 15
New Orleans 97
New York 96, 102
Newcastle 2, 172
Newmarket 32
Niksia 157
North Coates 125
North Foreland 48, 52
North Weald 27, 29, 79
Northampton 121
Northolt 7, 64, 161
Norwich 65
Old Sarum 138
Orkney Isles 59, 110, 132
Ostend 35
Ostri Point 153, 154
Oxford 133
Pajengo 158
Paleokastritsi 157
Palermo 152, 160
Panama Canal 97
Paris 23
Pasadena 97
Paxos 152
Pearl Harbor 96
Pegin 158
Penshurst 74
Pentland Firth 48, 132, 134, 135
Perranporth 106, 109, 110, 111, 113, 114
Peterhead 131, 132, 133, 134, 136, 137
Ploesti 143
Pluca 159, 160
Podgorica 158
Poix 126
Pol 115, 127, 128
Port Cruz 154
Portreath 110
Poulton 93
Predannack 121
Prestwick 109
Ragusa 154

River Clyde   48, 104, 105, 109
River Drin   155, 158, 159
River Mersey   48
River Severn   91
River Thames   48, 52, 80
Rochester   74
Rochford   30, 32, 36, 47, 48, 62, 63
Romford   37, 114
Rouen   127
Salisbury Plain   138, 164
San Diego   40, 95, 97
Sarande   153
Saseno   159
Scapa Flow   31, 110, 132
Schiphol   124
Scutari   154, 158, 159
Sealand   8
Selenica   154
Selmer   96, 97, 101
Serqueux   128
Shanghai   4
Sheringham   68
Shetland Isles   59
Shijati   155, 156
Shrewton   164
Skeabrae   122, 132, 133, 134, 135
Sofia   156
Sotta   154
Southampton   7, 48
Southend   32, 80
Southwold   68
St Agnes   111
St Brier Dren   127
St John`s, Newfoundland   96
St Mawgan   141, 161
St Omer   125, 127
Sumburgh   133
Sutton Bridge   12
Sutton`s Farm   8
Swanton Morley   120
Sywell   4, 5, 14, 173
Tangmere   109, 115, 120, 121, 124, 126, 127
Taranto   141, 149, 151

Tarrant Rushton   167
Tepelene   159
Termoli   154
Tern Hill   163
Texel   122
Thruxton   164, 167
Thurso   134
Tirana   144, 156, 160
Tivat Bay   153
Tripoli   141
Trubjela   158
Truro   110
Tunis   141
Turnhouse   132
Ulcinj   159
Upavon   91, 93
Uxbridge   104, 173
Valona   154, 159, 160
Valoria   151
Varrazan   153
Velican   160
Vis   142, 159
Vitry en Artoise   128
Washington   96, 103
West Malling   59, 74, 80, 84, 132
West Raynham   78, 79
Westcliffe   79
Westhampnett   109, 126, 127
Weybridge   89
Whitstable   59
Wick   137
Winsford   95
Wittering   38, 59, 60, 61, 63
Woendsrecht   126
Worcester   91
Worth   75
Wrexham   93, 112
Wright Field   97, 98
Yanina   159
Yeadon   14, 95
Ymerfindu   158
Zeebrugge   116